Information Studies
and Other Provocations

Information Studies and Other Provocations
Selected Talks, 2000–2019

Jonathan Furner

Library Juice Press
Sacramento, CA

Copyright 2020

Published in 2021 by Litwin Books.

Litwin Books
PO Box 188784
Sacramento, CA 95818

http://litwinbooks.com/

This book is printed on acid-free paper.

Library of Congress Cataloging-in-Publication Data

Names: Furner, Jonathan, author.
Title: Information studies and other provocations : selected talks, 2000-2019 / Jonathan Furner.
Description: Sacramento, CA : Library Juice Press, 2021. | A compilation of talks the author gave between the years 2000-2019. | Includes bibliographical references and index. | Summary: "Provides a look at some of the perennial questions facing the field of information studies through talks given at conferences, workshops, and other meetings over a two-decade period."--Provided by publisher. Provided by publisher.
Identifiers: LCCN 2020050433 | ISBN 9781634001182 (paperback ; acid-free paper)
Subjects: LCSH: Information science. | Library science. | University of California, Los Angeles. Department of Information Studies. | LCGFT: Speeches.
Classification: LCC Z665 .F974 2021 | DDC 020--dc23
LC record available at https://lccn.loc.gov/2020050433

Table of Contents

vii   List of Figures
1   Preface

A · Library and information science
    9   1 · Social justice at UCLA's iSchool
    15   2 · The humanistic iSchool: A manifesto
    21   3 · Fundamental research questions in information science
    27   4 · Shera's social epistemology recast as psychological bibliology
    39   5 · "A brilliant mind": Margaret Egan and social epistemology
    49   6 · Society, epistemology, and justice: Prospects for a critical LIS?

B · Philosophy of information
    59   7 · The Snowman of Jenna
    63   8 · Information, evidence, and recommendation
    73   9 · Response to Geoffrey Nunberg, "The informations"
    77   10 · Informatism and informatology
    81   11 · Interrogating "identity": A philosophical approach to an enduring issue in knowledge organization

C · Works, documents, records
    107 12 · The ontology of works
    117 13 · Two kinds of "work"
    127 14 · The ontology of documents, revisited
    151 15 · The ontology of subjects of works
    161 16 · "Records in Context" in context: A brief history of archival data modeling

D · Classification

- 179 17 · The Universal Decimal Classification and its historical relationship to the DDC
- 183 18 · The treatment of topics relating to people of mixed race in bibliographic classification schemes: A critical race-theoretic approach
- 197 19 · The Classification Research Group, 1952–2000: A citation analysis
- 213 20 · Knowledge organization, *Knowledge Organization*, and the Classification Research Group: A citation study
- 227 21 · New

E · Vocabularies and folksonomies

- 237 22 · International standards, national traditions: Vocabulary control in archival science
- 249 23 · Collaborative indexing of cultural resources: Some outstanding issues
- 261 24 · Social classification: Panacea or Pandora?
- 267 25 · User tagging of library resources: Toward a framework for system evaluation
- 277 26 · Twenty tall tales about tagging
- 287 27 · Children's tagging of artworks

F · Information retrieval and scholarly communication

- 295 28 · Bibliographic relationships, citation relationships, relevance relationships, and bibliographic classification: An integrative view
- 301 29 · A unifying model of document relatedness for hybrid search engines
- 313 30 · The serials crisis and what we can do about it: New roles for the library and for faculty

317 Index

List of Figures

96	Figure 11.1. The aboutness relation.
98	Figure 11.2. Inter-class relations in a hierarchical classification scheme.
119	Figure 13.1. CCO's entity–relationship model.
121	Figure 13.2. FRBR's entity–relationship model.
136	Figure 14.1. FRBR's Group 1 entities and primary relationships.
138	Figure 14.2. Chisholm's top-level ontology.
139	Figure 14.3. Lowe's top-level ontology.
139	Figure 14.4. Lowe's top-level ontology (amended).
141	Figure 14.5. Lowe's four-category ontology.
141	Figure 14.6. Smith's four-category ontology.
156	Figure 15.1. Lowe's four-category ontology.
157	Figure 15.2. A four-level semiotic ontology.
163	Figure 16.1. The most basic data model ever.
164	Figure 16.2. The most basic data model ever (amended).
164	Figure 16.3. The most basic data model ever (amended again).
165	Figure 16.4. An archival data model.
165	Figure 16.5. A model of the levels of arrangement of a fonds.
170	Figure 16.6. Four different ways of categorizing archival descriptions (every one of them excellent in its own way).
170	Figure 16.7. Archival content and encoding/structure standards.
171	Figure 16.8. FRBR's Group 1 entities and primary relationships.
171	Figure 16.9. FRBR's Group 2 entities and "responsibility" relationships.
172	Figure 16.10. FRBR's Group 3 entities and "subject" relationships.
172	Figure 16.11. Ultra-simplified CIDOC CRM.

Page	Figure
215	Figure 20.1. Citation analysis: Definitions.
246	Figure 22.1. TCS-8 example.
263	Figure 24.1. The old way.
263	Figure 24.2. The new way.
297	Figure 28.1. Citation; relevance; indexing.
298	Figure 28.2. Co-citation; co-relevance; co-indexing.
302	Figure 29.1. Example of a small document network.
303	Figure 29.2. Example of a small document network (augmented).
303	Figure 29.3. Example of a small document network (augmented again).
303	Figure 29.4. Matrix representation.
307	Figure 29.5. Similarity matrices (cosine) derived from adjacency data.
308	Figure 29.6. Proximity (distance) matrix derived from adjacency data.
308	Figure 29.7. Centrality scores (Google's idealized "PageRank") derived from adjacency data.
310	Figure 29.8. UCXtra: Initial screen.
311	Figure 29.9. UCXtra: "View the collection" pop-up.
311	Figure 29.10. UCXtra: Results screen.
312	Figure 29.11. UCXtra: "More like this" pop-up.

Preface

What is information?

Ah, that's a tricky one. Maybe best to save it for later.

What is the "Department of Information Studies"?

It's one of the two academic departments that make up the Graduate School of Education and Information Studies at UCLA[1]. There are lots of other departments and schools around the world that are like it. Not all of them are called departments (or schools) of information studies. Some of them are called iSchools. Some are called departments (or schools) of library and information science, or something similar. Most of them are quite different from departments (or schools) of computer science, or information systems, or IT, or management. The people in those other places are usually interested in quite different kinds of things.

What is information studies?

"Information studies" is just the name that some people use to refer to the area of inquiry that they're interested in. That might sound unhelpful, but the problem is that it has proven very difficult to find a definition of information studies that everyone in information studies agrees to. It's easier, and perhaps more accurate, to say that

---

1 See http://gseis.ucla.edu/.

information studies is what the community of people, who say they do information studies, do.

No, seriously, what is information studies? Surely, if you really are a professor of it, you can do better than that?

OK, I'll give it another go. Information studies is what you do if you ask interesting questions about the things that *people do*—or that they *could* do, or *should* do—with or to information. So it's about people just as much as it's about information.

Fair enough. But wait … What. Is. Information?

Well… different people have different ideas about the nature of information. Some of the ideas are quite narrow in scope. Others are quite broad. Some are about the kind of thing that information is. Others are about the properties of information—especially those properties that only information has, and those that all information has. Here are a couple of those ideas. Which one is better than the other? You decide.

One idea is that information is something that is contained in the things that people say, write, draw, and make. (Instead of "contained in," you might prefer one of these: "stored in," or "recorded in," or "encoded in," or "expressed by," or "carried by," or "meant by," or "communicated by," etc. Although, there are subtle and important differences among these different formulations.) Here's something that people occasionally say (too occasionally, actually): "Norwich City F.C. won the Milk Cup in 1985." The information contained in this statement is the information that Norwich City F.C. won the Milk Cup in 1985. In other words, information is *whatever something means*.

Another idea is that information is *whatever has meaning*. Here's something that has meaning: the statement "Norwich City F.C. won the Milk Cup in 1985." According to this second idea, then, it's the statement itself, and not its meaning, that is information. Things that have meaning include the things that people say, write, and draw, and some (if not all) of the things that people make.

Each of these ideas has many variants. For example, some people define information as whatever can be encoded in a sequence of binary digits (0s and 1s). That's a version of the first, information-*as*-meaning idea. Others say that it's the sequences of binary digits themselves, not what they encode, that are information. That's a version of the second, information-*has*-meaning idea. The most important variants are probably the ones in which it is understood that meaning is not literally contained in any given statement, but is at least partially determined by the *context* in which the statement is made—a context that encompasses the mental state of both speaker and hearer.

So you're saying that some people in information studies are interested in meanings, and others are interested in things that have meaning? That sounds really vague. (And also maybe a bit like semiotics?)

Ah, well, remember that information studies is about the things that people do with or to information. Create it and destroy it; collect it and scatter it; lose it and find it; preserve it and waste it; hide it and display it; remember it and forget it; fake it and verify it; steal it and give it away; and so on. In particular, information studies is about the reasons that people have for doing these kinds of things in the ways that they choose, and about the effects of those actions on the world. By studying such reasons, methods, and outcomes, we can figure out what people could and should be doing with or to information, and endeavor to change the world accordingly.

So, for example, you might be interested in the ways in which:

- **school librarians** can meet the needs of children and teens by providing access to wide-ranging collections of relevant materials
- **community archivists** can ensure the preservation of unique records that provide evidence of the activities of previously underrepresented groups
- **user-experience (UX) designers** can conduct evaluations of search-engine interfaces
- **special-collections librarians** can develop standards for the digitization of medieval manuscripts
- **media archivists** can establish workflows for managing an animation studio's digital assets
- **data scientists** can build platforms that enable physicists to participate effectively in the curation of their research data
- **digital-humanities researchers** can devise techniques for the visualization of temporal changes in the themes of literary works

- **information policymakers** can establish principles for the protection of personal data privacy

The best place to study any of these topics, among very many others, is a department of information studies. There happens to be an excellent one of these at UCLA—ranked #1 in *U.S. News & World Report*'s ranking of public research universities in 2020.

You say on your website that you study something called "philosophy of cultural stewardship." That sounds extremely pretentious. What does it even mean?

Broadly speaking, to be the *steward* of something means to be the person who is *responsible for preserving the value* of that thing.

By extension, *cultural stewardship* is the set of practices involved in taking responsibility, both for preserving the value of cultural works (e.g., works of literature), cultural objects (e.g., individual copies of sound recordings), and cultural events (e.g., individual performances of plays), and for providing the means by which people may take future opportunities to benefit from that value.

And then, if you do *philosophy of cultural stewardship*, you inquire into the basic properties of cultural works, objects, and events; you try to understand the nature of the interactions among the *stewards*, the *cultural resources* in their care, and the *contexts* in which stewardship takes place; and you study theories of value, perhaps distinguishing among informational value, evidentiary value, inspirational value, entertainment value, transformational value, etc. You try to understand what stewards *could* do, and what they *should* do, as well as what they *do* do.

Why do you insist on using the word "steward"? It sounds like you're talking about labor union representatives, or flight attendants...

I know what you mean. But I don't have a better alternative. Let me know if you think of one.

What are some of the kinds of things that you do if you're a cultural steward?

- You *acquire* or *receive* quantities of cultural resources (henceforth, "stuff"—an ancient technical term).

- You build and develop *collections* of stuff.
- You *take care of* stuff so that it endures.
- You find out what kinds of things other people (sometimes called "*users*") would like to do with that stuff.
- You design, develop, evaluate *tools* and *systems* that help people do what they want to do with that stuff, while helping you take care of it.
- You put stuff in *order*.
- You *describe* (i.e., create representations of) stuff—and the *contexts* in which it is created, cared for, and destroyed—so that it can be found, accessed, displayed, interpreted, used, and exchanged, and its benefits enjoyed.
- You come up with *theories* as to how to do any of these things more effectively, efficiently, and ethically. ("There's nowt so practical as a good theory!" as my grandmother used to say. Or would have done, if she (a) had thought of it, and (b) was from Yorkshire.)
- You identify *principles* and *policies* that guide the actions both of systems designers and of the people who are interested in finding out about stuff.

... Amongst other things.

What sorts of job titles do cultural stewards have?

First of all, it's probably worth pointing out that many members of the LAM (library, archives, museum) community are cultural stewards. At the same time, many cultural stewards are members of other professional communities. Many cultural stewards do not happen to work for institutions that are actually called things like "The Such-and-such Library," or "The Archives of So-and-so." Of those who don't, many nevertheless think of themselves as librarians, archivists, or museum professionals; whereas many others prefer to think of themselves in other ways.

So, any list of job titles to look out for, if you're interested in a career in (what I'm calling) cultural stewardship, should include the following at a minimum:

- *x* librarian, *x* archivist, *x* curator: where *x* might refer to the type of "parent" institution (e.g., school, academic, public); the form, genre, or subject of the stuff you'd be dealing with (e.g., rare books, oral history, web, digital); or the group of people you'd be serving (e.g., youth, community); and
- data *y*, metadata *y*, records *y*, information *y*, knowledge *y*: where *y* might suggest the kind of thing you'd be doing with the stuff, ranging from the very general (e.g., professional, manager), through the still-fairly-general (e.g., analyst, scientist), to the more specific (e.g., architect, preservationist).

What has this book got to do with information studies?

It's a compilation of the texts of various talks I've given over the years. Some of the talks are on topics that I've subsequently covered in papers published in peer-reviewed journals or edited volumes. Other talks weren't followed up in the same way. All of them except three (Chapters 15, 21, and 30) are published as talks for the first time. They're arranged in topical rather than chronological order: there are six sections, beginning with "Library and information science" and "Philosophy of information," moving through "Works, documents, records" and "Classification," and finishing up with "Vocabularies and folksonomies" and "Information retrieval and scholarly communication." Taken together, the areas indicated by the section headings comprise a fairly narrow slice of the information studies pie, reflecting my primary interest in the philosophy of cultural stewardship. As you'll see, one of the common themes is the use of conceptual analysis to evaluate the theoretical frameworks, data models, and metadata standards on which information access systems rely. The aim with this collection is to show how and why such an approach is productive.

Do you want to thank anybody?

Too many to list here. But a few people deserve special mention. First, I'd like to thank Rory Litwin for his support and encouragement in bringing this collection to print. Second, I'd like to thank all my colleagues in the Department of Information Studies at UCLA, past, present, and future, and in particular Greg Leazer for his friendship and collaboration. Thirdly and most importantly, I'd like to thank Natalie, Zak, and Lucas for their love and understanding. Thank you all!

A
Library and information science

1
Social justice at UCLA's iSchool

May 22, 2017

This talk was given at IACAL 2017: Identity, Agency, and Culture in Academic Libraries Conference (Los Angeles, CA, May 22–23, 2017) as part of a panel session on "Structures of interaction with academic library constituencies: Labor, community, bureaucracy, and social justice." The panel chair was Gregory H. Leazer, and speakers were Jonathan Furner, Gregory H. Leazer, Safiya U. Noble, and Sarah T. Roberts. A version of the talk was also given at CLA 2019: League of Extraordinary Librarians: California Library Association Conference (Pasadena, CA, October 24–26, 2019) as part of a panel session on "Critical librarianship: Communities, labor, bureaucracy, and social justice" with the same panel members.

In the Department of Information Studies at UCLA, we're interested in the things that people do with or to information, whatever the context. We're interested in how information is created, how it's collected, organized, preserved, and made accessible; but just as importantly, we're interested in how it's faked, how it's hidden, wasted, and destroyed. We're interested, not only in practices of speaking, hearing, and remembering, but in practices of silencing, erasing, and ignoring—practices of epistemic violence.

Now, it's not this set of interests that makes us unique. There are many so-called iSchools around the world, many of them having originally been established as library schools, or as schools of library and information science, and all of them doing great work.

What does make us unique, we think, is the worldview that's reflected in the mission statement of our parent school, UCLA's Graduate School of Education and Information Studies. Our work is guided by a mission statement that specifically invokes, and here I'm quoting, "the principles of individual responsibility and social justice, an ethic of caring, and commitment to the communities we serve."

There's no other library school or iSchool in the country that talks in the same way about responsibility and justice and ethics and community and service. Our goals are far different, dare I say far more humane, than those of many of our sister institutions.

I'm also fairly certain that the IS department at UCLA is the only one of its peers across the country or around the world to have a formal vision statement that values and promotes "equity, diversity, accountability, and intellectual openness" above all others.

Now, of course, these are mere words if we fail to translate them into action. What do these words mean in practice? They mean that we're committed to changing the world—

- in ways that reduce divides and disparities—inequalities between rich and poor, and between powerful and powerless,
- in ways that generate fairer distributions—of social and cultural and economic and political opportunities, and
- in ways that build and maintain thriving communities in which basic human rights and freedoms are respected.

We're committed to a future—

- where members of all social groups enjoy equitable access to the information they need to get their jobs done and live their lives to the full.
- A future where everyone, not just an elite minority, is empowered to preserve their own artifacts and stories and ideas, in the ways they wish and to the extent they wish.
- And a future where the actions of governments and corporations respect the rights of individuals and communities—to intellectual freedom, to privacy, and to cultural property.

I don't imagine I have to belabor the point that the need to determinedly pursue these goals is increasing in intensity on almost a daily basis.

In many respects, this picture of the future is one characterized by distributive justice—that is, fair distributions of resources and opportunities and freedoms of various kinds. But to focus on distributive justice alone would be to ignore one of the most prevalent kinds of injustice in our society, which is that caused by the systemic oppression of social groups (Young 1990).

Injustice occurs—

- whenever labor is divided in such a way that women work specifically in order to maintain the power, wealth, and status of men.
- It occurs whenever those who are old, or young, or poor, or disabled, or otherwise dependent on others, are thereby deprived of basic rights and freedoms.
- It occurs when working-class people find that they are unable to participate in making the decisions that have the greatest effect on their lives,
- when the very means of interpretation and expression and communication in our society are so completely controlled by white heterosexual men that the experiences and values of nondominant groups are rendered invisible,
- and when we choose to tolerate the fact of black people living their lives under the constant threat of harassment, intimidation, and physical violence simply on account of their group identity.

Working towards social justice as a goal therefore involves the basic reform of social practices and institutions, as well as the redistribution of resources. Among these practices and institutions are those by whose means we produce and consume information.

At UCLA's iSchool, the practical way in which we work towards social justice is by building educational programs that prepare graduates for participation in a workforce of information professionals who understand the needs and values of the communities they serve. These communities are wonderfully and richly diverse—in many respects, albeit to greater or lesser extents. But one thing they all have in common is that they need librarians.

Our communities need children's librarians, young adult librarians, school librarians, academic librarians, rare books librarians, manuscript librarians, corporate librarians, digital librarians, data librarians.

Our communities also need archivists, and museum collections managers, and information architects, and user-experience designers, metadata curators, and digital humanities analysts.

Where do all these people come from? Well, the very best—the leaders of their respective fields, designing, developing, and implementing new kinds of information services and systems that meet the needs of members of diverse communities in the most effective but also in the most ethical ways—these leaders graduate with a master's degree in Library and Information Science from the Department of Information Studies at UCLA.

At the UCLA iSchool, we recognize that we have a rather large responsibility. It's a duty, if you like—and it's a duty not just to the profession but to civil society as a whole, that we share with other iSchools. This duty is to make sure that we graduate cohorts that are successively more culturally competent than before … to make sure that our graduates have a deep understanding of the conditions and outcomes that are most valued in the communities that they serve—outcomes such as justice, diversity, and freedom—and highly skilled in the practices that are most generative of those values.

How can we discharge that duty? Well, at least in theory, it's rather simple. We have two main strategies.

The first is to design, develop, and conduct continuous reviews of a curriculum that is suffused by education for cultural competence. To that end, we have recently revamped the core curriculum of our MLIS program so that a course on "Values and Communities" accounts for a full 25% of the credit-units required for all incoming MLIS students, no matter what area of specialization they choose, whether that's library studies, archival studies, informatics, media archival studies, or rare books / print and visual culture.

At the same time, we strive to teach towards specific cultural competencies in every class we offer, whether required class or elective. A class on the technology of search encourages students to uncover the values reflected in the design of retrieval algorithms; a class on archival description requires students to engage in critique of universalizing standards that flatten local differences and silence the already-marginalized voices of members of source communities.

The second strategy we have for fulfilling our duty to civil society, is to try to make sure that we admit cohorts of students that are successively more diverse than before.

And to do that, we try to make sure that we select students from more diverse pools of applicants,

which we might attract if our faculty and staff are more diverse, so we try to make sure we have more diverse pools of applicants for those positions.

And, for faculty members, that tends to depend on how diverse cohorts of graduating doctoral students are, which tends to correlate with how diverse the pools of applicants for doctoral programs are, which tends to correlate with how diverse cohorts of graduating master's programs are, and so it goes … a continuous cycle, which of course we want to make virtuous rather than vicious.

There are all sorts of reasons for an individual's decision not to attend graduate school. The cost of the program, and more specifically the cost of the program relative to one's expected earnings upon graduation, is one such reason, of course. And so we're always seeking out new sources of financial support for our students. But another reason is that the individual doesn't know that a particular program exists or doesn't even know that a particular profession or field exists. There are lots more unbelievably talented people out there who could and would take the library and archives world by storm, if only they realized that we are here.

We're doing what we can. But we can always do better. Please help us do better. Please spread the word.

Reference

Young, Iris Marion. 1990. "Five faces of oppression." In *Justice and the politics of difference*, 39–65. Princeton, NJ: Princeton University Press.

2
The humanistic iSchool: A manifesto

October 29, 2007

This talk originated as a proposal for a paper submitted by Jonathan Furner and Anne Gilliland to the 3rd Annual iConference (Los Angeles, CA, February 28 – March 1, 2008). The proposal was rejected, but a version of the talk was given at ASIS&T 2012: 75th Annual Meeting of the American Society for Information Science and Technology (Baltimore, MD, October 26–30, 2012) as part of a panel session on "Humanistic information science." The panel chair was Jens-Erik Mai, and speakers were Jonathan Furner and Jens-Erik Mai.

When the topic is the state of the information schools (and of information studies in general) in 2008, what could conceivably be the point, almost half a century on, of invoking Snow's *The two cultures* (1959)? Who among us could possibly need reminding that our two imaginary friends—"the scientist" and "the humanist"—tend to go about their daily business in different ways, and frequently run the risk of talking past each other?

Of course, Snow's crude dichotomy is just one of a number of taxonomies of knowledge domains that have been proposed with the goal of distinguishing among fields of inquiry (or among communities of inquirers) according to their ontological, epistemological, and/or axiological commitments. Some such taxonomies are similarly unidimensional: Kuhn (1962), for instance, distinguishes between those academic communities whose members generally find themselves in agreement about the kinds of question that they ought to be asking (and about the kinds of method that they ought to be using to arrive at answers), and those "preparadigmatic" communities that presently lack such consensus (but that continue to strive towards it). Other taxonomies multiply the dimensions to allow for more subtle distinctions: Becher (1994) draws on Biglan (1973) and Kolb (1981) to develop a two-dimensional model that distinguishes between the "hard pure" (natural sciences and mathematics), "hard applied" (science-based professions, such as engineering), "soft applied" (social professions, such as education and law), and "soft pure" (social sciences and humanities).

In Becher's model and others like it, the hard–soft dimension roughly corresponds to Snow's scientific–humanistic distinction. "Hard" fields are restricted in scope, studying a clearly delineated range of physical phenomena with a limited range of tried-and-tested methods, with the positivist goal of establishing general, deterministic laws of cause and effect that can each be used to explain the occurrence of large numbers of discrete events. Members of "hard" communities tend to make objectivist assumptions about the nature of reality, of truth, and of knowledge: scientists typically proceed, for example, on the basis that it is possible to acquire knowledge of "the" truth about "the" real world. "Soft" fields, in contrast, are more open to the study of complex, messy, lumpy problems, using a wide range of exploratory methods to come to interpretative understandings, both of the unique constellations of factors that produce particular events, and of the meanings those events have for individuals and for groups. Members of "soft" communities typically allow that our knowledge of the world (if not the world itself) is both socially constructed, in the sense that our beliefs are shaped not only by the ways in which we directly perceive the world but also by the ways in which we interpret others' beliefs about the world, and perspectival or relative, in the sense that the "truth" (or goodness) of our beliefs may be evaluated differently depending on the evaluator's present point of view.

Several communities of inquirers that have self-identified with a focus on information and information-related phenomena also have a long tradition of soul-searching—some might call it navel-gazing—when it comes to locating themselves among the four quadrants of the Becherian model. Many commentators have drawn attention, in more or less exasperated tones, to the positivist nature of much of the research in information science (see, e.g., Ellis 1984) and in library science (see, e.g., Harris 1986), and such observations have usually been accompanied by impassioned calls for a "softening" (in the Becherian sense) of information research.

These days, we are more likely to read about information studies' hospitality to a plurality of approaches, the implication being that each of its different subfields can be comfortably located in different quadrants, or even that each of its topics or problem sets can be explored using multiple methods originating in different quadrants. Bates (2005), for instance, distinguishes nomothetic (hard, scientific, universal) from idiographic (soft, humanistic, particular) approaches, and describes thirteen separate approaches to library and information "science" (sic) that can be located along the nomothetic–idiographic spectrum. In more recent work, Bates (2007) goes so far as to differentiate between information-related subfields that "arise from" the sciences (viz., "the sciences of information," such as information science, information systems, and informatics) and those that "arise from" the humanities (viz., "disciplines of the cultural record," such as library science, archives, and museum studies). Bates makes it clear, however, that these two sets of subfields are not to be understood as corresponding to the poles of the hard–soft spectrum, since each of the methods that are typically used in any given subfield is "applicable to a much broader range of information solutions than its origins indicate." Nomothetic and idiographic approaches alike may be taken to any of "the sciences of information" or the "disciplines of the cultural record."

And yet. Here are some of the results of the simplest content analysis imaginable—a word frequency analysis—of the "Call for participation" of the 3rd Annual iConference (see https://ischools.org/resources/Documents/iconf%202008/CallforParticipation_R4.pdf). The six most frequently occurring content-bearing words are as follows: information, 17 occurrences; community (or communities), 6; management, 5; systems, 5; technology (or technological, technologies), 5; digital, 3. Here are some of the words that don't appear even once: archival (or archives); bibliography; document (or documents); genre (or genres); knowledge; library (or libraries); museum (or museums); record (or records). What are we to make of this? That there is suddenly no place, in the iSchools' vision for iStudies, for the "disciplines of the cultural record" that range across fully half of Bates' "spectrum of the information disciplines"? Are we simply to accept that some of the keywords traditionally used to describe these humanistic approaches were considered by the program committee to smack a little too much of professional practice, or to be too institutionally-bound for a supposedly wide-ranging call? Or that the omission of these words is part of a deliberate effort to distance the iSchools from stereotypes that are not considered appropriate to a "progressive" agenda driven by corporate and government priorities?

The iConference's tagline is "Information: The power to transform our world," and of course it is power that is the issue here: the power of particular groups of scholars to call the shots. In general, academics are empowered if they are able to self-identify with a field that (a) is clearly delineable from other fields, (b) has content whose importance is agreed upon and whose transmission to students is easily controllable, (c) produces knowledge that is seen to be cumulative rather than agglomerative, and (d) produces knowledge that is perceived by university administrators and potential funders to be immediately and widely applicable to the efficient production of commodities (Bernstein 1971; Becher & Trowler 2001). The benefits of using speech acts like the iConference's "Call for participation" to locate information studies at the "hard" end of the spectrum, and simultaneously to sweep "soft" approaches under the epistemological carpet, are presumably quite clear. What may be less apparent are the potential consequences of this strategy for the continued vitality of the field—a vitality that is ordinarily ensured by its multidisciplinarity and methodological pluralism. "Where academic power is under threat, for example in a highly market-oriented [higher education] system … what are superficially the same disciplines will take on different characteristics… . One consequence of academics' continued involvement in 'chasing the dollar' is that the dollar's involvement in shaping epistemological forms is becoming increasingly central …" (Becher & Trowler 2001, pp. 37–38). It seems as if we do need to remind ourselves, one more time, that information studies certainly *need* not be, often *is* not, and maybe *ought* not to be conceptualized as a science, nor even as a social science. The "soft"-spoken should not be reduced to searching for and squeezing into places at a table that they helped to build.

We need to address questions of the following kinds (among others):

What makes any field of inquiry a "humanistic" one? We need to consider characteristics such as subject matter (e.g., the particular kinds of problems addressed), research methods, metatheoretical assumptions (e.g., about the nature of reality, truth, knowledge, theory, research, and method), values, and goals. We need to discuss the emphasis placed by humanities-oriented scholars on the following (among others): the human condition; ideology, race, class, and gender; identity and diversity; interpretive, critical, and historical approaches; meaning, language, and discourse; narratives and stories; aesthetic value; and doing the right thing (prior to doing the thing right).

What would a humanistic iSchool be like? Specifically, what kinds of programs, courses, research projects, and service operations would a humanistic iSchool develop? What kinds of collaborative, transdisciplinary activities would be undertaken by members of a humanistic iSchool? We need to examine how the iSchools have traditionally distinguished themselves from other schools (e.g., schools of computer science, information systems, and communication/media studies) that do not self-identify with the iSchools but that are nonetheless concerned with information-related phenomena. How, precisely, would a humanistic iSchool distinguish itself from a traditional iSchool? How would a humanistic iSchool be different (if at all) from Buckland's conception (Buckland 1996) of a liberal arts iSchool? Might it be considered inappropriate or otherwise misleading for such a school to continue to focus on "i" rather than on alternatives such as "d" (document), "r" (record), or "c" (culture)?

Why should any iSchool strive to be humanistic? What kinds of benefits, intellectual or otherwise, would accrue (and for whom) as a result of the decision taken by any iSchool to distinguish itself as humanistic? More generally, why is it of significance or of interest to consider questions about the value of humanistic approaches or orientations to information studies? Even more generally, what is it about approaches or orientations of this kind that makes them good (or useful, or productive, or rational, etc.)? In particular, we need to emphasize the importance of understanding our field's social, cultural, and intellectual history.

We conclude by assessing the short- and long-term prospects for humanistic information studies in a disciplinary context that continues to be shaped by the iSchool community. We argue, with Albert Borgmann (1999), that information studies is properly about the relation between people and (not technology, nor even information, but) *reality*; that information studies is about understanding the nature of representation, of meaning, and of interpretation; that information studies is about documents and records, about remembering and forgetting, about sensemaking and storytelling, about testimony and ritual; that information studies is about the practices of everyday life. Information studies is humanistic information studies; information studies is cultural studies.

References

Bates, Marcia J. 2005. An introduction to metatheories, theories, and models. In *Theories of information behavior*, ed. Karen E. Fisher, Sanda Erdelez, and Lynne McKechnie, 1–24. Medford, NJ: Information Today.

———. 2007. Defining the information disciplines in encyclopedia development. Information Research 12, no. 4 (October). http://informationr.net/i/12-4/colis/colis29.html.

Becher, Tony. 1994. The significance of disciplinary differences. *Studies in Higher Education* 19 (2): 151–161.

Becher, Tony, and Paul R. Trowler. 2001. *Academic tribes and territories: Intellectual enquiry and the culture of disciplines*. 2nd ed. Buckingham, England: Society for Research into Higher Education / Open University Press.

Bernstein, Basil. 1971. On the classification and framing of educational knowledge. In *Knowledge and control*, ed. M. F. D. Young, 47–69. London: Collier Macmillan.

Biglan, Anthony. 1973. The characteristics of subject matter in different scientific areas. *Journal of Applied Psychology* 57 (3): 195–203.

Borgmann, Albert. 1999. *Holding on to reality: The nature of information at the turn of the millennium*. Chicago, IL: University of Chicago Press.

Buckland, Michael. The "liberal arts" of Library and Information Science and the research university environment. In *CoLIS 2: Proceedings of the Second International Conference on Conceptions of Library and Information Science: Integration in perspective* (Copenhagen, Denmark, October 13–16, 1996), ed. Peter Ingwersen and Niels Ole Pors, 75–84. Copenhagen, Denmark: Royal School of Librarianship.

Ellis, David. 1984. Theory and explanation in information retrieval research. *Journal of Information Science* 8 (1): 25–38.

Harris, Michael J. 1986. The dialectic of defeat: Antimonies [sic] in research in library and information science. *Library Trends* 34 (3): 515–31.

Kolb, David A. 1981. Learning styles and disciplinary differences. In *The modern American college*, ed. A. W. Chickering, 232–55. San Francisco, CA: Jossey-Bass.

Kuhn, Thomas S. 1962. *The structure of scientific revolutions*. Chicago, IL: University of Chicago Press.

Snow, C. P. 1959. *The two cultures and the scientific revolution*. Cambridge: Cambridge University Press.

3

Fundamental research questions in information science

October 10, 2011

This talk was given at ASIS&T 2011: 74th Annual Meeting of the American Society for Information Science and Technology (New Orleans, LA, October 9–12, 2011) as part of a panel session on "Fundamental research questions in information science." The panel chair was Sachi Arafat, and speakers were John Budd, Ron Day, Jonathan Furner, and Julian Warner.

I see one of the goals of this session—if not *the* goal—as being for participants (and that means all of us, not just the panelists) to think seriously about this question: "What *ought* information science to be like?" Or, to put it another way, and to avoid, for the time being, that loaded word "ought," "What would we *like* information science to be like?"

Taking that kind of question seriously, means taking a step back even before we ask it, and checking that it's a question worth asking and answering. On the face of it, it would seem like it would take quite a bit of time and effort for anyone to address that kind of question with the kind of rigor that it seems like it deserves. So, before we dive into the deep end, as it were, it seems to me that it makes sense first to consider what possible *reasons* we might have, both for asking it and for giving answers of the kinds that we typically give.

It also seems to me that there is one rather obvious reason for asking it, which is that we are unhappy, to a greater or lesser extent, with what we take information science to be like currently. In this scenario, we see information science as something that is, in certain or uncertain respects, not what it could be, and that we are hoping to persuade those who have the capacity to effect change (whoever they may be) to act in whatever ways are necessary to effect such change as will bring information science more in line with what we would like it to be. In other words, we might think that information science is somehow not doing its job as well as it could, but that if it was somehow better in the ways we think it could be, then everything would be okay. We might even have a more or less clear vision of what information science could be like, if only certain aspects of the enterprise were different in certain specifiable ways.

At this point, we might task ourselves not only to make sure that we are able to express, clearly and accurately, our judgments as to what those points of difference are, but also to make sure we are able to specify the *criteria* on which we base those judgments.

So, for instance, we might start by thinking like this: You know, information science would be a whole lot better if people started paying more attention to concepts of "document" or even "consciousness" or "intentionality" instead of "information." Or, information science would be a whole lot better if people stopped thinking about it as a means to the end of understanding the relationship between people, information, and technology, and started thinking about it as a means to the end of understanding the various ways in which people interact with reality by creating and using representations of that reality. Or, information science would be a whole lot better if people who design information systems put concerns about justice, and equity of access, above concerns about profit margins or about users' satisfaction with perceived levels of effectiveness.

Evidently, there are lots of possible points of difference between what information science is like now, and what we might like it to be. There are also lots of potentially useful ways of *categorizing* those particular points of difference into kinds. One way is this: we could sort those differences into differences in phenomena, questions, methods, and goals. In other words, we could distinguish among the following four categories:

- differences between the kinds of *phenomena* that currently form the subject matter of information science, and the kinds of phenomena that we would like to see form that subject matter;

- differences between the kinds of *questions* that are currently asked in information science and the kinds of questions that we would like to hear asked;

- differences between the kinds of *methods* that are used to answer the questions that currently arise in information science and the kinds of methods that we would like to see used; and

- differences between the kinds of *goals* or purposes that currently motivate people to engage in information science and the kinds of goals that we would like to see people be motivated by.

You get the general idea. I don't think it would take too much work to map this particular classification onto the one that Sachi developed in the panel proposal, which distinguishes among ontological, epistemological, and ethical categories, among others.

Now, I say that this is a *potentially* useful way of categorizing particular points of difference. And of course there are other ways, and we might want to debate the relative utility of those different classifications. But there is a general limit to the utility of such classifications. This limit is a function of the fact that such classifications have nothing to say about the kinds of *criteria* on which we might base our judgments either as to which *kinds* of difference—ontological, epistemological, ethical, and so on—are the important ones, or as to which *particular* differences are the important ones. In other words, even after selecting one such classification rather than another, we still don't have a way to evaluate or to choose among alternative suggestions as to what information science ought to be like. All we have is a way of categorizing individual people's personal preferences. We don't have a way of assessing the justifications or arguments that individual people may or may not provide in support of their expressions of those preferences. We don't even yet have a framework that will help us understand the criteria that individual people consider in order to arrive at those personal preferences.

So: What are some general criteria that we could use both to determine to our own satisfaction which possible states of information science are better than others, and to choose among the various proposals for revitalizing information science that are competing for our support at any given time?

Here I'll just say that I'm not at all sure that I have a particularly interesting or even informed answer to this question, but that I simply want to defend the view that this is a question (if not the question) that deserves our attention.

That said, I can imagine that any draft list of the criteria that we could use to choose between competing states of information science might include the following:

The degree to which the proposed state of information science is productive of theories that seek to *explain* information-related events, activities, and phenomena. "Why did event *x* occur?" strikes me as a reasonable question for a scholar to ask in a very wide range of conceivable circumstances. Can information science help us propose answers to questions of that kind? We might be moved to say that the more it does, the better it is. We might even want to specify some further criteria for assessing rival explanations, such as correspondence with observed data, consistency with prior theory, internal coherence—that kind of thing.

The degree to which the proposed state of information science is productive of theories that help us to interpret the *meanings* that information-related events, activities, and phenomena have for their participants. Again, "What does event *x* mean?" is another question that seems like it would be sensible for scholars of various stripes to ask. Can information science help us propose answers to questions of that kind? Conceivably, the more it does, the better it is.

The degree to which the proposed state of information science is productive of theories that help us *build systems and services* that are fit for purpose, that meet requirements, that are cheap and fast and easy to use—in other words, systems and services that work, and that allow people to get their jobs done. Similarly, we might want also to consider under this heading the degree to which the proposed state of information science is productive of theories that help us *create policies, regulations, and laws* that effectively balance the interests of different groups. And, as before, we might very well see value in going further and specifying sets of criteria for evaluating the products of applied information science.

And now I've reached what I think is an important part. The important point is this: It may very well be the case that, when we enumerate, explicitly or implicitly, the criteria that we use, consciously or subconsciously, to evaluate information systems, services, policies, laws, and so on, we end up specifying criteria that, by themselves, do *not* appear to have any kind of *ethical* or moral dimension. For example—we might compare two information retrieval systems, and decide that one typically retrieves records that are more relevant to users' queries than the other. On the face of it, at least, there doesn't seem to be any ethical dimension to the criterion of retrieval effectiveness. But, I want to point out that there *is* an ethical dimension to the *prioritization* of criteria—that there *is* an ethical dimension to the choice among criteria that pushes retrieval effectiveness to the top of the list and that pushes others such as fairness to the bottom. Does it matter, for instance, that retrieval systems typically participate in the creation of conditions for cumulative-advantage processes? Where resources are distributed and recommendations made not on the basis of desire (however that might be measured) but on previous popularity? I happen to think that it does matter, and not only that, but also that it matters that the decision that is routinely made among system designers to ignore the implications of these conditions is one that is just as routinely glossed over and forgotten once it has been made.

I'm not saying this is a new idea. But, I think we do sometimes need reminding that there are other kinds of criteria on which our judgments of the value or goodness of information systems, services, policies, etc., may be based, criteria other than simple effectiveness, or efficiency, or usability. These are criteria such as fairness, equity, and diversity. And our ranking or prioritization of such criteria amounts to an ethical decision, which itself is susceptible to evaluation against ethical principles, the identification of which is the result of the application of ethical theories.

So, we might be inclined to add a fourth criterion to our draft list of criteria that will allow us to assess different states of information science. And that fourth criterion is this: The degree to which the proposed state of information science is productive of theories that help us create systems, services, policies, and laws that themselves are productive of distributions of resources, such as access to information, that are *fair and equitable*, or otherwise judged positively on ethical dimensions.

Whether or not we are persuaded to make that addition, my position is that we need to make sure, in any discussion of what information science ought to be like, that we understand the importance of what is sometimes known as *information ethics*, not just for understanding the nature and scope of the various ethical issues that are raised in the everyday practices of information professionals, but more fundamentally, for understanding the ethical implications of any choices that are made in the course of developing or evaluating proposals for a better information science. For that reason, I would place information ethics at the very base of any foundations built for information science.

Now, I think that there are a number of possible approaches to building an information science that has information ethics at its core. These approaches may be distinguished by pointing out differences in the emphases they place on particular aspects of *ethics* as a field of inquiry.

For example, one approach would be to focus on the concerns of *applied ethics*, studying the ethical dilemmas faced by information professionals, clarifying the practical guidance that is provided in specific situations by various ethical principles, and perhaps simultaneously uncovering the values and ethical decisions embedded in information artifacts and practices.

Another approach would be to focus on what is sometimes known as *normative ethics*, studying the ethical *theories* (rights-based, consequence-based, and so on) from which different ethical principles may be derived, and clarifying the distinctions among the justifications for, and implications of, choosing any one of those theories to justify one's own ethical decisions.

A third approach—maybe the most interesting?—would be to focus on *meta-ethics*, studying those conceptions of information ethics such as Luciano Floridi's, in which information ethics is conceived not so much as a branch of applied ethics, but rather as an ethical theory in itself that has emerged as a result of an "informational turn" in ethics. Here the assumption is that the universe is most usefully considered at an *informational* level of abstraction, rather than at a biological or chemical level. On that informational level, all things in the world are treated as data structures consisting of sets of attributes and functions, rather than as aggregates of physical objects; and *all* these elements of the "infosphere"—not just people—have rights and responsibilities that should be considered when choosing among rival ethical principles.

Is Floridi right? I have no idea. But I think that to answer *that* particular question would be to place a stone of quite considerable weight among the foundations of information science. Apart from anything else, engagement with Floridi's argument might persuade us that, after all, it *does* make sense to ask, "What *ought* information science to be like?"

4

Shera's social epistemology recast as psychological bibliology

November 7, 2001

This talk was given at ASIS&T 2001: 64th Annual Meeting of the American Society for Information Science and Technology: Information in a networked world: Harnessing the flow (Washington, DC, November 2–8, 2001) as part of a panel session on "Social epistemology and information science." The panel chair was Jonathan Furner, and speakers were John Budd, Don Fallis, Jonathan Furner, and Leah Lievrouw. A paper with the same title as the talk was published in **Social Epistemology** *16, no. 1 (2002): 5–22.*

Jesse Shera, the library scientist, is often credited with introducing the term and concept of social epistemology; but his idea is most profitably viewed not as a contribution to epistemology or even to the sociology of knowledge, but rather as the forerunner of a document-focused strain of socio-cognitive psychology influential in the information sciences from the 1970s onwards.

What I'd like to do today is justify this claim, and also demonstrate that, in turn, the work of Shera and his colleague Egan is itself reminiscent of the psychological bibliology defined by the documentalists Otlet and Rubakin in the early twentieth century.

In the philosophical literature, a social epistemology is typically conceived as one that provides a "social" rather than an "individualistic" account of the conditions that must be satisfied before a given belief may qualify as knowledge. Such an account will identify properties of society, culture, or community, rather than properties of the individual knower, as primary conditions.

Perhaps uniquely for a term in common philosophical parlance, however, the expression "social epistemology" seems to have been first used in the literature of library and information science, in a landmark paper published in *Library Quarterly* in 1952. Margaret Egan was the originator of both the term and this particular conception of social epistemology; after her death in 1959, it was left to Jesse Shera to revisit and refine his colleague's ideas in a succession of papers before his own death in 1982.

One of these documents was the transcript of some lectures that Shera gave in 1967, which was published in 1970 with the title *Sociological foundations of librarianship*. It was Shera's intention that these lectures should point towards solutions of "certain problems ... fundamental to librarianship," one of the most pressing being that of identifying the intellectual foundations, the "core of fundamental theory," to which the profession may look for guidance. Shera's motivation for defining the boundaries of social epistemology lies in his perception that such a discipline could provide the source of "the theoretical foundations of the library profession," and thus of library science.

Since Shera's clear intention is that the practice of librarianship should be based on the theory of social epistemology, we may view his project as essentially a normative one. The primary task of social epistemology is to specify the strategies that we ought to take if we're to improve the effectiveness of library and information services. I'll return to this point later, but first I want to clarify Shera's distinctive conception of knowledge, since it's the communication of knowledge that is the object of librarianship.

At the heart of the librarian's activities lie what Shera calls "graphic records," which contain "recorded knowledge." We might now talk about documents rather than graphic records. Shera's emphasis is on the recordability and communicability of knowledge; knowledge is something that may be recorded (in documents) and communicated (to people).

Of course, knowledge is also something that may be stored in the memories of those individuals to whom it is communicated. On occasion,

Shera explicitly labels the contents of people's minds as subjective knowledge (to contrast with the recorded knowledge that is the contents of documents). He also uses terminology introduced by the economist, Boulding. He specifically equates subjective knowledge with the "image" of the world that a person constructs as a result of her interaction with that world, and with recorded knowledge.

This is like the usage of "knowledge structure" or "knowledge state" in cognitive psychology, and in the related LIS literature on information-seeking behavior. A more apt or less confusing term might be "cognitive state," since it refers to the complete personal set of beliefs held by an individual, as well as sundry thoughts, feelings, motivations, intentions, and emotions. For these things, truth and justification are entirely irrelevant evaluative criteria.

Part of the remit of epistemology has traditionally been to provide an acceptable answer to the question "What is knowledge?" and specifically to distinguish between knowledge and (mere) belief. Various kinds of response have been made, but most are similar in the sense that they rest on criteria such as truth, correspondence with reality, justifiability, relevance, and consistency. In the cognitive sciences, no appeal to any such criterion is made when identifying what is knowledge and what is not; knowledge is simply the propositional content of minds or of documents. We may thus distinguish between an epistemological conception of (roughly speaking) knowledge-as-truth, and a psychological conception of knowledge-as-information.

The psychological conception is central to models of information-seeking behavior developed by such LIS writers as Belkin, Brookes, and T. D. Wilson. Work of this kind in the information sciences is sometimes recognized as being a consequence of a paradigm shift known as the "cognitive turn," and draws much of its inspiration from cognitive and social psychology.

Shera also has a lot to say, not all of it clear, not all of it explicit, and not all of it consistent, about certain distinctions that may be made between various conceptions of personal and social knowledge, private and public knowledge, intrinsic and extrinsic knowledge, and so on. Some of the related terminological distinctions are summarized in Table 4.1; we could probably debate the subtle differences among the distinctions for a while. I'd be very happy to do that, but it's not really what I want to do today.

Type I	Type II
Private knowledge	Public knowledge
Personal knowledge	Social knowledge
Intrinsic knowledge	Extrinsic knowledge
Internal memory	External memory
Subjective knowledge	Objective knowledge
World 2	World 3
Image	Transcript
Tacit knowledge	Recorded knowledge
Minds	Documents, libraries
Mental	Physical

Table 4.1. Conceptions of knowledge

The trouble is, I would claim that, if we're going to properly understand Shera's account of the way in which librarians may benefit from studying SE, we have to have some idea of how important social factors are to Shera's conception of knowledge. So, this is what I'm going to do now. Firstly, I'm going to characterize what Shera says about the goals of the library profession. Then I'm going to paraphrase what Shera says about what librarians need to understand, if they're going to do their job well. And hopefully that paraphrase will give enough of a sense of the complexities, relating to social factors that are involved in Shera's conception.

For Shera, the role or function of the librarian is to serve society by bringing together, on the one hand, people, and on the other, the knowledge that's recorded and stored in the contents of libraries. This is to be done in such a way that the utility of libraries for library users is maximized. And using Boulding's terminology, we might say that utility is maximized if the library user is enabled to develop a useful image of the world.

For Shera, the "basic problem in librarianship" consists in determining what we can do (quote) "to match two patterns—the pattern of human thought to the pattern of organization of the Library." The value of the latter depends on the extent to which it mirrors the former: says Shera, "the degree to which these two patterns coincide will determine the effectiveness of the way in which the material is organised." The librarian's bibliographic systems should therefore be "structured to conform as closely as possible to man's uses of recorded knowledge."

Shera is well aware, of course, that different individuals organize their thoughts in different ways; and therefore that we should not hope that any given enumerative classification scheme could possibly simultaneously reflect the multiple cognitive structures of all its users. But he seems to say that librarians may successfully identify the structure, not of individuals' images of the world, but of the image constructed by the society in which the library is situated. The relationship that needs to be cemented is that between "the structure of knowledge as it has developed in contemporary Western civilisation and the librarian's tools for facilitating intellectual access to that knowledge."

Shera's most important claim is that, in order to achieve this goal of matching up knowledge structures, the librarian must understand at least two things: how people use documents, and how documents affect people. He must have understanding of the impact of documents on people, and understanding of the impact of recorded knowledge on behavior.

Actually, ideally, the librarian should understand the following (and Shera doesn't present it this way—this is my paraphrase that I was talking about earlier):

- the ways in which people construct physical artifacts (including documents);

- the ways in which people construct subjective knowledge—i.e., images, both (a) personal and (b) social, of the contents (i) of the physical world, (ii) of other people's minds, and (iii) of documents;

- the ways in which people construct recorded knowledge—i.e., "reflections," or expressions of thought, contained in documents, considered both (a) individually and (b) collectively, and as representations of (i) the physical world, (ii) the mental world, and (iii) other documents.

Shera's view of the task of the librarian may then be interpreted as a dual responsibility: (a) to produce, in the form of whatever classification scheme is used to organize the documents in a collection, an accurate reflection of his society's (or library-user group's) image of its recorded knowledge; and (b) to ensure, in the course of person-to-person "reference interviews" (or person-to-machine query-formulation sessions) in which library or retrieval-system users express their information needs, that those users are able to construct as accurate an image as possible of the structure previously imposed on the collection.

The promise of the "new discipline" of social epistemology is that it will allow the librarian to reach the understanding of various basic cognitive and socio-cognitive processes that they must have to carry out these tasks. Shera admits that scholars are a long way from understanding these processes, and says that all he can do is "suggest certain lines of enquiry" that may lead to scientific knowledge. One of his primary recommendations is that library scientists draw on the findings of other disciplines that engage in analysis of cognition.

A primary source of confusion for the reader of Shera's account of social epistemology lies in what may be viewed as his ambiguous response to the sociology of knowledge. On the one hand, Shera explicitly states that his new discipline should concern itself not just with the use of knowledge, but also with its production. For instance, he says that: "The focus of [social epistemology] should be upon the production, flow, integration, and consumption of all forms of communicated thought throughout the entire social fabric." And when he defines social epistemology generally, as "the study of knowledge in society," with a view to understanding the nature of "the intellectual process in society," it seems natural to assume that he would want to include under this rubric study of the ways in which such knowledge is produced (as well as the ways in which it is used).

Yet, elsewhere, Shera expressly protests that (quote) "social epistemology ... is almost the reverse of the sociology of knowledge." He says: "The sociology of knowledge deals with the impact of the social fabric upon ideas ... Social epistemology ... deals with the impact of knowledge upon society ... We are talking about the other side of the coin entirely." Shera appears to want to retain a distinction between one mode of inquiry—his social epistemology—that concerns itself with the influence of documents on people, and another—his conception of the sociology of knowledge—that concerns itself with the influence of people on documents.

Well, if we ignore some of Shera's more general claims, we can salvage that very distinction. Before I clarify how, I want to undertake a brief review of recent developments in related fields, beginning with epistemology itself.

The impact on epistemology of the successive paradigm shifts that have come to be known as the linguistic and cognitive turns is well documented. It's common, for example, to distinguish between, on the one hand, the post-Fregean epistemology pioneered by Russell, Wittgenstein, and the Vienna Circle of logical positivists in the early part of the twentieth century, and on the other, the naturalized epistemology emerging from the work in the 1950s and 1960s of Quine and Kuhn. Post-Fregean epistemology may be characterized by the use of logic and conceptual analysis; in contrast, naturalists argue for use of the concepts (and sometimes even the results) of psychology in solving epistemological problems.

In his 1992 review, Kitcher further distinguishes between two flavors of naturalized epistemology, one "traditional," another "radical." Kitcher roughly equates radical naturalized epistemology with the sociology of knowledge. He emphasizes its denial of the validity of the general normative project of epistemology. What is left for the sociologist of knowledge is a descriptive study of the ways in which people in various social groups actually generate knowledge in practice. Kitcher's conception of social epistemology is of a naturalized epistemology that admits sociological as well as psychological explanation, and that may be considered "traditional" or "radical" depending on its normativity.

Kitcher does not differentiate between the sociology of knowledge practiced in the contemporary era by (for example) Bloor and Latour and the sociology of science exemplified by Merton, but many others have provided compelling accounts of this distinction. On a typical reading, the sociology of knowledge is conceived as being primarily concerned with the "content" of knowledge—whether the theories contained in scientific documents, or the beliefs expressed by the members of a social group—whereas the sociology of science focuses to a greater extent on the institutional and disciplinary "contexts" in which knowledge is produced.

The sociologist of science studies the social processes by which scholars, subjects, and documents are positioned within networks. She asks: How are scholars evaluated and rewarded, and how are they stratified by status? How do scholars choose amongst subjects to write about, and what are the consequent rates at which different fields of knowledge grow? How are disciplines, and the relationships among subjects, structured and organized?

We would have good reason, given the common focus on knowledge of each of these fields, to consider the set as forming the core not only of a narrow "science studies," in which knowledge produced in the name of science is privileged, but of a broader "information studies" whose goal is to understand all aspects of the production, organization, and use of knowledge-as-information, and that includes library and information science. A promising strategy for the modern reader of Shera would appear to be to characterize his social epistemology as a conception of theoretical LIS-as-SE—in direct comparison with these other fields.

Okay, so in Table 4.2, some of the distinctions that I've made are summarized. The columns give answers to the following questions.

A. Naturalization. May the proposed solutions to knowledge-related problems admit concepts or results from the empirical sciences?

	A	B	C	D	E	F
Post-Fregean epistemology	No	Yes	No	Yes	Yes	No
Traditional naturalized epistemology	Yes	Yes	Maybe	Yes	Yes	No
Social epistemology	Yes	Yes	Yes	Yes	Yes	No
Radical naturalized epistemology	Yes	No	Maybe	Yes	Maybe	No
Sociology of knowledge	Yes	No	Yes	Yes	Maybe	No
Sociology of science	Yes	Maybe	Yes	No	No	Yes
LIS-as-SE	Yes	Maybe	Yes	No	No	Yes

Table 4.2. A modern view

B. Normativity. Is the recommendation and justification of strategies for improving knowledge-production processes a primary objective?

C. Socialization. Are social (as well as psychological) factors treated as a primary source of variance in knowledge-production processes?

D. Content vs. Context. Is the propositional content of belief treated as a variable for which explanation is to be found?

E. Knowledge-as-truth vs. Knowledge-as-information. Is truth considered as a primary criterion in assessments of the status of beliefs?

F. Subjective vs. Recorded Knowledge. Is the primary focus on the production, organization, and use of recorded expressions of belief?

You'll notice that LIS-as-SE and the sociology of science are presented as having identical characteristics. How do we separate them? Well, one key may lie in the extent to which each field is concerned to establish norms or specifications of how things ought to be done. Shera viewed LIS-as-SE explicitly as a normative project that would infer, from observations of the ways in which people access and use documents in practice, recommendations of ways in which collections of documents should be structured and organized. So, whereas study of the factors influencing the structure of document networks is often seen as part of the sociology of science, and study of the factors influencing the structure of bibliographic classification schemes is sometimes seen as part of the sociology of knowledge, information use studies—and the guidelines for the design of document access (i.e., information retrieval) systems that are derived from the conclusions of such studies—are the core of LIS-as-SE.

A second and probably more crucial point of differentiation lies in the extent to which each field is interested in document use as opposed to document production, and it is here that we can resuscitate Shera's argument for drawing a line between LIS-as-SE and (what he called) the "sociology of knowledge." "Information use studies" is commonly used as a convenient label for all kinds of studies of the needs and behavior of information-seekers and the users of libraries, information services, and information systems: precisely the kinds of studies, in other words, that Shera saw as informing the practice of retrieval-system design and reference work. The sociology of science, on the other hand, insofar as it is concerned with recorded knowledge, is not typically motivated by the goal of understanding how scholars (let alone non-scholars) use documents, but rather how they generate them.

In conclusion, given (a) Shera's motivation to establish a new name for his (and Egan's) "new" theoretical discipline that was to underpin library science, (b) the lack of a distinctively epistemological aspect to his work, (c) the affinity of that work with the emerging cognitive sciences in general and cognitive psychology in particular, and (d) its obvious concern for social factors, I present four suggestions for disciplinary labels that may be used to distinguish Shera's "social epistemology" from the social epistemology that will be more familiar to readers of the journal of that name, and from the sociology of knowledge.

It might be argued that neither "socio-cognitive psychology" nor "cognitive sociology" gives sufficient indication that the practitioners of the new discipline are concerned primarily with the cognitive effect of documents (as opposed to that of sense-data). "Information use studies" conveniently and accurately describes the extensive and valuable work on the usage of documents and libraries that has been carried out in LIS, with or (mostly) without citing Shera, over the last half-century.

A more intriguing possibility is suggested by an appreciation of Shera's oversight when he fails to distinguish effectively between knowledge-as-information and knowledge-as-structure. (We might instead wish to contrast knowledge-as-data and knowledge-as-metadata.) Just as (it may be argued) the creation of a narrative text is not the same kind of act as the creation of a classification scheme, neither should the use of a conventional document be viewed in the same way as the use that is made of a classification scheme. Shera distinguishes between knowledge production and use, but does not consider that knowledge organization may properly be viewed as a third category, and that the study of social factors influencing the ways in which existing indexing languages and metadata schemes are used by people might be an area of inquiry—"metadata studies"?—with its own unique challenges.

Finally, mindful of our desire to emphasize both cognitive factors and documentary objects, we might otherwise be persuaded to turn to either of Rubakin's neologisms, "bibliological psychology" or its abbreviated form "bibliopsychology." I should confess a personal preference for "psychological bibliology," Otlet's turnaround of Rubakin's term, originally introduced in its French form by Otlet in 1919. Shera's account of the need for a theory of social epistemology to act as a foundation for the practice of librarianship is reminiscent of Otlet's promotion of the science of "bibliology" as "a general theory of the Book and the Document."

If Otlet's work had been disseminated more widely, perhaps we would now enjoy the precision not only of psychological bibliology rather than user studies, but also of linguistic bibliology instead of knowledge organization, computational bibliology instead of information retrieval, and so on.

This parlor game of terminological "what-if?" may reasonably be interpreted as pointless whimsy. In the present context, the more important point is this: If we understand Shera's conception of social epistemology in any of the five ways described above, we point ourselves in directions taken neither by contemporary social epistemologists nor by sociologists of knowledge. We need to recognize both (a) that Shera's work does successfully indicate where a theory of librarianship may be found, and (b) that much progress toward this goal has already been made—thanks to the "cognitive turn" in LIS that is typically dated to the work of such authors as Brookes, Belkin, and T. D. Wilson, but that was heralded by Egan and Shera, and by Otlet and Rubakin before them.

5
"A brilliant mind": Margaret Egan and social epistemology

October 19, 2003

This talk was given at ASIS&T 2003: 66th Annual Meeting of the American Society for Information Science and Technology: Humanizing information technology: From ideas to bits and back (Long Beach, CA, October 19–22, 2003) as part of a panel session on "Pioneering women in information science." The panel chair was Shawne D. Miksa, and speakers were Laurie J. Bonnici, Jonathan Furner, Alexander Justice, Kathryn La Barre, Shawne D. Miksa, and Helen Plant. A paper with the same title as the talk was published in **Library Trends** *52, no. 4 (2004): 792–809.*

In the April 1952 issue of *Library Quarterly*, Margaret Egan and Jesse Shera of the University of Chicago's Graduate Library School co-published what came to be regarded as a seminal article in the history of library and information science. Seven years later, Egan had died, and Shera was left to develop the arguments begun in 1952. Over the last half-century, citations have occasionally been made to the original article; more often than not, however, the citations have been to Shera's sole-authored publications in which he refines the ideas presented in 1952. It is Shera's name that seems to have become associated in common consciousness with the ideas contained in the original article. Yet there are indications—deriving in part from Shera's own statements—that Egan deserves rather more credit than that she has historically received. In this talk, I examine the hypothesis that it is time for the balance of credit to be redressed. I will briefly summarize the contributions made in the 1952 article; I will outline the methods that may be used in determining the nature and extent of Egan's intellectual influence on Shera; and I will conclude with an evaluation of Egan's oeuvre.

Essentially, what Egan and Shera do in "Foundations of a theory of bibliography" (or FTB as I'll call it from now on) is to identify a gap in the disciplinary landscape, and fill it with the "new discipline" that they call "social epistemology." They situate social epistemology on the one hand in relation to economics, and on the other in relation to sociology, psychology, and traditional epistemology. Just as economics emerged as a theoretical framework for the study of the production, distribution, and utilization of various kinds of material products, Egan and Shera propose social epistemology as a framework for the study of intellectual products. They also invoke Parsons' structural-functionalist analysis of individual action in terms of three "modes of orientation"—the cognitive, the goal-directed, and the affective—to conclude that no existing field has attempted to study cognitive behavior at the social level.

The object of study of the cognitive mode is the process by which the actor attempts to know the particular situation in which the action takes place. They thus define social epistemology as "the study of those processes by which society as a whole seeks to achieve a perceptive or understanding relation to the total environment … ."

Because I know many of you will be more than familiar with FTB, I'll summarize by identifying the following major contributions:

- The ultimate goal or end of library service—informed social action—is explicitly identified, and the extent to which bibliographic services contribute to this end is established as the primary criterion by which they may be evaluated.

- A theoretical framework is sketched out for the study of information-seeking behavior, knowledge organization, and bibliometrics, setting the scene for the subsequent treatment of that framework as a theoretical foundation for library and information science.

- The term "social epistemology" is used in the published literature for what appears to be the first time—a full thirty-five years before philosophers such as Goldman and Fuller will reclaim the term from the librarians.

I've already noted that Shera is often credited for the idea of social epistemology, to the extent that Egan is occasionally written out of citations to the 1952 article entirely. It sometimes seems as if Shera was himself only too conscious of this injustice. In particular, he is careful in his entry on Egan for the *Dictionary of American Library Biography* of 1978 to credit Egan for the idea that underlay their jointly-authored paper. "'Social epistemology,'" he says, "both the term and the concept, were hers, but because I have given it wide currency, despite frequent disclaimers, it has generally been attributed to me."

A quick look at the citation indexes can help us here. Data on publications that cited FTB during the years 1952 through 1955 is unavailable since the coverage of ISI's Social Sciences Citation Index (SSCI) extends back only to 1956. But we can draw a fairly accurate picture of the extent to which FTB has been cited since 1956 by making combined use of the print and online versions of SSCI.

In its form as a journal article in *LQ*, FTB has been cited in the literature indexed by ISI on 17 occasions. In 13 of these instances, Egan was correctly cited as the primary author; on the remaining four occasions, Shera was incorrectly cited either as the primary author or indeed the sole author of FTB. These data, however, do not provide a complete picture, since FTB was reprinted in at least two collections. One of these is much more widely cited than FTB itself; this is the collection of Shera's essays edited by D. J. Foskett and published in 1965 as *Libraries and the organization of knowledge* (LOK). In LOK, FTB is presented as a work of Shera's, with a footnote explaining to the reader that it was written "with Margaret E. Egan."

Unsurprisingly, perhaps, given this slightly misleading mode of presentation, many of the authors who have chosen to cite FTB in its LOK form do not mention Egan's contribution in their citations. I have identified nine items that specifically cite FTB in its LOK form. The authors of every one of these nine citing items credit Shera as the primary, if not the sole, author of FTB. Of a total of 26 citations to FTB, then, fully 50%—a remarkable percentage in the circumstances—do a disservice to Egan.

What of Shera's claims that he has always been careful to credit Egan for her origination of social epistemology? Well, sometimes he was, and sometimes he wasn't. In his *Sociological foundations of librarianship*, the transcripts of the Ranganathan lectures that he sent to India in 1967, Shera says: "I have called this new discipline 'social epistemology,' a term which was, if I remember correctly, originally devised by my former associate Miss Margaret Egan … ." More typically, however, in his papers on "Social epistemology, general semantics, and librarianship" from 1961, and "An epistemological foundation for library science" from 1965, both themselves highly cited, Egan's name is nowhere to be found.

As a footnote to this analysis, we should also observe that Egan herself, in both of the articles of her own in which she mentions the 1952 work, cites it by the self-effacing form "Shera and Egan."

Meanwhile, those authors in the philosophical community who are busy constructing their own version of social epistemology are usually satisfied, when it comes to establishing intellectual primacy, with a quick nod to Shera alone (if, of course, they feel the need to nod to library science at all). For example, Steve Fuller, perhaps the most well-known philosopher with an interest in social epistemology, cites Shera and LOK in a 1996 review article. Egan is nowhere to be seen.

It is clear, then, that despite Shera's best efforts Egan has, to a substantial extent, been written out of the history of the development of the idea of social epistemology.

It is my perception, however, that Egan left us with a legacy that deserves rather better treatment, and in the rest of this paper I'm going to examine how she did so.

Margaret Elizabeth Egan was born in Indianapolis in 1905. She was employed as readers' advisor at Cincinnati Public Library from 1933 to 1940, before going on to do graduate work at Yale and in the Graduate Library School (GLS) of the University of Chicago. In 1943, Egan joined the Industrial Relations Center of the University of Chicago as librarian, and began teaching part-time in the GLS. She was appointed by Ralph Beals as a full-time assistant professor in the GLS in the fall of 1946. Shera brought Egan to join him in the School of Library Science at Western Reserve University in Cleveland, OH, in 1955, initially as a research associate of the newly-formed Center for Documentation and Communication Research (CDCR). Egan died of a heart attack on January 26, 1959, at the age of 53.

It is instructive to compare Egan's career trajectory with that of her friend and colleague. Shera graduated from Yale University with a master's degree in English language and literature in 1927, before returning to his home town of Oxford, OH, just outside Cincinnati for 11 years. Shera attended Chicago's GLS as a doctoral student between 1938 and 1940, and was appointed by Ralph Beals, a friend from student days, as the university's associate director of libraries in 1944. Egan had already begun to teach on a part-time basis in the GLS, and Shera was to do the same from 1944, becoming full-time in 1947. I haven't found any evidence to indicate that their two paths crossed before that time, despite their geographical proximity and similarity of professional interests between the years of 1930 and 1938.

In 1952 Shera was appointed dean of the School of Library Science at Western Reserve, where he was to establish the CDCR in 1955. Egan was apparently instrumental in his deciding to leave Chicago for Cleveland. In a 1968 interview, Shera recalled: "I went back to my office—at that time [the spring of 1952], Margaret Egan and I shared an office because of the shortage of space—and I was talking to her about it and she was sort of encouraging me to apply, and I said, 'I don't know.' And finally, after two or three days of talking … , she just pushed the typewriter over and said, 'Here, write, go ahead and write. Apply.' And I said, 'Okay, I'll go ahead and apply.'" Within a few years, Shera had brought Egan to join him in Cleveland; it was at that point that, as he remembered later in a 1970 interview, "we really thought we were going to get down to things." The shock of Egan's death in 1959 affected Shera greatly: "I felt as just half of me had gone. How do I go on without this gal?" Shera retired as dean in 1970. He died on March 8, 1982, at the age of 78.

In attempting to determine the nature and extent of Egan's intellectual influence on Shera, we can treat the idea of social epistemology as a kind of case study. But there are several difficulties inherent in conducting intellectual history of this kind.

Suppose that we wished to gather evidence that would allow us either to press or to comfortably ignore the claim that it is Egan rather than Shera whom we should thank for originating the concept of social epistemology. On the one hand, we have Shera himself graciously deflecting the credit in Egan's direction. We also have what we may simply infer from the order of names in the statement of authorship attached to the *LQ* article. Shera and Egan co-authored eleven publications, and took care in three cases to specify Egan as first (and, by implication, primary) author. On the other hand, we have the fact that it was Shera, not Egan, who was to revisit and develop the themes of the *LQ* article on multiple subsequent occasions. What methods do we have at our disposal that might provide further clues as to the nature and relative extent of the debt that library and information science owes to Egan for her contribution to the discipline's theoretical foundations?

One possibility is to take a quantitative approach. Today, however, I'd like to move briskly to consideration of more-qualitative approaches. In the first place, we may consult the existing archival record, in the form of the collections of personal papers, correspondence, and institutional records that are stored in the archives associated with Egan's places of work.

Two of the richest sources of data are oral interviews conducted with Shera towards the end of his deanship at Case Western. The tapes of these interviews, together with written transcripts, are available in the University Archives at CWRU.

Firstly, in an interview with Shera conducted in 1968 by Mrs. Gerald Ruderman, then a student in the library school at Kent State University, Shera identifies the three people who are, as he puts it, "unquestionably, the ones who have done the most" to stimulate his thinking. These are the demographer Warren Thompson, who was Shera's boss at the Scripps Foundation; the librarian Ralph Beals; and Margaret Egan.

The importance of Egan's influence even among this exalted group is confirmed in a second interview with Shera conducted in 1970 by Ruth Helmuth, the university archivist at Case Western. Shera says to Helmuth: "… a lot of my thinking even today is colored by Margaret's thinking. Brilliant gal really, almost a genius in some ways. And I owe her a tremendous debt, because … her influence on my thinking is probably greater than any other. Certainly it's greater than any other about library problems; sure, there's no question about that."

At the time he made these comments, Shera was 67 and Egan had been dead for 11 years. We can readily assume that Shera knew personally most if not all of the finest minds that had emerged in library and information science in the mid-century period. His singling out of Egan from this pantheon remains a striking tribute.

Shera went on to write the entry on Egan that appeared in the *Dictionary of American Library Biography*. Here he states: "Even today, on those rare occasions of contemplating what I have published, I am amazed to find how much of it is her speaking through my own halting prose." He also quotes from a letter he received from Ralph R. Shaw at the time of Egan's death: "Hers was one of the truly great minds of American librarianship." Winifred Ver Nooy, writing to Shera at the same time, concurs: "She was such a grand person, with such a brilliant mind … ."

I recently spent a week sifting through multiple series of boxes of Shera's personal papers in Cleveland, and saw at first hand how Shera built his reputation as a correspondent of remarkable wit, honesty, and energy. Yet I was confounded by how few references to Egan appear in these papers. When Shera does make reference to Egan—for instance, in the oral interviews of 1968 and 1970—he invariably introduces her as "my old friend and former associate." But among thousands of letters sent to and received from Shera's associates, covering all periods of his professional life, not a single one is addressed to or signed by Egan. One might expect to have encountered at least a few dating from the period 1952–55, when Egan was in Chicago and Shera in Cleveland; but if, indeed, any ever existed, they were not deposited in the archives. I have not been able, as yet, to find out where, if anywhere, Egan's own papers have been kept.

In the second place, we may consider that interviews may be conducted with people who knew Egan and Shera, and who can comment on the dynamics of their intellectual relationship. Since Egan died almost 45 years ago, it is not getting any easier to identify contemporaries willing to speak on the subject. I have nevertheless compiled lists of Egan's colleagues and students, and would be very grateful to receive any help that members of the audience might be able to provide in this respect.

A qualitative approach of a third kind is potentially the most productive approach of all, and it is that which involves close reading and content analysis of the texts of Egan's works.

A review of Egan's first-authored publications, which set of 21 includes four full-length journal articles and eight substantial conference papers, reveals Egan as a central player in the popularization amongst North American library scientists of the motives, concerns, and research results of the European documentation movement. The late 1940s and early 1950s, of course, were the time of the publication of Bradford's collection of papers simply called *Documentation* (which Egan reviewed favorably, and together with Shera wrote an introduction for that was reprinted in later editions); the revitalization of the American Documentation Institute, later to be renamed ASIS; and the launch of the journal *American Documentation*.

The question posed by those many, including Egan, who recognized the value to society of specialized information in technical fields in science, industry, and commerce, was whether the library profession could refine the traditional bibliographic tools and techniques for application to the new specialized requirements, and in support of scientific research and managerial decision-making as well as cultural enrichment. Were the problems faced by special libraries the same as those addressed in general librarianship or must a new profession emerge? Egan believed firmly in the unity of the profession; that the library, in its role as a social agency, must surely change as the needs of society change, but that its general functions of information provision and bibliographic control are the same whatever the content, structure, purpose of that information.

Trained as a political scientist at Yale, and with a lifelong interest in sociology, Egan was an expert on the history of the development of the behavioral sciences. The references in her writings to Parsons, von Neumann, Simon, and so on, are no idle name-drops. The pervasive influence of the pragmatist philosophers and Parsons' structural-functionalism on Shera's work is no doubt mediated by Egan's interpretation of those writers. Central to the pragmatist ideal are two related claims associated with John Dewey: firstly, that ideas are valuable only in terms of their instrumentality to an active reorganization of the context; and secondly, that different groups of people classify ideas differently depending on what they want to do with them. Dewey concludes from these: "Things have to be sorted out and arranged so that their grouping will promote successful action for ends."

From this simple theoretical framework and her interpretation of European documentation, Egan derived the following:

- an assumption that no communication has value unless it stimulates behavior that has a social impact;
- the view of the library as a social agency, and more specifically of bibliographic service as an instrumentality in support of the general process of graphic communication, and ultimately in support of the smooth functioning and continued progress of society through its promotion (and, ideally, maximization) of the effective utilization of society's graphic records;
- a macrocosmic view of the development of bibliography, such that individual bibliographic tools are integrated and coordinated both

in a coherent pyramid that may easily be accessed at any level of generality and in a network that allows movement between subject fields as well as within them;

- a recognition that different types of bibliography serve different purposes for different groups, suggesting the need for studies of what kinds of bibliography there are, and what kinds of readers there are;

- a recognition of the need for the application of subject analysis to the bibliographic control of units smaller than books;

- an appreciation of the importance of library schools in educating the future producers and managers of bibliographic services in the methods of dealing with social change. Here, Egan develops a model of the profession of librarianship as art not science, as one that crucially involves the use of judgment in the application of its body of principles;

- finally, a recognition of the importance, since there is no basic science underlying LIS as biology underlies medicine, of creating a theoretical framework for it rather than borrowing one or several from other fields.

Those who are familiar with Shera's later work will notice that each of these is a conspicuous element of the intellectual legacy that is more usually attributed to him.

Shera wrote that it was in her position as librarian of the Industrial Relations Center in Chicago that Egan "began seriously to develop her philosophy of special librarianship and documentation." "Philosophy" is a word that is often used to describe the mode of Egan's thought. Whether it is considered appropriate or not to evaluate her conception of social epistemology as a philosophical theory, we can surely conclude that, despite the small number of formal citations to Egan's work, the influence that her ideas had on the development of LIS as a discipline, largely through Shera's mediation, was great in both quantitative and qualitative terms. The life and work of this pioneering woman of information science clearly warrants further attention.

6
Society, epistemology, and justice: Prospects for a critical LIS?

August 16, 2017

This talk was given at a workshop on Social Epistemology as Theoretical Foundation for Information Science: Supporting a Cultural Turn (Copenhagen, Denmark, August 16–17, 2017).

In efforts to construct theoretical foundations for library and information studies, scholars have drawn variously on conceptions of social epistemology, social justice, and epistemic justice (among other ideas). Is it possible to untangle the relationships among these conceptions, in order to arrive at a compelling justification for a distinctively "critical" LIS? The following remarks are divided into four parts. First, I have some things to say about epistemology, then I'll talk about justice, thirdly society, and lastly critical LIS.

OK then, *epistemology*. I'd like to consider, just for a moment, the relationship of epistemology, as a field of inquiry, to philosophy of "information," where "information" is in scare quotes because of course as we all know there is no such thing. It seems to me that the subject matter of philosophy of "information" is exhaustively comprised of elements of three more-traditional branches of philosophy that we might conveniently label philosophy of *mind*, philosophy of *language*, and philosophy of *belief*, or "epistemology"—which term one might argue is somewhat of a misnomer given the availability of the Greek root "doxa," but there you go, people like to privilege a particular kind of belief, namely knowledge, and that's why we have "epistemology" rather than "doxology" or "credology" or something like that.

It also seems to me that theories of belief come in two generic flavors. On the one hand, there are *truth*-oriented theories, and on the other hand, there are *relevance*-oriented theories.

One approach to explaining the difference between the two categories involves first making an ontological commitment to at least two categories of abstract objects, namely *attitudes* and *propositions*, and then conceiving of beliefs as attitudes towards propositions. You may well prefer to make a different set of ontological commitments, but my hunch is that regardless of your choice, we would still find it a relatively straightforward matter to draw the distinction between truth-oriented and relevance-oriented theories.

Truth-oriented theories are theories of belief that distinguish between *true* and *false* beliefs, that is, between beliefs that true propositions are true, and beliefs that false propositions are true, respectively. Note the assumption made here, that it is possible to determine whether a proposition is true or not. In fact, according to truth-oriented theories, the most important feature of any proposition is its truth-value.

Relevance-oriented theories are theories of belief that distinguish between *relevant* and *non-relevant* beliefs, that is, between beliefs that relevant propositions are relevant, and beliefs that non-relevant propositions are relevant. Note the assumption made here, that it is possible to determine whether a proposition is relevant or not. In fact, according to relevance-oriented theories, the most important of any proposition is its relevance-value.

One of the interesting things about this distinction between truth-oriented and relevance-oriented theories of belief is that we can use it to express a historical disconnect between epistemology as a subfield of what has come to be known as analytic philosophy, and other fields such as library and information science. LIS is not a subfield of analytic philosophy. But that doesn't stop some of its affiliates from engaging in theorizing about belief. Typically, the resulting theories are relevance-oriented.

(Just parenthetically here, there is a corollary to all of this that, as far as I'm aware, hasn't been fully explored in the literature, which is that, if knowledge is to be characterized in a truth-oriented system as some sort of justified true belief, then in a relevance-oriented system what is it that should correspondingly be characterized as some sort of justified relevant belief? But maybe that's for another day.)

Moving along a little, let's take a look at some high-level branches of epistemology. I don't think it's controversial to suggest that there's a difference between *pure* epistemology and *applied* epistemology, even if those labels are seldom used in practice. I'm thinking here of the distinction between theories that are "merely" *descriptive* of the nature of doxastic and epistemic concepts and practices, and those that are *normative* in the sense that they seek to specify the practices that are most conducive to believing true or relevant propositions.

Regardless of whether one's objectives are descriptive or normative, one's approach or methodology may be more or less *rationalistic*, and more or less *naturalistic*, depending on one's readiness to admit different kinds of evidence in support of one's conclusions. Similarly, one's interests may be more or less *individualist*, and more or less *social*, to the extent that one chooses to focus on interpersonal interaction as a factor in the formation of beliefs.

Which brings us to a simple, if fairly narrow characterization of what we might call applied social epistemology, which is the study of *normative* questions about the *social* practices that are most likely to generate true or relevant beliefs. So, for example, we might ask, on what kinds of grounds should we assign positive evaluations to testimony? Under what kinds of conditions should we believe that what we read is true, or that what we're told is relevant?

OK, so far, we have a conception of social epistemology. We might also have at least an inkling of how that conception might be related to a certain conception of library and information science, given some common intuitions we might share about the goals of library service including support for the acquisition of knowledge. But before we look a little more carefully at that relationship, let's turn to the second of the three concepts mentioned in my title, which is *justice*.

Like truth and relevance, and other concepts like beauty and freedom, justice is a *value*—a more-or-less desirable feature of the outcomes of people's decisions and actions. The nature of justice has of course been the subject matter of a huge body of philosophical literature spanning ethics, social and political philosophy, and jurisprudence, with both descriptive and normative dimensions. Simplifying greatly, one theme that has attracted much attention is the idea of justice as *fairness*, with its corollary that the kinds of practices that generate states of justice most effectively are those in which people are treated fairly. Simply substituting "fairness" for "justice" does nothing to explain the concept or to suggest what kinds of criteria can be used to evaluate how fair or just a particular treatment might be. But typically justice is seen to be done when people are treated in accordance with their just deserts, on their merits or needs, without prejudice or bias or discrimination, without violation of their human rights, without limitation of their freedoms, and without the exercise of any form of oppression stemming from asymmetric power relations. Different theories of justice account for the relationships between notions of desert, merit, bias and so on in different ways.

In contrast to what we might call theories of *discriminatory* justice, theories of *distributive* justice focus on the outcomes of actions taken to distribute quantities of resources among the members of given populations. Theories of *social* justice, which may or may not simultaneously be theories of distributive justice, highlight the importance of individuals' identifying with certain groups—races, genders, and classes, for example—and of ensuring that such memberships are taken into appropriate account in any calculus of justice. Different theories of social justice work with different ideas about how "appropriateness" in accounting can be determined.

Theories of *epistemic* justice are special in the way that they focus on the fairness of our treatments of people in their capacity as believers and as knowers. These theories, too, may or may not be theories of distributive justice, depending on whether or not they suggest how quantities of what we might call epistemic resources, such as data or knowledge, or opportunities to access data, may be distributed fairly. Similarly, they may or may not be theories of social justice, depending on whether or not they emphasize people's affinities with social groups as factors to be weighed when determining the fairness of particular treatments.

Now, the interesting thing is, whereas the goal of social justice has, over the last decade or so, become quite a commonly articulated objective for the providers of library and information services, at least at the more activist or progressive end of the spectrum of views about the proper role of LIS institutions, the notion of epistemic justice has not been taken up by LIS scholars or practitioners to anything like the same degree. This is odd, I would argue, given the magnitude of the overlap that may be discerned in the respective concerns of LIS and epistemology, especially applied social epistemology.

To bolster this point, I'd like now to turn to the third concept on our agenda, which is *society* ... which gives us the chance to consider the role of library and information services in society just a touch more carefully. Many of us in LIS education avow a commitment to social justice in *distributive* terms, which means that in general our goal is to change the world in ways that include (1) reducing divides, disparities, and inequalities between rich and poor, and between powerful and powerless, (2) generating fairer distributions of social, cultural, economic, and political opportunities, and (3) building and maintaining thriving communities in which basic human rights and freedoms are respected.

Translating that specifically into a vision of the future of library and information services, we say that we are working towards a society (1) where members of all social groups enjoy equitable access to the knowledge they need to get their jobs done and live their lives to the full, (2) where everyone, not just an elite minority, is empowered to preserve their own artifacts and stories and ideas, in the ways they wish, and to the extent they wish, and (3) where the actions of governments and corporations respect the rights of individuals and communities to intellectual freedom, to privacy, and to cultural property.

Yet, to focus on distributive social justice alone would be to ignore one of the most prevalent kinds of injustice in our society, which is that caused by the systemic *oppression* of, or discrimination against, specific social groups. Iris Marion Young distinguishes between what she calls the "five faces of oppression," pointing out that injustice is manifested as *exploitation*, whenever labor is divided in such a way that women work specifically in order to maintain the power, wealth, and status of men; as *marginalization* whenever those who are old, or young, or poor, or disabled, or otherwise dependent on others, are thereby deprived of basic rights and freedoms; as *powerlessness* whenever working-class people find that they are unable to participate in making the decisions that have the greatest effect on their lives; as *cultural imperialism* when the very means of interpretation, expression, and communication in our society are so completely controlled by white Christian heterosexual men that the experiences and values of nondominant groups are rendered invisible; and as *violence* when we choose to tolerate the fact of black people living their lives under the constant threat of harassment, intimidation, and physical violence simply on account of their group identity.

Working towards social justice as a goal therefore involves the basic reform of oppressive, discriminatory social practices and institutions, as well as the redistribution of resources. Among those practices and institutions are those by whose means we produce and consume knowledge—the practices and institutions, in other words, of library and information services.

So here we've reached the crux of my argument today. I want to advocate for the recognition of *epistemic* justice as the principal goal of library and information service. The pursuit of social justice is incontrovertibly laudable, but to present it as the primary end to which library and information service is directed is to undermine the unique character of such service. That unique character is captured in the idea that the librarian's mission is to provide access to the world's recorded knowledge: in other words, to support us in our acquisition of true beliefs. And access to knowledge is optimized under conditions of minimal epistemic *in*justice.

Miranda Fricker distinguishes between two kinds of epistemic injustice, discriminatory and distributive. *Distributive* injustice occurs whenever epistemic resources, "goods such as education or information," are distributed unfairly. *Discriminatory* injustice, which she might just as well have called oppressive injustice, occurs whenever wrong is done to an individual either as a testifier or as a sensemaker—that is, either as a potential source of evidence, or as a potential acquirer of true belief. *Testimonial* injustice happens "when a speaker receives a deficit of credibility owing to the operation of prejudice in the hearer's judgment" (and Fricker gives the example of a police officer not believing the testimony of a young black male), whereas *hermeneutical* injustice happens "when a subject who is hermeneutically marginalized (that is, they belong to a group which does not have access to equal participation in the generation of social meanings) is thereby put at an unfair disadvantage when it comes to making sense of a significant area of their social experience" (and Fricker gives the example of a female victim of domestic violence unable to process the reality of their situation).

So now I'd like to conclude by mentioning a few ways in which my preceding remarks point to a potentially innovative mode of *critical* library and information science.

Firstly, we have the identification of epistemic justice rather than social justice as a goal that is specific to the library and information profession. This also serves as a timely clarification of the nature of the relationship of applied social epistemology to LIS. Using Fricker's terminology, we've suggested how the goals of library and information service may be viewed as the result of applying the normative theory of a particular flavor of social epistemology.

Secondly, we have an opportunity to articulate a *right to be believed*, a right to testimonial justice, to set alongside the rights to free thought and free expression that are already encapsulated in the UN's Universal Declaration of Human Rights and in IFLA's Code of ethics for librarians and information workers.

Thirdly, we may have an opportunity to proclaim a *veritistic* turn, in the course of which the centrality of epistemological concerns to LIS is recognized, and truth supplants relevance as a core value. Given the historical attachment of LIS to relevance-oriented service, the influence of postmodernist denials of the possibility of objective knowledge, and the maintenance in IFLA's Code (among many others) of a statement of librarians' commitment to "neutrality," perhaps this is the most controversial of conclusions? Then again, in the era of Trump, fake news, and "alternative facts," maybe it's to be welcomed.

Once again simplifying greatly, it seems to me that it's possible to distinguish between relevance-oriented and truth-oriented characterizations of the mission of the librarian, along the same lines on which we earlier differentiated between two families of theories of belief. Relevance-oriented librarianship is that which seeks to evaluate its practices, institutions, and products on the basis of the extent to which the desires of library users are satisfied. Truth-oriented librarianship is evaluated on the basis of the extent to which the beliefs acquired by library users are true.

You might say, well this is just a manifestation of the age-old debate between the "give them what they say they want" brigade and the "give them what we think they need" faction. Not quite. I suggest that the most critical task facing LIS theorists today is to recognize the moral emptiness of *both* of those positions and provide a justification for a librarianship that is consistent with contemporary, pluralist conceptions of truth.

References

Coady, C. A. J. 1992. *Testimony: A philosophical study*. Oxford: Oxford University Press.

Craig, Edward. 1990. *Knowledge and the state of nature*. Oxford: Oxford University Press.

Fricker, Miranda. 2007. *Epistemic injustice: Power and the ethics of unknowing*. Oxford: Oxford University Press.

———. 2013. "Epistemic justice as a condition of political freedom?" *Synthese* 190, no. 7: 1317–32.

Goldman, Alvin I. 1999. *Knowledge in a social world*. Oxford: Oxford University Press.

International Federation of Library Associations and Institutions. 2012. *IFLA Code of Ethics for Librarians and Information Workers*. The Hague: IFLA. https://www.ifla.org/publications/node/11092.

Roberts, Sarah T., and Safiya Umoja Noble. 2016. "Empowered to name, inspired to act: Social responsibility and diversity as calls to action in the LIS context." *Library Trends* 64, no. 3: 512–32.

United Nations. General Assembly. 1948. *The Universal Declaration of Human Rights*. Paris: UN. http://www.un.org/en/universal-declaration-human-rights/.

Young, Iris Marion. 1990. "Five faces of oppression." In *Justice and the politics of difference*, 39–65. Princeton, NJ: Princeton University Press.

B
Philosophy of information

7
The Snowman of Jenna

October 11, 2011

This talk[1] was given at ASIS&T 2011: 74th Annual Meeting of the American Society for Information Science and Technology (New Orleans, LA, October 9–12, 2011) as part of the panel session on "Metatheoretical snowmen II." The chair was Jenna Hartel; speakers were Marcia J. Bates, Nicholas Belkin, Jonathan Furner, Michael Olsson, and Soo Young Rieh; and discussant was Andrew Dillon. The talk was a revised version of one called "Philosophical analysis as an approach to information studies" given at CoLIS 2010: 7th International Conference on Conceptions of Library and Information Science (London, England, June 21–24, 2010) as part of the panel session on "Metatheoretical snowmen." The chair there was Jenna Hartel; speakers were Birger Hjørland, Jonathan Furner, Jens-Erik Mai, Ross Todd, and Siobhan Stevenson; and discussant was Steve Fuller.

Did you ever hear about the Snowman of Jenna? Wasn't he the one who led a very uncertain kind of life, a life of existential torment, in which he never quite managed to clarify to his personal satisfaction precisely in what his snowmanity consisted?

For did he not have cousins in Denmark who weren't even made out of snow?

---

1 See slides at https://litwinbooks.com/books/information-studies-and-other-provocations/.

And wasn't he the one who never quite understood precisely where *he* stopped and the rest of the snow began? For did not the wind continuously add particles to and take particles away from his body in a frighteningly arbitrary manner?

And wasn't he the one who could never come to terms with the idea that he could possibly cease to be?

For, as surely was his fate, would he not gradually melt, until some point in the future when the Snow-Gods would fashion new snowmen out of the very stuff of snowmen past?

In fact, wasn't he the one who counted among his closest peers not just the Ship of Theseus, but the Temple of the Golden Pavilion, Menudo, and George Washington's Axe, which had had three new handles and two new heads?

What can be said about the Snowman of Jenna, and about the reality that is the context *both* for the Snowman of Jenna himself and for whatever can be said about him? Can we at least assume that he is cold, whether he feels it or not? What if we said that "The Snowman of Jenna is cold"? Would we be talking *about* the Snowman of Jenna? In other words, would it be appropriate to say that the *subject* of that utterance or sentence or proposition (or document, or text, or work) is the Snowman of Jenna?

Well, what do we really mean when we say that a given sentence s is *about* a given thing z? For one thing, what *kind* of thing is subject z? Is sentence s literally about the Snowman of Jenna, the actual snowman that exists in space-time? Or is it about some *idea* or concept of the Snowman of Jenna? Or is it about the *name* "Snowman of Jenna" that is used to refer either to the actual Snowman of Jenna or to a concept of the Snowman of Jenna?

Meanwhile, is the Snowman of Jenna (actual or conceptual or linguistic) the *only* thing that sentence s is about? Or is it possible that sentence s is simultaneously about coldness, or cold things in general? Could it simultaneously be about the class of *non*-cold things (because sentence s_1, "The Snowman of Jenna is cold," is logically equivalent to sentence s_2, "Non-cold things are non-Snowmen of Jenna")? Wouldn't that mean that sentence s, like *every* sentence, is about *everything*?

Even more generally, what constitutes information for the Snowman of Jenna? Is the expression "The Snowman of Jenna is cold" an instance of data, or an instance of semantic information, or an instance of factual information?

Or, looking at it a slightly different way, is the expression "The Snowman of Jenna is cold" an instance of encoded, embodied, experienced, enacted, expressed, embedded, or recorded information? Or an instance of Information 1 or Information 2? And how can we tell without asking Marcia?

Or, looking at it a slightly different way again, does it make sense to distinguish between the *work* constituted by the proposition *p* that the Snowman of Jenna is cold, the *text* constituted by the English sentence *s* "The Snowman of Jenna is cold," and the *item* constituted by any utterance of that English sentence? Which of these classes of phenomena is the one whose instances have *subjects*? And are those subjects themselves items, texts, or works, or are they instances of some other class of phenomena?

What if our starting point were the Snowman of Jenna *himself*, rather than the proposition that he is cold? Isn't the Snowman of Jenna, like the legendary Antelope of Suzanne, a document? Then wherein lies *his* itemhood, his texthood, his workhood? And can we say that *he*, rather than any depiction or representation of him, has subjects? Or are those subjects properties of the *contexts* in which he is represented rather than properties of the snowman himself?

Now, doesn't all this just go to show …

… that it is precisely by taking a philosophical approach to the study of information that we are able to evaluate metatheories, that we are able to identify the very criteria that we may use to choose among them, that we are able to choose among the very criteria that we may use to judge this very competition?

And doesn't all this just go to show …

… that we can do philosophy of information in our heads, while we sit in our comfy chairs, rather than having to go out into the cold and wet? Isn't that rather fantastic?

And, most urgently, will Jonathan ever answer any of these questions?

8
Information, evidence, and recommendation

November 20, 2002

This talk was given at ASIS&T 2002: 65th Annual Meeting of the American Society for Information Science and Technology: Information, connections, and community (Philadelphia, PA, November 18–21, 2002), as part of a panel session on "Conceptions of information as evidence." The panel chair was Jonathan Furner, and speakers were Jack Andersen, Marcia J. Bates, Michael Buckland, and Jonathan Furner.

In this talk, I'd like to examine a particular conceptualization of "evidence," clarify the relationship between "evidence" and "information" that is implicit in such a conceptualization, and identify an assumption about the nature of information that is also implicitly made by holders of this view of evidence.

I'd then like to examine certain implications of this conceptual framework for our ideas about the nature of information. Specifically, I'll identify a number of aspects of information that typically are not considered in library and information science, but that are pushed to the foreground if we accept the view of information implicit in the common view of evidence. Secondly, I hope to establish a link between conceptions (in library and information science) of a distinction between information-as-thing and information-as-knowledge, and conceptions (in philosophy of language) of a distinction between proposition, statement, sentence, and utterance. I'll suggest furthermore that such a distinction maps fairly precisely to that between work, expression, manifestation, and item, proposed in IFLA's Functional Requirements for Bibliographic Records. And finally, I'd like to draw attention to the value of examining conceptualizations of evidence in this way for the design of information retrieval systems, which identify items for recommendation to the searcher on the basis of evidence of the worth of those items.

A conception of evidence

So, to begin, and in order to explain a conception of evidence that, in its barest outline, is common to several fields of inquiry, including the legal, historical, and scientific disciplines, I'm going to describe a pair of hypothetical situations.

The first of these is a situation also described by both Hacking and Schum, in which you are asked to imagine that you are living in an apartment block where pets are not allowed. You suspect, however, that your neighbor is keeping a dog. You have not seen a dog in your neighbor's apartment, but when you have been in their apartment, you have noticed an opened can of dog food on the kitchen counter, and what appear to be dog hairs on the sofa. You have also heard, at night, barks coming from the direction of your neighbor's apartment. In other words, you might say you have evidence that your neighbor keeps a dog.

The second situation is one in which you are asked to imagine that you are working as the doorperson of a nightclub where alcohol is served. You suspect that one of the people attempting to enter the club is under the drinking age of 21. You inspect the driver's license that this person gives you, and you notice that the birthdate stated on the license is more than 21 years ago. You admit this person into the club, since (you might say) you have evidence that they are over the age of 21.

Premises and conclusions

We can view this conclusion that we draw from the evidence as a proposition p_1 expressible in the form "x is a"—for example, as the proposition that, at a given time and location, your neighbor is a dog-keeper, or that the clubber is over the age of 21.

Similarly, we can view each piece of evidence, or premise, as a proposition p_2 expressible in the form "y is b"—for example, the proposition that, at a given time and location, a dog is barking, or that a person was born.

Propositions, events, and records

Propositions have truth-value. A proposition may be evaluated as being either true or false. There is some controversy about the nature of truth, but let's assume for the sake of argument that we agree on a particular conception of truth—for example, the idea that the truth-value of a proposition depends on whether or not it corresponds to reality. (Of course, acceptance of this definition holds us in the first place to evaluating as true the proposition that reality exists, but we'll skip over that today.)

Another way of talking about the correspondence of a proposition to reality is to talk about the accuracy with which the proposition represents the occurrence of an actual event. In our hypothetical situation, proposition p_1 may be viewed as a representation of an event e_1, and p_2 as a representation of an event e_2.

Such representations are abstract or mental; it is not necessary that they have physical form. If a proposition is expressed at a particular time and location by a particular person, in the form of a spoken or written statement, that event may be represented in physical form as a record.

Evaluating the truth of a conclusion

Let's suppose that you wish to evaluate or judge the truth of p_1. Is your neighbor a dog-keeper, or not? According to one common theory of evidence, it is possible, in principle, to calculate the *probability* that a "rational" person will evaluate a conclusion to be true — or alternatively the degree of *certainty* with which a rational judge may evaluate the truth of a conclusion—by examining the premises that are entertained by that judge. (Note the assumption of rationality on the part of the judge.)

The degree of certainty that a rational judge has in evaluating the truth of a conclusion p_1 is assumed to depend on two things:

- Partly, it depends on the degree of relevance that the judge perceives each p_2 to have to p_1. For instance, in the hypothetical situation about the dog, it may seem to you that p_1 is a necessary condition of p_2, and thus that p_2 entails p_1. In that case, we may say that, for you, p_2 is highly relevant to p_1. Alternatively, you may believe that it is possible, for instance, that your neighbor has a friend who visits him, often at night, together with that friend's dog — in which case, you might perceive p_2 as being less relevant to p_1. Of course, there are many other propositions, such as the proposition that the sky is blue, that you may perceive as having no relevance at all to p_1, since your evaluation of those propositions' truth has no bearing on your evaluation of the truth of p_1. Similarly, in the hypothetical situation about the club, it may seem to you that p_2 entails p_1. But you might instead believe that it is possible, for instance, that the license being offered to you does not belong to the person offering it, but to an older person—in which case, you might perceive p_2 as being less relevant to p_1.

- The degree of certainty that a rational judge has in evaluating the truth of p_1 is assumed also partly to depend on the degree of certainty with which the judge evaluates the truth of each p_2.

Before we start worrying that, by identifying this latter dependency, we are locking ourselves into a never-ending cycle of having to establish the relevance of a p_3 to a p_2, and of a p_4 to a p_3, we need to understand the idea of *admissibility*, and recognize that, in many practical situations, only propositions of certain kinds—specifically, those that have been stated in a certain way—are admissible as evidence.

In the law, for example, a proposition p_2 is admissible as evidence if it has been stated, either in speech or in writing, by a person who claims to have been a direct witness to the event e_2 (of which p_2 is a representation).

As I noted earlier, the event of making such a statement may be represented in physical form as a record. In the first case, if you were particularly aggrieved by the barking, we might imagine your making a written statement to the police, and this statement would be the record of p_2; in the second case, the license is the record of p_2.

Evaluating the truth of a record

As judges, we may evaluate the truth of a *record* in either or both of two senses.

- Firstly, we may evaluate the truth of the *propositions stated in the record*. For instance, we may ask: Is it true that a dog barked (at time t_1 and location l_1)? Is it true that the person named on the license was born at time t_1 and location l_1?

  Our evaluation of the truth of these propositions will depend primarily on our evaluation of the *trustworthiness* (i.e., *credibility* or *reliability*) of the *speaker*. (In the first case, the speaker is you; in the second case, the speaker is the person whose photo appears on the license.) Did the speaker actually witness the event—the dog's barking at a particular time, or the speaker's being born on a particular date—that they claim to have witnessed? We might choose to infer an answer to this question from the evidence that would be supplied by a historical record of the speaker's prior performance at truth-telling. Does the speaker normally not lie? Even when the speaker's intention has been to tell the truth, have they actually told the truth?

- Secondly, we may evaluate the truth of the *record qua record*—that is, as an accurate representation of statements. For instance, we may ask: Is it true that "A dog barked" was stated (by speaker s_2 at time t_2 and location l_2)? Is it true that "My date of birth is 10/10/80" was stated (by speaker s_2 at time t_2 and location l_2)?

  Our evaluation of the accuracy of these representations will depend partly on our evaluation of the *trustworthiness* (i.e., credibility or reliability) of the *witness* to the statement. (In the first case, the witness to the statement is the police officer. In the second case, the witness to the statement is the DMV officer.) If the record-creator claims to have directly witnessed the event—the statement—in question, are they telling the truth? What is their prior truth-telling performance like? If the record-creator claims merely to certify or authorize such a claim (i.e., the claim to have witnessed a statement) originally made by a third party, on what basis does this certification or authorization rest? What is the prior truth-telling performance of that third party?

  Our evaluation of the truth of the record qua record will also depend partly on our evaluation of the *authenticity* of the record. Did the record originate in the manner that is claimed for it in its associated metadata? Has the procedure that produces the metadata been certified by a witness to that procedure? How authoritative is that witness? In the second case, for example, we may ask whether the license was indeed produced by the DMV, and remains untampered with. Moreover, if the record is a copy of an original, is it a true copy in the sense of being identical in content to the original? Has the procedure that produces the copy been certified by a witness to that procedure? How authoritative is that witness?

Our evaluation of the truth of a record's content and the accuracy of its representation of statements—based on our evaluation of its authenticity and the reliability of both speaker and record-creator—all these assessments have a bearing on the likelihood with which a rational judge will determine a conclusion relevant to the premises contained in a record to be true.

Evidence: Definition and characteristics

What, then, is evidence? We might propose a definition, and identify some important features of evidence and of the process of evaluating evidence, as follows.

If, in an argument, a proposition is treated as a premise for another proposition treated as a conclusion, and if evaluating the premise as true increases the probability that a rational judge will evaluate the conclusion as true, then we can say that the premise is evidence for the conclusion.

Some important features of evidence are these.

Evidence is propositional.	Propositions are what we examine when we evaluate evidence.
Evidence is relational.	Evidentiariness—the property of being evidence—is not inherent in individual propositions, but is a property of pairs of propositions. We can't say that a particular proposition is always evidence; its evidentiariness derives from its use as the premise in an argument. Evidence, in other words, is a relationship—like relevance.
Evidence is inferential.	Making the claim that there is indeed an evidentiary relationship between a pair of propositions is a step in a process of

	reasoning, inference, or argument. The function of this step—our goal in taking this step—is to persuade, to convince the listener of the truth of our conclusion.
Evidence is truth-revealing.	We're concerned about evidence because we're concerned about truth. The reason we evaluate evidence is to determine the truth of a conclusion. Our goal is to determine what actually happened.
Evidence is quantitative.	Evidence is a quantitative property. We can talk about the strength or amount of evidence for a particular conclusion. We can talk about weighing or evaluating the evidence for a particular conclusion. We can talk about combining the evidence that multiple premises supply for a particular conclusion.
Evidence is probabilistic.	Evaluating evidence is a probabilistic process. Evaluating evidence allows us to establish the probability that a conclusion is true, given an estimation of the probability that a premise is true.

Information as evidence

How does this characterization of evidence affect our understanding of information?

The suggestion is sometimes made—in the archival-science literature, for instance—that one of the ways in which people use the term "information" is to mean something that has specifically evidentiary qualities. In other words, "information-as-evidence" is suggested as a category on a par, for example, with the categories of "information-as-thing" and "information-as-knowledge" familiar from Michael Buckland's work. Given our characterization of evidence, what are we to make of this?

The simplest interpretation involves looking to our assertion that evidence is propositional, and equating information with propositions—that is, with claims about the world. Then, just as we say that propositions have evidentiary value only when considered as premises for others, we might say that *information is potential evidence*, in that its evidentiariness depends on its usage in an argument.

How does this characterization relate to the categories of information-as-thing and information-as-knowledge, however? It might seem as if information-as-evidence exhibits the properties both of thing and of knowledge—as if, in other words, we might be able to distinguish information-as-evidence-as-thing (the physical record of a proposition) and information-as-evidence-as-knowledge (the proposition itself).

A distinction in philosophy of language

Here, a distinction commonly made in philosophy of language may prove helpful in illuminating these distinctions we have already made. This new distinction is that between proposition, statement, sentence, and utterance.

An example of an *utterance*, or sentence-token, is the individual, unique instance of the words "A dog is barking," spoken or written by a particular person at a particular time in a particular location. This utterance is an instance of a *sentence* (utterance-type) made up of a particular sequence of words in a particular language; which is in turn an instance of a *statement* (sentence-type) conveying a particular attitude toward a proposition; which is in turn an instance of a *proposition* (statement-type) about the world. Given the proposition that a dog is barking, many different statements indicating different degrees of belief in this proposition may be made; many different sentences, in many different languages, may be constructed to express each statement; and each of these sentences may be uttered on many different occasions.

This hierarchy of categories may be mapped not only against the information-as-thing / information-as-knowledge dichotomy, but also against the signal / message dichotomy familiar from information theory. The point is that any individual utterance or speech-act may be considered at any of four different levels—as a unique event, or as an instance of a sentence (signal, document/data, information-as-thing), statement, or proposition (message, content/meaning, information-as-knowledge).

A distinction in library science

Moreover, the same hierarchy of categories may be mapped directly against the four-fold hierarchy identified in IFLA's influential report on Functional Requirements for Bibliographic Records. We might consider that propositions are equivalent to FRBR's works, statements to expressions, sentences to manifestations, and utterances to items. In the FRBR model, works and expressions are purely abstract categories; manifestations and items are physical. An example of a *work* is that set of propositions which Shakespeare gave the title *Twelfth Night*; many different *expressions* of this work have been imagined by Shakespeare and other interpreters as scripts, performances, pieces of music, etc.; many different physical *manifestations* of each expression have been produced as books, plays and movies, sound-recordings, etc.; and many different copies of each manifestation are published as unique *items*.

Conclusion: Evidence theory and information retrieval

From another perspective, we might argue that, if we are to take our characterization of information-as-evidence seriously, we should attend to certain properties of information that are not always taken into account in explorations of the nature of information. We have suggested that evidence is propositional, relational, inferential, truth-revealing, quantitative, and probabilistic. Concern for some of these properties is explicitly avoided in information science. The truth-value of information, for example, is seldom considered in discussions of how information is created, stored, retrieved, transferred, and used; the means by which truth may be evaluated, and the effects of evaluating truth, are usually viewed as appropriate subject-matter for logic and epistemology, but not for information science.

Yet, the process that we have described—the process of evaluating the relevance of certain propositions to others, and of evaluating the truth of relevant premises in order to determine the truth of conclusions, and thus to persuade other people to accept those conclusions—this process would seem to be analogous in some important respects to the process, carried out by information retrieval systems, of recommending documents to information-seekers [Slide 14]. Maybe this is where evidence theory can really be, and in fact has been for many years, a helpful resource for information studies.

In *evidence theory*, a judge evaluates the probability that a conclusion is true, given an estimation of the probability that a premise is true, and of the degree of relevance of the premise to the conclusion. In *information retrieval*, a retrieval mechanism evaluates the probability that an as-yet-unretrieved document will be approved by an information-seeker, given an estimation of the degree to which a previously-retrieved document was approved by the information-seeker (or an estimation of the degree to which the seeker's query accurately represents the seeker's need), and an estimation of the degree of relatedness of the previously-retrieved document (or query) to the unretrieved document.

In *evidence theory*, the goal is to determine the likelihood that a rational judge will approve—that is, evaluate as true—a proposition. In *information retrieval*, the goal is to determine the likelihood that a rational judge will approve—that is, evaluate as retrieval-worthy—the set of propositions making up a document.

This conception of information retrieval is, of course, hardly original; research on probabilistic IR has been making advances since the early 1960s. But I suggest that there is still a need for those who seek to understand information-as-evidence to examine the substantial body of literature on the use in IR of Bayesian probability, inference networks, and techniques for combining evidence of document retrieval-worthiness from multiple sources. It's in the field of IR that the significance of the evidentiary properties of information has been appreciated for some time.

9
Response to Geoffrey Nunberg, "The informations"

February 9, 2012

This talk was a response to the keynote address, "The informations," given by Geoffrey Nunberg at iConference 2012: Culture | Design | Society (Toronto, Canada, February 7–10, 2012). The moderator was Brian Cantwell Smith. Nunberg's slides are available at http://people.ischool.berkeley.edu/~nunberg/IConfTalk2-8.pdf.

It's splendid, of course, to have a keynote that focuses so incisively on one of those questions that are so central and foundational to the work that we all do. It's a question that each of us has to grapple with sooner or later, but it's also one that we do frequently find one reason or another to save until later, or to leave to others—and this is the question of what it is that we're talking about when we talk about information.

So, from a presentation that was evidently replete with highlights, I believe it's my role very briefly to pick out a few talking points that I think are particularly interesting, and I'm going to do that and then move toward a single request for clarification, before opening up the question-and-answer period to the floor.

I love the title, by the way, "The informations,"—in itself, a critique not just of James Gleick, but of Martin Amis, and Beck, too—now there's a triumvirate to be reckoned with—but the implication is clear: To talk about "The information," singular, is both misguided and misleading. In the first place, there are several, if not many, senses in which this term is used, not just technical senses but multiple senses in ordinary language, too, and it is imperative, if we're not to talk past one another, to distinguish precisely and clearly among those senses.

In the second place, an important one of those senses is in several languages other than English assigned consistently to the plural form, so the potential for miscommunication seems like it might even be somewhat greater in English.

I think it's clear that one of the major contributions of Geoff's presentation is to demonstrate very effectively how illuminating and instructive it can be to take an approach to conceptual analysis that is essentially historical—a diachronic approach in which it is recognized that the relationships between senses (or concepts) and terms change over time. Words are trickling down and percolating up and circling around in complex ways and on a continuous basis. It's very difficult to take a snapshot of any part of the current structure, let only tell the whole story about how we got here. So it's a real treat and a surprise, I think, to learn that the sense that Geoff labels "information-s," "information-as-substance," has its origins not in the concept of propositional information as one might expect but in the separate "Bildung/education" sense.

Independently and secondly, it's important for us to be reminded that one of the drivers of change in the ways terms are ordinarily interpreted is ideology, and certainly that information is one of those words whose senses have been especially directly shaped by professional ideologies. In turn, one of the measures of success of the iSchools movement may actually turn out to be the degree to which it contributes to the hardening of one or other of those ideologies, so in a way we need to be very careful what we wish for. And we all have to thank not only Geoff, of course, but also our colleague Phil Agre for making these insights plain.

Thirdly, I love the comprehensive accounting of the candidate conditions for informationhood—propositionality, veridicality, informativeness, quantifiability, autonomy, fungibility. So much food for thought there. I do feel like, at the very least, my vocabulary has been very usefully enhanced.

And fourthly, I think Geoff is doing us all a great service in re-problematizing that tired old saw of the information pyramid that purports to distinguish among "data," "information," "knowledge," and "wisdom"—of all the textbook clichés, that has to be one of the least helpful, right? I have an idea that, given the concepts of "data" and "knowledge," we can actually do without "information" completely. But that doesn't go down too well in information science.

So now, my request for clarification has to do with the taxonomy of information concepts that Geoff is presenting here, and specifically with the basic distinction that's being made between propositional information and information-as-substance, which I understand in the past you've also labeled "information-in-the-mass" or "autonomous information" or "abstract information." My immediate reflex reaction to any such taxonomy, and maybe this is shared by others in the audience, is to try to map it to others that I already have some familiarity with, not necessarily because I think those others are any good, but just so that I can orient myself and get clear about the distinctive aspects of the new taxonomy. So, for example, I might start thinking about Michael Buckland's information-as-thing and information-as-knowledge; Marcia Bates' Information 1 and Information 2; Luciano Floridi's semantic information and factual information; and maybe even Karl Popper's World 2 and World 3, or Bertie Brookes' version of them—and, of course, in each case those categories are just two of a larger number of categories identified by their respective authors, and there are important differences between the frameworks thereby established.

But there are several distinctions that do recur quite frequently from conceptual framework to conceptual framework. One is a distinction between signal and message, container and content, document and text, vehicle and meaning, sentence and proposition, term and concept even. Another is a distinction between type and token, or universal and particular. And then there are others, emphasized sometimes to a greater, sometimes to a lesser extent, between recorded and ephemeral, public and private, published and unpublished, concrete and abstract, objective and subjective, linguistic and mental, material and immaterial, true and false.

So, I'm looking at information-p and information-s, and I'm thinking, okay, so information-p is whatever is expressive of propositions, or more broadly representations, or maybe it's those propositions or representations themselves; and information-s is whatever is expressive of propositions or representations that happens to also have been recorded in documentary form.

Now, you say that information-p is different in kind from information-s—it can't be that the universal set of instances of information-s is simply a subset of the universal set of instances of information-p. So I'm inclined to think of information-p as what is expressed by information-s. But then some of the characteristics of information-as-substance are propositional. So I've got the nagging feeling that I'm missing something really important. It may have something to do with the way in which the distinction between data, information, knowledge, and wisdom doesn't make a lot of sense, but I can't put my finger on it. So maybe you can help me out. Basically I'm wondering about the ontological status of information-p and information-s. I guess to turn this into a concrete question would mean my asking questions about both information-p and information-s, and starting with something like, is an instance of information-p or information-s something that *is* propositional or representational or semantic content, or is it something that *has* propositional or representational or semantic content? Geoff, what do you think? If that's a blind alley, just put me out of my misery.

10
Informatism and informatology

March 27, 2018

This talk was given at iConference 2018: Transforming Digital Worlds (Sheffield, England, March 25–28, 2018) as part of a panel on "Curators of the infosphere: What's the good of the philosophy of information for library and information science (and vice versa)?" The panel chair was David Bawden, and speakers were Luciano Floridi, Jonathan Furner, Ken Herold, Lyn Robinson, and Betsy Van der Veer Martens.

Sometimes it's suggested not just that LIS can learn from PI, but that in fact PI can serve as a theoretical foundation for LIS, and it's that strong version of the claim that there's a productive relationship between PI and LIS that I'd like to focus on. What I'd like to do in the next few minutes is try to clear up a misunderstanding that has the potential to derail conversations about PI as a theoretical foundation for LIS.

That such a misunderstanding is possible is the result, I think, of a situation that may be summarized as follows.

- Firstly, there's a difference between (what I'm going to call) Isms and (what I'm going to call) Ologies.
- Secondly, Luciano Floridi's upper-case PI is an instance of an Ism; instead of calling it upper-case PI, we might conceivably refer to it as informatism, or something like that.

- Thirdly, there's a danger, when we ask the question "Is informatism the best theoretical foundation for LIS?" that we make the category error of treating informatism as an instance of an Ology rather than as an instance of an Ism, with unfortunate consequences.

So, what is the essential difference between Isms and Ologies? Well, it's very simple.

An Ology is a branch of philosophy in which fundamental questions raised in a specific, more-or-less well-defined area of shared concern are studied. Examples are ontology, epistemology, and axiology, and also philosophy of language, philosophy of mind, and "lower-case" philosophy of information—what we might call informatology.

An Ism is a particular set of assumptions, arguments, and claims about answers to the fundamental questions raised in a specific area of shared concern. Examples are realism, idealism, and "upper-case" Philosophy of Information—what we might call informatism.

When we ask a question of the form "Is X the best theoretical foundation for Y?" we need to clarify whether we're asking about an Ism or an Ology. Is Informatism the best Ology for LIS? Is Informatology the best Ism for LIS? Neither of those questions makes sense. We'd be committing a category error if we asked either of those.

The two questions that do make sense are: Is Informatology the best Ology for LIS? And is Informatism the best Ism for LIS? I think that there's a relatively straightforward way of answering the first of these, but that it's not so obvious how to answer the second.

What criteria could we use to judge how good an Ology informatology—lower-case PI—is for LIS? I suggest that the primary criterion is simply the degree of overlap between the areas of concern. Is information the main topic of concern for LIS? Is it the main topic of concern for lower-case PI? If we answer "Yes" to both questions, then we're well on the way to making a case for lower-case PI as an appropriate, if not "the best" Ology for LIS.

My personal view is that, in fact, information is not the main topic of concern for LIS. Topics such as collection, preservation, and access are more important to LIS than information is. (These all happen to be intentional activities, by the way, carried out by people, interacting with one another and continuously making choices about how to act.) Even if it's the case that, when we talk about PI, we're talking about lower-case PI as a branch of philosophy, I don't think we should be looking primarily to that branch of philosophy to learn more about the theoretical foundations of LIS.

What about the question of whether Informatism—upper-case philosophy of information—is the best Ism for LIS? Again, what criteria could we use to judge how good an Ism upper-case PI is for LIS? Remember that I'm defining an Ism as a set of assumptions, arguments, and claims. How do we normally evaluate assumptions, arguments, and claims? Variously, by their correspondence with external reality; by their internal coherence and simplicity, their soundness and validity; by their practical utility or productivity; and so on.

My view is that it makes most sense to ask about the value of an Ism for an area of inquiry like LIS if the criterion we have in mind is the last of these: Utility (however that may be operationalized). For example, we might be tempted to compare the utility for LIS of the set of assumptions, arguments, and claims that make up upper-case PI with that of Egan's Social Epistemology (i.e., upper-case SE) or Brookes' Fundamental Equation of Information Science. Which is something that David Bawden and Lyn Robinson and others have done very well. I have three further remarks on efforts of this kind.

One is that all three of these Isms—Egan's, Brookes', and Floridi's—have, to different extents, received disproportionate attention on account of their authors' explicit, self-conscious identification and naming of their Ism. Many other authors (and Patrick Wilson, Seymour Lubetzky, and Elaine Svenonius come to mind, and that's just late-twentieth-century California) have constructed Isms of comparable power and interest, and we can move forward with the comparative evaluation of Floridi's PI only to the extent we're able to broaden the scope of that inquiry.

My second comment has to do with the complexity of all these Isms. They are aggregates of assumptions, arguments, and claims, often spanning multiple Ologies—ontology, epistemology, axiology, and so on. It can be difficult to compare Isms without analysis, without breaking them down into their components. We might look at Floridi's PI, for example, focus on its ontological claim about the nature of information, and evaluate that small part of the whole structure, without necessarily committing ourselves either way to any of the rest of that structure.

Once we start taking this analytical approach, we quickly realize that our work in LIS already has theoretical foundations. It's just that those foundations are unacknowledged, unexpressed. In LIS, we need to do a better job of making our own Isms more explicit. Any Ism like upper-case PI is most useful, not as a sort of package that we can choose to take off the shelf and plug in or not, but to the extent that it helps us become more aware of the assumptions that we actually make when we do our own work.

My third and final comment has to do with the ethical aspect of PI—what we might call upper-case Information Ethics. Many of us find at least some of the moral principles that are derivable from PI to our liking. But we need to be careful not to use the fact that PI produces acceptable moral principles as a justification for PI—because there may be other sets of assumptions, other Isms, from which the same moral principles are derivable. For example, take the idea of a duty to preserve cultural heritage. PI derives such an idea from the idea that artifacts have rights to persistence. But we can imagine an alternative Ism that proposes instead that future generations have rights to the use of resources produced by past generations. Different assumptions, same result. Just because we like IE doesn't necessarily mean that we should accept PI.

11
Interrogating "identity": A philosophical approach to an enduring issue in knowledge organization

August 6, 2008

This talk was given as the keynote at ISKO 2008: 10th International Conference of the International Society for Knowledge Organization (Montréal, Canada, August 5–8, 2008), and was published in slightly different form in **Knowledge Organization** *36, no. 1 (2009): 3–16.*

The motivation for choosing today's topic is the theme of the conference, which is "Culture and identity in knowledge organization." One claim that's implicit in that choice of theme is that there is an issue, or maybe a number of issues, to do with identity, that impact the goals of knowledge organization (KO) researchers or the results of their work. I'm going to take the liberty today of suggesting one way in which that claim may be interpreted.

Which is that the primary issue is one of *evaluation*. There is a strong claim there that you may or may not agree with, and I'll do a little more to argue for it later. The strong claim is that, ultimately, as KO researchers, it's our responsibility to figure out how to build KO systems that work *well*. And to figure out how best to *go about* determining how well KO systems work.

Anyway, in this context, the issue is specifically one of evaluating how KO systems do at handling *identity*. Now, as we shall see, there are many ways in which that word "identity" may be understood, and part of the challenge is untangling all those different senses in which the word may be used. But there are two things we can do immediately to clarify certain aspects of the issue.

One of those is to specify that when we talk about how well KO systems deal with identity, we're really talking about one in particular of the functions of KO systems, which is that of *representation*. KO schemes are representations or models of reality. We may disagree vehemently about what things, or what kinds of things, count as real things; but I would be surprised to encounter a conception of KO schemes that doesn't include the representational function as a necessary condition for being a KO scheme. So, the question becomes: How well do KO systems represent identity?

Secondly, and I'll have a lot more to say about this later, there seems to be an important sense in which we can distinguish between identity singular and identities plural. On the face of it, even though the situation turns out to be a little more complicated than this, it seems as if there's a distinction to be made between identity as a relation between things, in the sense in which something might be said to be identical with or the same as something, and identities as properties of things, in the sense in which something might be said to have a particular identity.

There appears to be a way of breaking down the basic question, How well do KO systems represent identity?, into two separate questions that correspond respectively to senses of identity as relation and identity as property.

In the first place, we might ask, How well do KO systems represent relationships of identity between classes of documents? And how well do KO systems help indexers *and* searchers explore those relationships?

In the second place, we might ask, How well do KO systems help indexers, classifiers, catalogers organize knowledge about the personal or social identities of members of social groups? How well do KO systems help people find the right labels for classes of documents that are about those identities, and help people find those documents?

Even though both of these kinds of question are about identity, they are often treated quite separately in the KO literature. Sometimes the relationship between them is emphasized, but certainly not always. One of the objectives of this talk is to demonstrate that it is at least somewhat helpful to emphasize the relationship by considering the two questions in tandem. And a subsidiary objective is to show that it's at least possible, if not desirable, to do this using a conceptual framework that looks to philosophy on the one hand, and information retrieval on the other, for inspiration.

The primary objective, though, is to defend a series of related propositions. These are as follows:

- firstly, that identity is analyzable in a way that can inform our decisions about how to analyze two other relations that have historically been considered very important in KO, and they are aboutness and relevance;

- secondly, that the *production* of identity, in a sense that I'll explain later, could usefully be considered to be the ultimate goal of KO;

- thirdly, that achieving the effective representation in KO systems of personal and social identities is a complex special case of a general challenge facing some traditional KO techniques; and thus

- that the concept of identity is central to KO, possibly even more central than its selection as this particular conference's theme indicates.

Hopefully this will set the scene for some of the sessions that are coming up over the next few days that I know will be taking ideas about identity and identities in many more fascinating directions certainly than I'm capable of taking them.

On that note, just as an aside, my worry at this point is not so much that you might very well be thinking that this is all wrong or misguided. I actually see the task of any keynote as just being to *avoid* being boring-but-right. If it were boring-and-wrong, at least we'd have something to talk about. And interesting-but-wrong would be better still! I'm not sure that being interesting-and-right is an option for me at this point. Certainly, if you're looking for right answers, there are two people in particular I'd recommend turning to for guidance in that respect.

One of those, of course, would be Poly Styrene, singer in the late, lamented X-Ray Spex, who realized over 30 years ago that identity is the crisis. "Can't you see?" asked Ms. Styrene. "Identity! Identity." You can't argue with that.

And then, sharing the same haircut, there's Gottfried Leibniz, whose lyrics were a little more obtuse, but no less persuasive: "$\forall x \forall y[\forall P(Px \leftrightarrow Py) \rightarrow x=y]$." In other words, for all objects x and all objects y, if, for all properties P, x has P if and only if y has P, then x is identical to y. Can you argue with *that*? Well, maybe you can, actually. But that doesn't diminish Mr. Leibniz's genius nor, indeed, the luxuriance of his cascading locks.

Both Ms. Styrene and Mr. Leibniz were fans of a particular kind of philosophical approach to examining the pressing issues of their respective times. This is the approach that I'll be taking today, and it's one that involves analysis of the *concepts* that we use to talk about those issues. In my characterization of the main issue as one of determining how well KO systems do at representing identity, there are four core concepts, and if we had time I'd be looking closely at all four.

The sense of goodness I'm using here is just the sense in which some KO systems are good, some are bad, some are better than others, at doing certain things, and this is very similar to the sense in which María López-Huertas uses "quality" in her wonderful contribution to the latest issue of the journal *Knowledge Organization*, which I'm sure you've all seen, but if you haven't it's highly recommended. María explicitly identifies "quality" as something to aim for in the design of KO systems, and the implication is that evaluation of quality is an absolutely necessary component of the KO system design process.

So, first, to *identity* itself. The magnitude of the challenge here might be demonstrated simply by listing some of the kinds of identity that are dealt with in the various literatures. I did make some effort to be exhaustive with this listing, but I still have the feeling that this is really just the tip of the iceberg.

In the first place we have various conceptions of individual, personal, or self-identity, to be distinguished from various conceptions of group, collective, or social identity. We can distinguish the different kinds of identity defined in different domains of theory and practice, such as cultural, economic, and psychological identity. If we focus on personal and social identity, there are all sorts of dimensions on which different identities may be distinguished, so that we talk about racial, sexual, and linguistic identity, and so on. If we take a metaphysical or logical approach to identity, we find that it's possible to distinguish numerical and qualitative, relative and absolute, synchronic and diachronic identity.

And then there are a whole slew of related concepts. These aren't *kinds* of identity, so much as concepts whose meaning could usefully be clarified in any analysis of identity. There are concepts that seem to have very similar meanings to identity, such as sameness, identicality, similarity, and indiscernibility. And then there are concepts that seem to have sort of opposite meanings, such as individuality, uniqueness, distinctness, difference, and diversity. And then there are lots of things that can be done to and with and by and through identity and identities—including organization, classification, and categorization, of course. So, it's a conceptual minefield!

Even if we limit ourselves to looking at philosophical approaches to the study of identity, the literature is enormous and varied and scattered very widely. Different analytical approaches have been taken in philosophy of logic, metaphysics, social and political philosophy, philosophy of technology, and philosophy of art, as well as in what you might call philosophy of documentation or even philosophy of knowledge organization, although as far as I know there's not a soul who consistently uses those terms.

All right, let's go back to that basic distinction made earlier, between identity conceived as a relation and identity conceived as a property. Sometimes we talk about the identity of x and y; sometimes we talk about the identity of x. What's going on here?

Taking identity as a relation first. Here are definitions of two senses of identity. First of all, we say that object x and object y are *numerically* identical if x is the same object as y. Notice that it does sound a little odd if we say "two objects, x and y, are identical." Because in the case of identity, we don't have two objects. The whole point is, we just have one. In fact, more generally, we might say that x and y are identical if they are countable as one thing. This is why identity in this sense is sometimes known specifically as numerical identity.

Secondly, we can contrast numerical identity with qualitative indiscernibility. We say that x and y are qualitatively indiscernible if x has all and only the same properties as y. And here's some more terminology: If x is not the same object as y, then we say that x and y are numerically distinct or individual. And if x does *not* have *all and only* the same properties as y, then we say that x and y are qualitatively discernible or dissimilar.

So we've introduced two kinds of relation here: there are continuous relations and binary relations. Continuous relations are ones like indiscernibility and similarity, where we can happily talk about indiscernibility as a matter of degree. Two things can be more or less indiscernible, more or less similar. In contrast, binary relations are ones like numerical identity. Two things are either identical (in which case they're actually one thing) or they're not.

Now, here we come back to Leibniz's Law. This is what he said (in translation): "No two substances resemble each other entirely and differ in number alone." (Leibniz 1686, *Discourse on metaphysics*). From that, modern metaphysicians have derived two principles or theories, the principle of the identity of indiscernibles, and the principle of indiscernibility of identicals, which have mesmerized philosophy students for generations, and you know, I guess I was a philosophy student once, and I'd love to spend the rest of the week talking about this stuff but I rather doubt anyone else would share my enthusiasm. It would involve ps and qs as well as xs and ys. But the basic theory is that x and y are identical *if and only if* they share all and only the same properties, and vice versa.

Suffice to say, even though they look kind of reasonable, tautologous even, both of these principles have actually turned out to be fairly controversial. *Some* people argue that it *is* possible for two things to resemble each other entirely, thus denying the principle of the identity of indiscernibles; and *many* people argue that it is possible for x and y to be numerically identical but qualitatively discernible—for example, when x is me-before-this-talk, and y is me-after-it. Actually the problem of identity over time, diachronic identity, is a live one, and I'm sure everyone's familiar with the paradox of the ship of Theseus, you know, where Theseus's ship is in the harbor, and every day a single plank gets replaced, until after a few years not a single original plank remains. Is it still the ship of Theseus? And suppose meanwhile they've been building a new ship out of the replaced planks? Is *that* the ship of Theseus?

Now, I have to admit something. I thought, when I first started thinking about this talk, I thought, right, I get to talk about the identity of indiscernibles, and whether I'm the same person as I was yesterday, and the ship of Theseus and all that, and some grand theory of identity in knowledge organization will just emerge out of that. I've got to let you know that, well, no such grand theory emerged. At least,

I'm still thinking about it and maybe I'll get a chance to let you know when I'm done.

On the other hand, this is all excellent material for a discussion about identity conditions or identity criteria. The questions here are about two kinds of conditions, in fact. They're questions about the conditions under which x should be considered the *very same thing* as *y*, and about the conditions under which *x* should be considered an instance of the same *kind* of thing that *y* is an instance of. Or, if you like, criteria for *individuation*, and criteria for *instantiation*. Although that terminology isn't really standardized, it's clear that these are very different questions. And in fact they're questions that lots of people in KO and in the information sciences more generally are interested in because they're exactly the kinds of questions that need to be answered if we're going to do a good job of designing systems that can determine mechanically whether one document is an instance of the same work or class or kind or type as another document. Allen Renear and Richard Smiraglia and others, of course, are authorities in this area.

Some of Allen's work aims to establish identity conditions for digital objects and clarify, for instance, what it means to say that one version of an electronic document, such as its XML code, is an instance of "the same" document as another version, such as its rendering in a browser. This work has ramifications for Richard's studies of workhood, and what a FRBRized conception of the relations between works and expressions and manifestations and items means for attempts to specify identity conditions for works, where the main question is, given two items, how can we tell whether they're instances of the same work or of different works? As an aside, there's a school of thought that these kinds of problems are less problems of identity, as such, as they are problems of workhood, since different kinds of things are going to have different identity conditions, and the interesting thing about works is not *that* they have properties that serve as identity conditions, but whatever it is that those properties are, that literally define what it means to be a work.

Now, just as there are many different philosophical, rationalist approaches to the a priori study of identity, of course there are many psycho-socio-cultural approaches to the empirical study of identity, too. People working in developmental psychology, social psychology, cultural anthropology, cultural studies, and political science, as well as in social and political philosophy, have much to say about various aspects of personal and social identity, and these are themselves based on some fundamental assumptions about the metaphysical nature of identity, which actually turn out to be quite different from the ones we've just looked at, so it would be worth examining these even if it were just for the purposes of comparison.

Just to kick things off, here's a proposal of a primitive definition of personal identity. According to this definition, the identity of a person is the property or set of properties that a person has, that individuates that person, that distinguishes that person from another, or at least that instantiates that person, that identifies that person as an instance of the same kind of person that other persons are instances of, or as a member of the same social group that other persons are members of.

Here's a similar definition of social identity. According to this definition, the identify of a social group is the property or set of properties that a social group has, that identifies that group, that distinguishes that group from another.

Now, there are many different kinds, or facets if you like, of personal and social identity. Here's a non-exhaustive list of some that are considered important by different agents engaged in the process of identification at different times. I'm sure we could come up with many more. They're listed in alphabetical order. Because, who's to say which is more important than another?

age; ancestral territory; ancestry/genealogy; class; community; culture; discipline/field; ethnicity; family; gender; group; history; hobby/interest; home/birthplace; language; mental ability; mythical origin; nationality; organization/department; physical ability; political party; profession/occupation; race/phenotype; religion; sexual orientation; skin color; society; subculture.

So, maybe it will be clear by now that in this discourse, we've started to look at identity more as a property than as a relation. And there's an interesting thing that happens when we start to look at identity as a property rather than as a relation. There's a kind of inversion whereby identity is equated not with sameness but with the opposite of sameness, that is, with difference. Here, the idea is of identity as the property or set of properties that x has, in virtue of which it is different and thus distinguishable from y. In other words, the identity of x is whatever property that x has that makes x individual, that identifies it.

This basic idea of identity as what makes something individual is pretty simple right? But, well, it turns out we can make it quite complex if we want to.

And we might have good reason for wanting to conceive the identity of *x* as whatever it is that person *a* thinks is the property that makes *x* individual, or indeed whatever it is that person *b* (who may or may not be the same as person *a*) projects to others as an image of the property that person *a* thinks is the property that makes *x* individual, or whatever it is that person *c* (who may or may not be the same as person *b*) thinks is the image projected by person *b* of the property that person *a* thinks is the property that makes *x* individual … . Oh my goodness.

One thing that all this highlights is that the process of identification is an active process that is always the result of human intentionality and subjectivity. It's carried out by an agent on an object (where object here just means the object of the act).

And sometimes, very frequently in fact, the agent is the same person as the object. In which case, identification is a process of self-categorization, or affiliation with a particular group or category. By the way, it might be helpful to assume that, in this process, an agent acts more or less autonomously, that is, free of any *logical* constraints, in the sense that an individual is essentially free to choose whatever identity they want. From a human rights perspective, it could be argued that to be in that position of choice, to define one's identity in whatever way one wishes so long as the rights of others are not thereby infringed, is a basic human right.

The complexities don't end there. It seems as if there are at least eight dimensions on which we can simultaneously locate any given act of identification.

In the first place there's the degree of subjectivity assumed to be involved in any act of identification. For example, let's say the object of identification is me. We might allow that it's possible to talk meaningfully about what the identity of me actually, objectively is, about how I really am. We might deny that that's possible, even if we accept that there is a way in which I really am, because it's not clear how any one of us might be able to know how things really are. We might be most interested in talking about what most people think is the case. But then again we might be interested in talking about what one particular person (e.g., me) thinks is the case, or what that particular person thinks most people think is the case, or even what that particular person thinks another individual thinks is the case.

Secondly, we can distinguish between an act of identification whose object is a single thing, and one whose object is a collection or group made up of multiple things. Thirdly, we can distinguish between an act of identification whose object is a person or group of persons, and one whose object is not a person or group of persons. Fourthly, we can distinguish between an act of identification whose subject—the agent doing the identifying—is a single thing, and one whose subject is a collection or group made up of multiple things.

Fifthly: As we saw just now, we can look at the relation of the subject to the object. The agent who's doing the identifying—are they identifying their self, or something other? And sixthly, we can look at the power of the agent who's doing the identifying relative to that of the object. Is the subject in a position of domination over the object, or in a subordinate position?

Seventhly, an act of identification could be one in which one particular thing is distinguished from another particular thing, or it could be one in which one kind of thing is distinguished from another kind of thing. And eighthly, it could be one in which the identifying property is considered to be intrinsic to the object, or one in which the identifying property is considered to be extrinsic.

Different fields have different kinds of interest in personal and social identity, but it's possible to identify some general categories of empirical research questions that consistently attract cross-disciplinary attention. Such as, what kinds of processes are involved in individuals' affiliating with and prioritizing particular identities? What kinds of factors affect individuals' affiliating with and prioritizing particular identities? And in what ways and to what extents do individuals' affiliations with and prioritizations of particular identities affect the other kinds of decisions and actions taken by those individuals? And a large part of that third question relates to the kinds of decisions and actions that are taken that result in the representation, expression, or reflection of individuals' identity affiliations in symbolic form, in documents. The challenge for KO, as I'll have more to say about, is how to make sure that such expressions of identities are represented in KO systems in ways that serve the users of those systems.

Okay, so I'm done with identity for a bit, and now I'd like to say some more about the other three of the four core concepts that I mentioned earlier. Want a definition of KO? Look no further than Joe Tennis in the latest issue of the *KO* journal, who says that "KO … is the field of scholarship concerned with the design, study, and critique of the processes of organizing and representing documents that societies see as worthy of preserving." (Tennis 2008).

Here's another, slightly different take on a definition of KO—see what you think: KO is the practice (and the theory) of building KO systems that work well. Now, you might be thinking, well that's just circular. And I might say, What's wrong with circles, you anti-circulite? Actually, if we can get past the circularity problem, the point here is to make a point that's possibly a little more controversial than it might at first seem, which is that KO *systems* don't support KO: they're the product of KO.

So we seem to have two rival conceptions of KO: one that sees KO as a bunch of processes (organization, representation, and so on) that are ends in themselves (or the study of those processes), and another that sees KO as the means to a variety of ends, including not only retrieval and access and preservation but also learning and understanding and mapping and modeling. In practice, of course, the distinction between these two conceptions is fuzzy—it's more like there's a continuum of conceptions ranging between the two poles.

There are two central research questions in this KO. The first is the design question. How ought subjects, and the relations between them, to be represented in a KO system? The answer to this is, well, in whatever way that evaluations tell us is best. But then there's the evaluation question, which is, how do we evaluate? *How do we decide* how subjects, and the relations between them, ought to be represented in a KO system? Let's be clear about it—*this* is the big one. Answer that one, and everything follows.

I think it's possible to distinguish two conceptions of the goal of the practice of KO, and this distinction corresponds roughly to the one Raya Fidel (1994) draws between two conceptions of the goal of indexing. On the one hand, Raya says, we have the document-centered view that indexers should aim to assign index terms to documents (or documents to index terms) in whichever way it is that produces the most accurate representation of that content. On the other hand, there is the user-centered view that indexers should aim to associate documents with those terms that are most likely to be used by searchers looking for those documents.

Similarly, I think that, on the one hand, we have a *description-oriented* conception of the goal of KO, being to build systems that do well at helping people produce accurate descriptions and representations of documents. And on the other hand, we have a retrieval-oriented conception of the goal of KO, being to build systems that do well at helping people find the documents they think they want to find.

Looking more closely at the description-oriented conception first, we might see that it assumes that a necessary condition for a system doing well at helping indexers and classifiers produce accurate representations of documents is that the system itself incorporates an accurate representation of the universe of knowledge that can be used by indexers. We might choose to evaluate that representation or model by assessing how it stacks up against internal criteria like coherence, richness, simplicity, or elegance. But, more likely, we would choose to evaluate it by comparing it with the way things really are (or with the way somebody thinks things are), and seeing what the degree of correspondence or match is. That's how we would decide how "accurate" a representation is.

Let's just take a quick further look at that last criterion: "Correspondence with the way someone thinks things are." We need this criterion as an alternative to "Correspondence with the way things really are" because, even if there were a way in which things really are, nobody, not one of us, could have knowledge of it. This, of course, is an epistemological argument that has excited many people over the years, and we probably shouldn't get into it now, so I'm just going to assert that different people see reality in different ways, and draw the conclusion from that that every KO system is necessarily and unavoidably "biased," in the sense that every KO system reflects the view of reality of its designers.

Now, to say the least, this is a bit of a problem. Because we seem to be saying that it's impossible for any KO system either to simultaneously reflect the views of everybody, or even to simultaneously reflect the views of all of its users. Which is a bummer, because we'd rather like it *not* to be impossible. In fact, many of us would argue that, even if—actually, *especially* if—we accept this description-oriented conception of the goal of KO, then there's another very significant external criterion that should be brought into play when evaluating how well any KO system meets that goal. And that criterion is justice or fairness.

There are a number of rival conceptions of social justice—of what it means for any policy or action that affects the multiple members of any group to be evaluated as "just." One category of conceptions is called "communitarian."

If we apply a communitarian conception of social justice as a criterion for evaluating KO systems, then this is how it plays out. We can say that the just KO system is one that supports the distribution of cultural resources without violating the rights or liberties of particular groups or communities and their members—especially minorities and other groups that have historically been oppressed by the dominant groups in power. In other words, the just KO system is one that supports equitable access to an exhaustively comprehensive range of documents for all members of society, no matter what their motivations are (unless those motivations infringe upon the rights of others).

So a just KO system is what we wish for. Unfortunately, just because we know we want it, doesn't mean that it's possible to get it.

Now let's have a look at the retrieval-oriented conception of the goal of KO. Here the goal is conceived as one of helping users of KO systems—both indexers and searchers—improve the quality of their and other users' access to documents, and benefit from that access. In general, the criteria that we might use to evaluate KO practice might at first sight look quite different under this conception than the ones we looked at a couple of moments ago. This time it seems like we're not so concerned about correspondence with reality or internal coherence. We're more concerned with the degree to which KO practice produces KO systems that enable access to documents in an effective, efficient, and easy manner. These are criteria that have been examined every which way in tests of IR systems.

Effectiveness is usually highlighted as the most important of these retrieval-oriented criteria, and it's worth taking a closer look at the factors that have been identified in IR tests as the ones that have the greatest influence on levels of effectiveness. You wouldn't believe it, but, yes, there are two conceptions of the priority of these factors. There's an objectivist conception and a user-oriented conception.

In the objectivist conception, the factor that has the greatest influence on levels of retrieval effectiveness is the degree of correspondence between the model of reality constructed by the KO system designer, and reality itself.

Now, this is interesting. Because, even though we're adopting a retrieval-oriented conception of the goal of KO at this point, one that suggests that the best way to evaluate KO practice is to determine how well it produces KO systems that enable effective retrieval, we're now saying that the best way of ensuring effective retrieval is to make sure that the model of reality enshrined in the KO system is an accurate representation of reality. In effect, we'd be using the same criterion to evaluate KO as we did under the description-oriented conception of KO.

In the user-oriented conception of the priority of factors affecting retrieval effectiveness, the key factor is the degree of correspondence between the model of reality constructed by the KO system designer, and the mental model of the world that the KO user has, whether indexer or searcher. The idea is that, if there's any sort of mismatch between the way the world's represented by the KO system and the way the user expects it to be represented, then there's a problem. It doesn't make any difference how the world actually is: it's all about matching people's images of that world.

This is an idea that's very similar, of course, to the claim that indexing should only be evaluated on the basis of the extent to which the terms assigned to documents by indexers match those that are used by searchers for whom those documents are relevant. It doesn't make any difference what the documents are actually about—there isn't really a way in which it makes sense to say that a document is about anything in particular anyway—all that matters is that indexers are able to predict how searchers will describe documents.

Right. Remember what I said at the beginning about there being two conceptions of identity, one of identity as a relation between things, and another of identities as properties of things? We need to talk about relations in general. Yet another wonderful contribution to that special issue of *KO* makes it clear: "Relationships are at the very heart of knowledge organization," says Rebecca Green (2008). Absolutely. Now, there are two ways of distinguishing relations: either we can identify distinctive properties of the entities being related, or we can identify distinctive properties that are intrinsic to the relations themselves.

In the quaintly-named bibliographic universe, the one that we all visit from time to time, there are a number of different kinds of entities that are capable of entering into relations with one another. We might find it convenient to distinguish in some way between worlds, works, words, persons, and so on. (It doesn't really make much difference whether we decide to treat these entities as substances that somehow exist separate from their properties, or simply as bundles of properties.) Whatever system of fundamental categories of entities we settle on, we can also use it as the basis of a taxonomy of relations between entities. Depending on our purposes, we might want to distinguish relations between works and people from relations between works and other works, for instance.

Or, we could look at properties of the relations themselves, rather than properties of the entities being related. For instance, we could distinguish between kind/instance relations and whole/part relations, and so on. Lots of people have done this. Rebecca, of course, and Elaine Svenonius does a great job of this kind of analysis in her book.

So let's take a look at the relation of aboutness. It's quite simple, right? Say we have two documents, Doc 1 and Doc 2. If I decide that Doc 1 is about Subject A, what that amounts to is a judgment, an entirely subjective judgment made by me on a particular occasion, that Doc 1 has the property of being about Subject A, that Doc 1 is a member of the class of documents that share the property of being about Subject A, that Doc 1 instantiates Subject A—all those are different ways of saying exactly the same thing.

There are many different ways of modeling that relation, and there many different ways of visually depicting it, and we would use different modeling techniques depending on whether we were working within a philosophical framework, or a computer science framework, or a library and information science framework. We would come up with different models depending on whether we wanted to emphasize aboutness as a property, with subjects treated as attributes of documents, or aboutness as a relation, with subjects treated as classes of documents. But this diagram (Figure 11.1) tells the basic story. We can also say that Doc 1 and Doc 2 are similar in the sense that they share the same property or that they are members of the same class. Doc 1 and Doc 2 are not the same document, but they are the same kind of document.

Another thing we can say is that, if it turns out that Subject B has exactly the same extension as Subject A does—in other words, if it turns out that all and only the documents that are about Subject A are about Subject B—then we can say that Subject A is the same subject as Subject B. They're not just similar; they're identical. In fact, there's only one subject, not two.

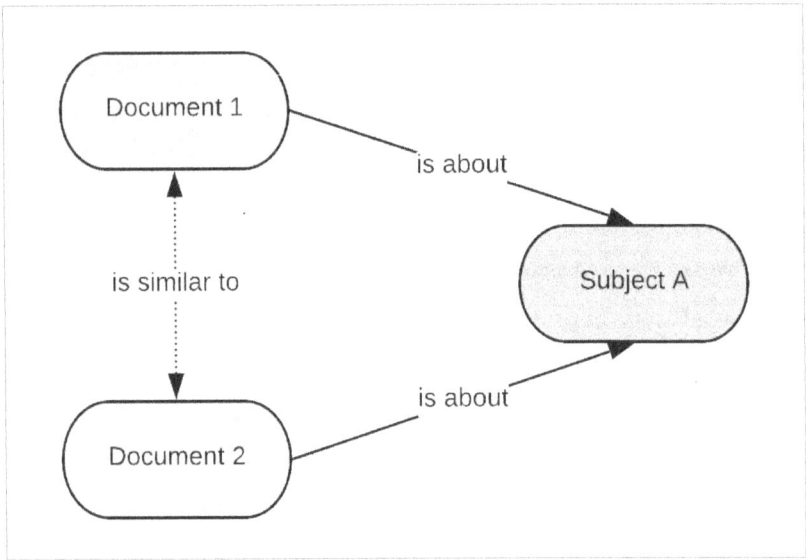

Figure 11.1 The aboutness relation.

It's important to realize, I think, that the structure of the relation of work-instantiation is exactly the same. If I decide that Doc 1 instantiates Work A, what that amounts to is a judgment, an entirely subjective judgment made by me on a particular occasion, that Doc 1 has the property of being an instance of Work A, that Doc 1 is a member of the class of documents that share the property of instantiating Work A. Again, these are just different ways of saying the same thing, and again we can also say that Doc 1 and Doc 2 are similar in the sense that they share the same property or that they are members of the same class. And again, if it turns out that Work B has exactly the same extension as Work A does—in other words, if it turns out that all and only the documents that instantiate Work A instantiate Work B—then we can say that Work A is the same work as Work B.

Relevance works the same way. If I decide that Doc 1 is relevant to Subject A, what that amounts to is a judgment, an entirely subjective judgment made by me on a particular occasion, that Doc 1 has the property of being relevant to Subject A, that Doc 1 is a member of the class of documents that share the property of being relevant to Subject A. And if all and only the documents that are relevant to Subject A are relevant to Subject B, then we can say that Subject A is the same subject as Subject B.

Okay, so that's the sense in which aboutness and relevance, and incidentally work-instantiation, are equivalent in structure. And an understanding of identity, and the difference between similarity and sameness, is obviously helpful in analyzing that structure. Meanwhile, we should note the assumption here that subjects (and works) are not natural kinds, they're human artifacts—social constructs. Subjects don't somehow inhere in documents. Judgments of aboutness, work-instantiation, and relevance are arbitrary and subjective. Whenever somebody, anybody, says, this document is about x, all they mean is, I currently think this document is a member of the class I currently call x.

Now, the main claim I'd like to make about the importance of identity for KO is not that an understanding of identity is helpful in analyzing the structure of aboutness and relevance. It's that there's a sense in which identity is actually the goal of KO. This is how we get there.

There's a view, and it's a useful view I think, that the aim of information retrieval system design is to produce identity, to produce matches or correspondences, between sets of aboutness judgments and sets of relevance judgments. If the system retrieves all and only those documents that are judged by the searcher to be relevant, then the system is successful. In this view, it's just the judgments made by the system, as to whether given documents are members of the classes named in the user's queries to the system, are being characterized as aboutness judgments.

In this account, the aim of indexing, the aim of making aboutness judgments in fact, is to achieve consistency between the aboutness judgments made by indexer a with respect to subject x at time t_1, and the relevance judgments made by searcher b at time t_2.

And the aim of KO in general is to achieve consistency, to produce identity, between the KO system designer's representation of reality, which basically amounts to the aggregate of the extensions of all subject classes and the relations between them, and the KO system user's model or image of the world.

Now, the challenge for KO is simply that there are many different views of the world. It's not just that there isn't one, but that there at least six billion! So, there can be no doubt. If KO systems are to work well, then they have to be dynamic and adaptive in whatever ways are productive of consistency between the system and each individual user.

I've talked about aboutness and relevance as different relation-types. These two relation-types are similar in the sense that they are themselves instances of the same broad class of relation-types, and that's the class formed by relation-types whose own instances relate classes on the one hand and the instances of those classes on the other.

There's another broad class of relation-types, and that one is made up of relation-types whose instances are class-to-class. This is the class of relation-types whose instances relate subjects in KO systems such as faceted, hierarchical classification schemes. In this example of such a scheme (see Figure 11.2), there's a broader-narrower relationship between Subject A1 and Subject A11, and another one between Subject A1 and Subject A12.

Notice three things here:

- Docs 2 and 3 are instances of subjects both in Facet A and in Facet B, but Doc 1 is an instance only of subjects in Facet A. That's okay, of course.

- Docs 1 and 2 are instances of both Subject A1 and one of its two sub-classes, but Doc 3 is an instance only of Subject A1. That's okay, too.

- Note that we're not saying anything about the semantic relations among the things or concepts that are represented by whatever terms are used as the labels for these Subjects. The relation between Subject A1 and A2 is simply a class-to-class relationship. The thing or

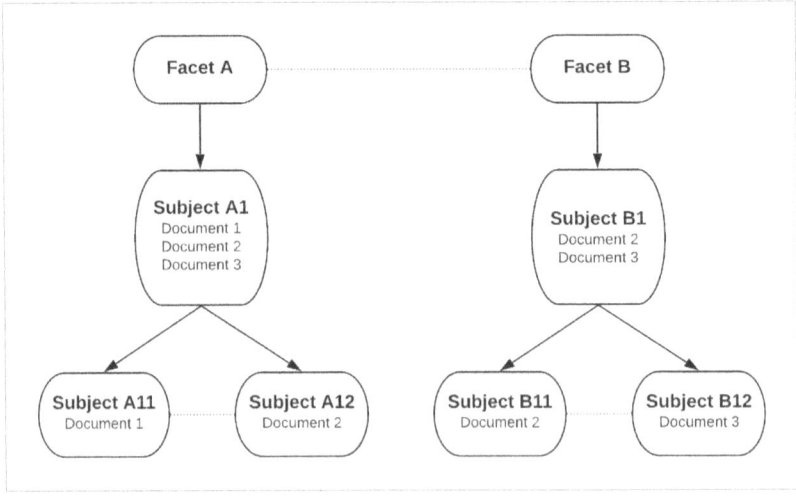

Figure 11.2 Inter-class relations in a hierarchical classification scheme.

concept represented by the term used as the label for the narrower class may be an instance of the kind that is represented by the term used as the label for the broader class, or it may be a subclass of the class that is represented by the broader term.

These are the kinds of relations that have historically been put to use in faceted, hierarchical classification schemes. The question I'm asking today is, Is this small set of relation-types, together with the rules of logic that constrain how particular subject-classes may be instantiated in relation to other subject-classes—is this particular set of relation-types adequate for the representation of relationships between classes of documents about people?

Now I have to admit a couple of things, just to dampen down your palpable excitement: (a) Obviously I'm not the first to ask this question—and the work of people like Hope Olson, Joan Mitchell, Rebecca Green, Barbara Tillett, and Elaine Svenonius takes this question in all sorts of fascinating directions. And (b) I'm actually not going to answer this question, because, well, apart from anything else it's quite hard. But I do think that it's worth posing in the present context, because I think it's helpful to think about it as a special case of the general question of how well KO allows for the construction of system/user identity.

Okay. Classes of documents about people. The thing to be made clear at this point is that some subjects of documents are the identities of the persons to whom the documents are relevant. That bears repeating: Some subjects of documents are the identities of the persons to whom the documents are relevant.

As we saw earlier, one way in which different persons' views of the world vary is the way in which different persons have different views of their own and other people's personal and social identities. In fact, the phenomenon of personal identity is fairly complex, and the challenge for KO is the possibility that this complexity of identity relations can't be represented by simple hierarchical class divisions.

Quick recap of a couple of things we covered earlier. Remember how there are two central research questions in KO, the design question and the evaluation question? Now, we can translate these general research questions into a couple of specific research questions that relate to KO's handling of identity.

The first is the design question. How ought identities-as-subjects, and the relations between them, to be represented in a KO system. Again, the answer to this is, well, in whatever way that evaluations tell us is best. But then there's the evaluation question, which is how do we evaluate? *How do we decide* how identities-as-subjects, and the relations between them, ought to be represented in a KO system?

And here's a bit of a recap of some of the things we said about evaluation earlier. We took a look at some of the criteria we can use to decide whether a particular representation of reality is any good or not. We said that it's possible to take a description-oriented view or a retrieval-oriented view of which are the most appropriate criteria to use.

We talked about effectiveness as the most important of the retrieval-oriented criteria, and we looked at some of the factors that affect levels of effectiveness. One of those factors was indexer–searcher consistency. Now, we can say that one component of any strategy that's intended to maximize the degree of consistency between categorizers—between indexers and searchers, for instance—is to ensure that categorizers' self-identities are reproducible in the KO system.

What does reproducible mean here? Well, one way of clarifying that might be to draw up a kind of bill of rights for KO system users. Ask yourself, intuitively, should our opportunities to do these things with KO systems be conceived as rights that should be protected like other basic human rights?

Don't I have the right to find documents that are relevant to any one or any combination of my multiple personal identities—1. as effectively, efficiently, and easily as I would find documents about any *other subject*, and 2. as effectively, efficiently, and easily as *anyone* would find documents about any of *their* personal identities?

Don't I have the right to use, and expect others to understand, my own vocabulary in communicating about identities-as-subjects—without hurting effectiveness, efficiency, or ease of retrieval in any way?

And don't I have the right to describe identities-as-subjects, including my own, differently in different situations and at different times—again, without hurting effectiveness, efficiency, or ease of retrieval in any way?

Now, there are a number of complexities in this account of what it means to have an identity, and each of the complexities poses a challenge of a different kind for the designers of KO systems used to support the provision of access to documents about identities.

I'm going to take a brief look at five of these in turn, that I'm calling multifacetedness, differences in prioritization, mixedness, multidimensionality, and vagueness. Each of these ideas on its own is quite straightforward, but put them all together and you have quite a complex situation.

Multifacetedness is quite simple. The idea is that every person may have multiple identities, in the sense that each person may simultaneously affiliate with multiple classes, each of which is defined by a property instantiating a different facet. So, for example, I might simultaneously identify with forty-somethings, with males, with Brits, and so on.

Not only that, but different persons prioritize their affiliations in different ways, at different times. Different persons who have the same set of multiple affiliations may have different "defining characteristics," or identities that they consider to be the most important, or the most strongly influential on their decisions and actions.

There's another sense in which a person may simultaneously or diachronically have multiple identities. This is the sense in which a person may affiliate with multiple classes defined by different properties in the same facet, so that for example somebody who self-identifies as racially mixed may self-identify with one racially-defined population at one time and another racially-defined population at different times, or even with multiple racially-defined populations at the same time.

And here it's instructive to refer to Maria Root's "Bill of Rights for Racially Mixed People," which includes the rights to self-identify with more than one group of people, to self-identify differently at different times, to self-identify in ways that may be contrary to other people's expectations or wishes, and to use one's own vocabulary to communicate about one's multiraciality or mixedness.

The fourth source of complexity is intra-facet multidimensionality. The idea here is simply that some facets aren't unidimensional. Take sexual orientation, for instance. Is it really the case that all sexual orientations can be located on a single dimension with homosexuality at one pole, heterosexuality at the other, and bisexuality in the middle? Or should we be thinking about sexual orientation as a two-dimensional thing, where different orientations can be located on a graph with degree of attraction to members of the same sex on one axis, and degree of attraction to members of a different sex on the other?

Fifthly and finally, we have the observation that the boundaries of the classes with which persons affiliate are themselves vague. These classes are not natural kinds; they're not classes whose definitions are somehow discoverable through scientific enquiry. They're nominal kinds or artifactual kinds whose memberships are determined over time by convention. Not only that, but these are classes whose members are identified as being members of those classes not because they share certain specified properties that are somehow known to all agents doing the identifying, but because they resemble, more or less closely, certain prototypes known from experience to have been identified by others as core exemplars of those classes.

Of course, a lot of work, theoretical and empirical, has been done in the last hundred years or so that has had the general effect of changing our understanding of how people categorize in general, and I'd just like to throw in the name of Timothy Williamson here as an example of the work being done in mainstream philosophy on the implications of vagueness for traditional Aristotelian theories of logic that tend to rely on assumptions about the reality of binary dichotomies. And many voices in KO have been arguing for a long time that, if the design of KO systems is to improve, then we somehow have to start taking seriously these ideas about how categorization actually proceeds, and of course Hope Olson and others are the authorities here.

That is all a statement of what should happen, of what we might wish for. Of course, we all want to respect the rights of users. I shouldn't think anyone would want to come up here and start arguing that in fact we've got it all wrong when it comes to protecting basic rights and promoting the just KO system, and that KO systems would be better if they were unjust and so on. I know I'm preaching to the choir here.

But here's the issue. We *want* our KO systems to represent all identities-as-subjects in a just manner that respects everyone's rights. But how *can* they—given the multifacetedness, and the differences in prioritizations, and the mixedness, and the multidimensionality, and the vagueness of identities-as-subjects?

I'll give you a clue about how I think you *can't* do it. And that's through traditional library classification—that is, through hierarchies of classes that are divided up one dimension at a time. Or even through facet analysis, and this is where I very much agree with Birger Hjørland's comments in *his* paper in the latest issue of *KO*.

I think we need to look at the very methods we use in our current systems to represent the relations between classes, and take a critical, questioning perspective on those methods that ask, Is that all there is? Because if it is, then we're doomed! Doomed I tell thee. I think there's got to be a third way, and it's probably a way that takes what we've learnt from IR approaches and takes what we've learnt from folksonomic approaches, and applies that with the intention not of adding to the fuel of those age-old arguments about who should do the indexing, people or machines, experts or hoi polloi, but with the intention of discovering literally, new ways of adequately allowing for the representation of the multiprioritizability, the mixedness, the multidimensionality, the vagueness, as well as the multifacetedess of identities as subjects.

To emphasize: This isn't about removing people from the process and replacing them with machines. It's not about rejecting vocabulary control. It's about advocating for a new kind of structure for representing the relations among documents. It's about encouraging people to look at different kinds of relationships from the ones that perhaps they're used to looking at, looking carefully at the similarities between those relationships, similarities in structure and similarities in role, and determining the implications of those discoveries of similarity for the design of representational structures. And it's about engaging seriously with the challenges for KO that are presented by analyses of identity and identity-forming processes. And I know that's what we'll be doing this week. So let's wish ourselves the best of luck!

Finally, I just have a few remarks about the prospects for a fully-fledged philosophy of documentation or philosophy of knowledge organization. Several authors have recently picked up on Margaret Egan's social epistemology, or at least the version of it promoted by Jesse Shera, as a good source of ideas about what the philosophical foundations of the information sciences are, or what they could be. The general idea seems to be that it's possible to move from an understanding of the social processes by which we most reliably acquire true or useful or relevant beliefs, to recommendation of the ways in which our information services can best support those processes, and Don Fallis is one of the people who's doing a lot to show how this move works.

But Luciano Floridi and others have suggested that this kind of social epistemology can't on its own provide a complete philosophy of information, since it focuses, obviously on knowledge acquisition processes and doesn't deal directly with metaphysical questions about the nature of information, the nature of documents, the nature of our interactions with those kinds of things and so on. Not only that but it doesn't deal directly with ethical questions about the kinds of justification that might be required of calls for the just information service or the diverse information service, and so on. In this context, maybe a metaphysics and an ethics of identity is just what is needed to augment the social epistemological approach to a philosophy of KO.

References

Egan, Margaret E., and Jesse H. Shera. 1952. Foundations of a theory of bibliography. *Library Quarterly* 22: 125–37.

Fallis, Don. 2006. Social epistemology and information science. *Annual Review of Information Science and Technology* 40: 475–519.

Fidel, Raya. 1994. User-centered indexing. *Journal of the American Society for Information Science* 45: 572–76.

Green, Rebecca. 2008. Relationships in knowledge organization. *Knowledge Organization* 35: 150–59.

Hjørland, Birger. 2008. What is knowledge organization (KO)? *Knowledge Organization* 35: 86–101.

López-Huertas, María. 2008. Some current research questions in the field of knowledge organization. *Knowledge Organization* 35: 113–36.

Olson, Hope A. 2002. *The power to name: Locating the limits of subject representation in libraries*. Dordrecht: Kluwer Academic.

Renear, Allen H., and David Dubin. 2007. Three of the four FRBR Group 1 entity types are roles, not types. In *Proceedings of the 70th ASIS&T Annual Meeting* (Milwaukee, WI, October 19–24, 2007), ed. Andrew Grove and Abebe Rorissa. Medford, NJ: Information Today.

Root, Maria P. P. 1996. A bill of rights for racially mixed people. In *The multiracial experience: Racial borders as the new frontier*, ed. Maria P. P. Root, 3–14. Thousand Oaks, CA: Sage.

Smiraglia, Richard P. 2001. *The nature of "a work": Implications for the organization of knowledge*. Lanham, MD: Scarecrow.

Svenonius, Elaine. 2000. *The intellectual foundation of information organization*. Cambridge, MA: MIT Press.

Tennis, Joseph T. 2008. Epistemology, theory, and methodology in knowledge organization: Toward a classification, metatheory, and research framework. *Knowledge Organization* 35: 102–12.

Tillett, Barbara B. 2002. Bibliographic relationships. In *Relationships in the organization of knowledge*, ed. Carol A. Bean and Rebecca Green, 19–35. Dordrecht: Kluwer Academic.

Williamson, Timothy. 1994. *Vagueness*. London: Routledge.

C
Works, documents, records

12
The ontology of works

November 6, 2006

This talk was given at ASIS&T 2006: 69th Annual Meeting of the American Society for Information Science and Technology (Austin, TX, November 3–8, 2006) as part of the panel session on "Philosophy and information science: The basics." The panel chair was Jonathan Furner, and speakers were Don Fallis, Jonathan Furner, Kay Mathiesen, and Allen Renear.

My aims today are to give the broadest of outlines of a particular subfield of philosophy—specifically, a subfield of the philosophy of art known as the ontology of art—and to identify a few of the opportunities that seem to exist not only for information science to learn from philosophy of art, but also, conversely, potentially for philosophy of art to learn from information science.

Two separate literatures

Here's a funny thing (see Table 12.1). On the left is an alphabetical list of thirteen authors noted for their contributions to the ontology of art. On the right is a list of thirteen authors similarly noted for their contributions to the literature on the Functional Requirements for Bibliographic Records (FRBR), its historical precursors, and related topics in library cataloging theory. These lists are separate, in that authors within one list cite others in that list frequently, but cite authors in the other list never (or as good as never). I did a quick and dirty citation

Carroll	Carlyle
Collingwood	Delsey
Currie	Lagoze
Davies	Leazer
Goodman	Le Boeuf
Howell	Lubetzky
Ingarden	O'Neill
Kivy	Smiraglia
Levinson	Svenonius
Margolis	Tillett
Thomasson	Vellucci
Wollheim	Yee
Wolterstorff	Zumer

Table 12.1. Two separate literatures

analysis in the Web of Science. Question 1: Are any of the authors on the right cited in journals categorized by Thomson ISI in the "Art" subject category (which includes the *Journal of Aesthetics and Art Criticism* and the *British Journal of Aesthetics*) or the "Philosophy" subject category? Answer: No. Not one single citation. Svenonius, for example, is cited in 306 articles, but not once in any art or philosophy journal indexed by Thomson ISI. Over 10% of the citations to Smiraglia and Vellucci are in journals categorized under "Music"—but these are all either in *Notes* (the journal of the Music Library Association) or in *Fontes Artis Musicae* (the journal of the International Association of Music Libraries). Question 2: Are any of the authors on the left cited in articles in journals categorized by Thomson ISI in the "Information Science & Library Science" (IS&LS) category? Answer: Yes, but only very occasionally. Some of these authors have each been cited more than 1,000 times in journals indexed by Thomson ISI. But the only citations I could find in IS&LS journals are a few to Goodman by the Berkeley pair of Patrick Wilson and William Cooper, and a single citation to

Wollheim in an article in the *Journal of the American Society for Information Science and Technology* in 2005. (One factor I should point out that lessens the impact of these results is the fact that Thomson ISI doesn't index two of the three main journals that carry articles relating to FRBR—it does index *Library Resources & Technical Services* [*LR&TS*], but not *Cataloging & Classification Quarterly* [*C&CQ*] nor *International Cataloguing & Bibliographic Control* [*IC&BC*]—and I've found several citations in *C&CQ* from Smiraglia to, for example, Stephen Davies. But still these amount to a vanishingly small proportion of the citations made by the citing authors.)

And yet, you'd think that, given the descriptions of goals emanating from representatives of the two groups, they would at least be on speaking terms! Yee asks "What is a work?" in the title of her series of papers from the mid-nineties. The first sentence of Smiraglia's book is "What is the nature of a work?" The first sentence of Thomasson's overview of the ontology of art is "The central question for the ontology of art is this: What sort of entities are works of art?" You might say, well, hang on, not all works considered as works in the bibliographic universe are works of *art* (which is an issue for debate in its own right), but I think most people would allow that at least some bibliographic works are works of art, and on that basis alone it would be interesting to see what the philosophers have to say.

Ontology of art

Philosophy of art in general seeks a theoretical understanding of the phenomenon of art. Some of the key questions considered in philosophy of art are about the nature of the practice of art itself—and about the ways in which art is or can be or should be valued, and about the ways in which art is or can be or should be interpreted. Another key question is the ontological question: What sorts of things are artworks? Ontology is the field whose goal is to identify the fundamental categories of things that exist in the world. An ontology is a list of the basic sorts of things there are, together perhaps with a description of the sorts of relationship that exist between those fundamental categories. Aristotle and Kant, for instance, had famous ontologies. Aristotle's included ten categories such as substance, quantity, quality, relation, place, time, and so on. Ontologies of art tend to define fewer than ten categories. Many get by with just two or three, as we'll see. Specific ontologies have been proposed for specific art forms. The ontology of music asks, what sorts of things are musical works? The ontology of literature asks, what sorts of things are literary works? And so on.

Now, you might be thinking, I don't need a philosopher to tell me what a work of art is—I know one when I see one (and someone else might disagree with me, and that's okay)—and what can possibly be the problem here, anyway? Well, here are a few things to think about. Firstly, we need to be clear here about the difference between this question of what sorts of things works of art are, and the separate question of what it is about art that makes it art. We may well disagree about whether a given work is a work of art, at the same time as agreeing that it's a work. Secondly, it really isn't immediately clear what the answers to questions about the nature of works are. Take a literary work like *Don Quixote*, for instance. Is the work the copy of the particular edition of the English text that I have at home? No. Is it that edition? No. Is it that text? Hmm, maybe …. But if not, what exactly is it? It's not a physical object, obviously. So is the work a mental object, existing only in Cervantes' head? Well, he's dead now, so quite frankly nothing exists in his head. So does that mean that the work doesn't exist any more? Well, no …. So things aren't quite as simple as we might initially think, even for literary works. In the case of musical works, or any works that are specified by sets of instructions like scores, the situation is even more complicated. Is the score the work? Is a given performance the work? No, and no. So the question remains: What sort of thing is a musical work?

An even better reason to worry about this stuff is the realization that any answers we can give to these kinds of question are just preliminaries to other questions—questions, for example, about the nature of the various kinds of relationship that exist between works and things of other sorts. For instance, we might decide that there's a distinction to be made between the score of a given musical work and a performance of that work. What if the performance doesn't accurately follow every single instruction given in the score? Does that make it a performance of a different work? How badly would it have to be performed to make it a performance of a different work? Or consider a translation of a literary work. How loose would the translation have to be to make it a version of a different work? And what would be the nature of the relationship between the old work and the new work? These are questions about how works and their related entities can or should be individuated, and philosophers ask the same kinds of questions about director's cuts, colorized movies, cover versions of pop songs, and so on.

How do philosophers approach these problems? There are two broad alternatives. One is to engage in rational introspection—to think hard and logically about the issues. Lots of philosophers do that very well. The other is to conduct an empirical survey—to go out, have a look around, gather some data, and come back and see where that gets you. In general, philosophers of art are very good at that, too, using real-world examples of things that are (and things that aren't) commonly considered as works (or versions, or copies, and so on), both as guides to improving their philosophical theories, and sometimes as indications of occasions where our commonsense understanding of the nature of works needs to be revised.

Ontology of documentation

Now I'm going to describe a field that no-one else really calls the "philosophy of documentation," but I'd like to try to persuade you that nonetheless it exists, and that it corresponds quite neatly to the conception of philosophy of art that I just presented. Some of the key questions asked in philosophy of documentation are about the nature of the practice of documentation itself, and about the ways in which documentation is or can be or should be valued, and about the ways in which documentation is or can be or should be interpreted. Another key question is the ontological question: What sorts of things are documents? Specific ontologies might be proposed for specific documentary forms—ontologies of musical documents, moving-image documents, or textual documents, and so on. Sound familiar?

You might be thinking, I don't need a philosopher to tell me what a document is—I know an antelope when I see one—and so on. Why worry? Well, it really isn't clear what the answers to questions about the nature of documents are. And any answers we can give to these kinds of questions are just preliminaries to other questions, for example about the nature of the various kinds of relationship that exist between documents and things of other sorts, and about how documents and their related entities can or should be individuated. Déjà vu?

When it comes to finding good approaches to tackling these problems, documentalists are pretty good at thinking hard and well, but they're even better at going out and asking other real-life documentalists how they think document records should be grouped so that catalog-users can easily find documents of the sorts they want. The people behind FRBR, for instance, did a massive survey of that kind.

And the FRBR model, essentially, was the result: an ontology of documentation that, among other entity-types, defined Works, Expressions, Manifestations, and Items, related to each other in distinctive ways. Taking the example of *Don Quixote* again, we can distinguish between *Don Quixote* the work by Cervantes, the various texts of *Don Quixote* in different languages at the expression level, the various editions of each text at the manifestation level, and the numerous copies of each edition at the item level.

Ontology of literature

An enormous variety of answers to the question "What sort of thing is a work of art?" have been proposed in the literature. One simple way of classifying the answers is first to determine whether they conceive works as concrete particulars or as abstract universals, and secondly (if works are conceived as particulars) to determine whether they are physical objects or mental objects. The work-as-physical-object thesis might seem sensible initially. But, as Wollheim puts well, "there is no object existing in space and time (as physical objects must) that can be picked out and thought of as a piece of music or novel." So that answer fails for literature and music, even though, on the face of it, it might still seem like an option for visual arts such as painting or sculpture. The work-as-mental-object thesis advanced by Croce and Collingwood seems like it fails because, among other things, it can't account for works surviving beyond the death of their authors. The work-as-set thesis claims that a novel is the set of all its copies, or that a piece of music is the set of all its performances, and has been criticized (a) because it leads to the possibly counterintuitive result that any given work is never complete, (b) because it doesn't provide a straightforward means of establishing that a given copy is a copy of work x rather than work y, and (c) because none of a set's properties are necessarily shared with its members, since sets do not somehow transmit properties to their members. The work-as-type thesis is often advanced as an alternative to the work-as-set thesis that doesn't face these objections. Here the idea is of a type in the Peircean sense, to be distinguished from its tokens, i.e., its occurrences or instances.

Back to *Don Quixote* for a moment. One of the paradigmatic problems in the ontology of literature is how to deal with the imaginary example, found in one of Borges' short stories, of the novel *Don Quixote* by the twentieth-century French author Pierre Menard, which has an identical text to that of *Don Quixote* by Cervantes. It's written by a different person with different intentions in a different context. Is it a different work, even though its text is the same?

Different answers would be given by proponents of different versions of the work-as-type thesis that is most common in ontology of literature. For Goodman, a work is a fixed sequence of words in a given language; for Wolterstorff, a work is a "norm kind," i.e., a fixed sequence of words specifying what counts as a correct instance; for Levinson, a work is a fixed sequence of words "indicated" by a given author at a given time; for Currie, a work is an "action type," i.e., a fixed sequence of words arrived at by an author's following a given set of contextual influences. Goodman and Wolterstorff would argue that a copy of Cervantes' work and a copy of Menard's work are tokens of the same type. Levinson and Currie would argue that the two copies are tokens of two different types.

One theory advanced by Stevenson in the fifties, but that has received minimal attention since, is nonetheless interesting for the parallels that may be drawn between it and the recent direction taken by ontology of documentation. Stevenson's idea was to propose a three-level hierarchy of megatype, type, and token, in which types (i.e., sequences of words) that have the same propositional meaning are said to instantiate the same megatype. Thus, works of literature may be conceived to correspond to megatypes. This introduction of a three-level as opposed to a two-level ontology appears to help out on the question of how we determine whether two tokens that don't share the same sequence of words (perhaps one a translation of the other) are instances of the same work. Ontology of art has for so long been focused on investigating the viability of a two-level ontology for various art forms, that the full implications of Stevenson's ideas are only just recently beginning to be worked out, for instance in Stephen Davies' forthcoming paper on versions of musical works.

Trends and issues

Here are a few trends occurring in ontology of art that I think are notable for people working on ontology of documentation:

- Philosophers of art are starting to generalize the questions they're asking to cover entities of related kinds—not just works of art, but human artifacts in general. The results of their investigations can only become more interesting for documentalists.

- The pluralist approach has long been in the ascendant, meaning that different ontologies have been worked out for different art forms. This is in direct contrast to the uniformist approach taken by FRBR.
- A consensus seems to have been reached that the only entities that are concrete are tokens, and that types are not sets.

Looking in the opposite direction, a couple of trends occurring in ontology of documentation that I think are notable for people working on ontology of art:

- It has been shown to be possible, even desirable, to determine the validity of a given ontology by evaluating its practical utility—in FRBR's case, its utility as the conceptual model underlying the design of effective library catalogs.
- The type/token model can be extended beyond two levels, and indeed beyond three levels. The implications of that move are still being worked out by people like Allen Renear, but this certainly seems to be an instance of philosophy of documentation being ahead of the curve.

To conclude, here is a brief shopping list of outstanding issues specifically for the philosophy of documentation. None of these will be unfamiliar to FRBR aficionados, but the list might serve as a snapshot, for what that's worth.

- The first three issues—How should FRBR handle seriality, aggregation, and aboutness?—are well-known and well-discussed in the FRBR community. The third one we talked about yesterday [in the panel session on "Theoretical topics in FRBR"].
- The fourth problem—What criteria should be used for individuation?—has recently been identified by Allyson Carlyle as an implementation issue, meaning that the way FRBR is implemented in different systems and different cultures may conceivably embody variations in the criteria that are used for individuating works and other entities.

- The question, How many ontological levels?, has been a source of great debate over many years and shows no sign of going away just yet.

- The question about the nature of the relationships between entity-types at different levels—how exactly works are realized, expressions embodied, and so on—hasn't received as much attention as it perhaps should have had.

- And the final question about the prospects for FRBR's uniformism in the face of calls for pluralism is perhaps the most interesting of all.

13

Two kinds of "work"

March 29, 2007

This talk was given at VRA 2007: 25th Annual Conference of the Visual Resources Association (Kansas City, MO, March 27–31, 2007) as part of a panel session on "What is a work?" The chair was Richard Urban, and speakers were Sherman Clarke, Jonathan Furner, and Tammy Moorse.

I'm going to address the theme of this session—the inquiry into what kind of thing is to be denoted by the word "work"—by clarifying two different, separate senses in which the word "work" happens to be used in the broad context of cultural informatics. Sometimes, in that context, the term is used to refer to one kind of thing, sometimes it's used to refer to another, and it seems as if it would be useful to distinguish those two referents as clearly as we can. Specifically, it's important to recognize that "work" is used in quite different ways in *Cataloging Cultural Objects* (and by extension the VRA Core) on the one hand, and in IFLA's Functional Requirements for Bibliographic Records (and by extension *Resource Description and Access*) on the other.

Works in CCO

So let's take a look at *Cataloging Cultural Objects* (CCO) first. The fundamental kind of thing that CCO is concerned with is the "cultural object," and CCO defines what that category includes by specifying various subsets of the universal set of cultural objects. At the highest level, the set of cultural objects is divided into two subsets: (i) the set of works, and (ii) the set of documentary images—the use of "documentary" here indicating that not *all* images are to be considered as cultural objects, but only those that are images *of works*. (Note also that there is no suggestion that these two subsets are mutually exclusive, since some cultural objects—some photographs of works, for instance—can be considered to be both work and image, simultaneously.) In CCO, the category of works is further subdivided into three main subcategories: (i) works of visual art, such as paintings and sculptures; (ii) built works, such as buildings; and (iii) cultural artifacts, such as decorative and functional objects.

There are two characteristics that are obviously shared by all cultural objects (in the CCO sense of that phrase), whether they are ultimately treated as works or as images. Firstly, cultural objects are objects: they are physical, they are concrete; whether they exist in analog or in digital format, they exist in the external world; they are particulars that are datable and locatable in space-time. Secondly, cultural objects are cultural: they are made by people; their existence is the result of human activity.

So, when CCO explicitly considers the question "What is a work?" the answer given is that works are "distinct intellectual or artistic creation[s] limited primarily to objects and structures made by humans." The modifier "physical" isn't used in this definition, but it might as well be. When CCO goes on to separately characterize works of visual art, built works, and cultural artifacts, it is made clear at that point that such objects and structures are assumed to be physical, concrete particulars. Explicitly *excluded* from this definition of "work" are literary works, musical works, works in the performing arts, and other "intangible" culture.

The answer that CCO gives to the corresponding question "What is an image [of a work]?" is that an image of a work is "a visual representation [or, to use a term that is commonly used elsewhere in CCO, a depiction] of a work." In other words, an image of a work is something that can stand as "a [visual] surrogate for a work" that "documents" it, visually—just as a textual description can be thought of as a verbal representation of (or surrogate for) a work, that documents it verbally. As CCO says, images of works typically exist in photographic, photomechanical, or digital format. Of course, images of works are precisely the things that are held in visual resource collections.

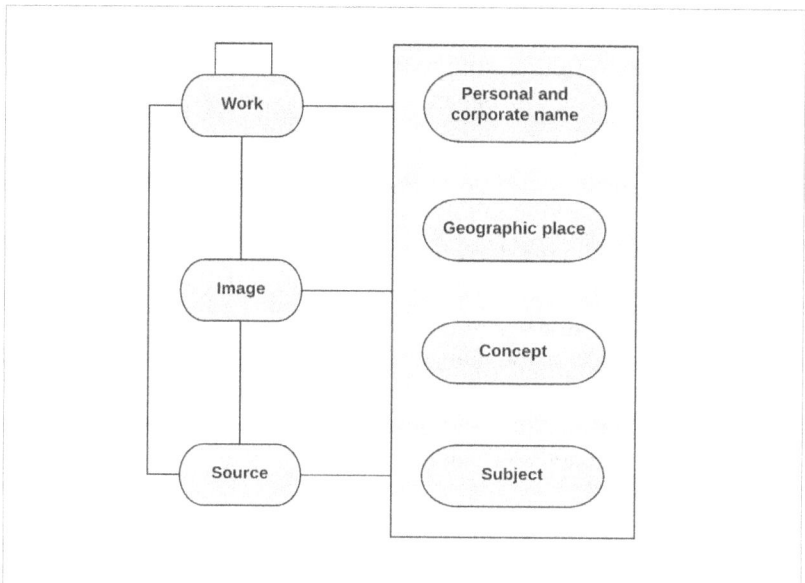

Figure 13.1 CCO's entity–relationship model.

Specifically excluded from the CCO definition of "image of a work" are those things that, while they are indisputably visual representations of works, are also indisputably intellectual or artistic creations, and are therefore works themselves. So, according to CCO, paintings and drawings that happen to depict other works are never to be considered as images of works, but as works. (In actuality, a painting that depicts another work is *both* an image of a work and a work-in-itself.)

Photographs of works form a category of objects that are sometimes to be treated as images of works, and sometimes as works-in-themselves. The decision about an individual photograph should be made on the basis of "the stature of the photographer and the aesthetic or historical value of the photograph"—in other words, on the basis of the significance of the photograph, as an intellectual or artistic creation that itself may require documentation of the kind that works get, and that images do not.

Figure 13.1 is a simplified visual representation of (i) the entity-types (or entity-classes) that are defined in the conceptual model underlying CCO, and (ii) the types of relationships existing between those entity-types. Seven entity-types are represented here. Five of them are entity-types that we're not too concerned about today. The important thing is to note that entities of the type "Work" may be related both to entities of the type "Image" and to other entities of the type "Work." In other words, any individual work may be depicted both by images and by other works.

When it comes actually to creating database records that describe entities and relationships of these types, CCO recommends that the work depicted in an image should be treated as a "Related Work" of that image. Similarly, any image depicting a work should be treated as a "Related Image" of that work. If the work being cataloged is a work that happens to depict another work, the depicted work should be treated as a "Subject" of the work being cataloged. But if the depicted work is itself also described in its own catalog record, then it should also be treated as a "Related Work" of the work being cataloged—just as if the object being cataloged were an image.

CCO gives some very clear examples of how certain kinds of "problem cases" should be dealt with. One such example is the common case of a photograph of a work where the photograph itself has artistic significance. In the case of a photo by Durandelle of the Eiffel Tower, both the work depicted in the photograph, and the photograph itself, should be treated as works. A Work record should be created at least for the photograph, and ideally also for the work depicted (in this case, the Eiffel Tower).

Another example is the case where there are two separate images in the collection: one of a particular building, and one of an architectural plan for the same building. The CCO recommendation is to create Work records for both the building and the plan, each Work record related to each other and to a corresponding Image record.

And a third example is the complex case where there exists a 35mm slide copied from a lantern slide of an artistically significant photograph of a work that itself depicts another work. There are at least two different solutions here—one resulting in two Work records, the other in three—the choice between them being made on the basis of whether it's the work depicted in the photograph, or the photograph itself, that has more significance, either in the context of the collection, or to the collection's users.

Works in FRBR

The foregoing is an account of the sense in which "work" is used in CCO. It's a quite different sense from the way in which "work" is used in

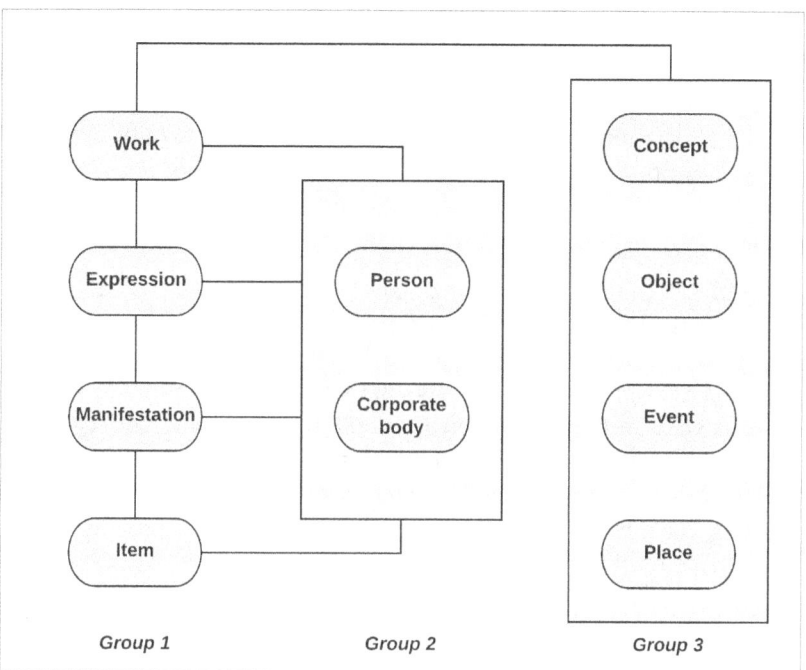

Figure 13.2 FRBR's entity–relationship model.

IFLA's Functional Requirements for Bibliographic Records (FRBR). The difference is clearly noted in CCO itself, albeit in a footnote. "*Work* in CCO is more concrete than *work* as defined in FRBR … . The work in CCO is usually a physical entity, whereas that in FRBR is an abstraction or intellectual entity, such as a literary work or a musical composition."

Here (Figure 13.2) is a much simplified version of FRBR's entity–relationship model, for direct comparison with the one underlying CCO that we looked at a minute ago. Two important things to note here are (i) the distinction made in this model that isn't made in the CCO model, between works and the kinds of things that FRBR calls expressions, manifestations, and items, and (ii) the distinction made in the CCO model that isn't made in this one, between works and images.

So let's take a closer look at the definitions provided in the FRBR report of its so-called Group 1 entities. A *work* is "a distinct intellectual or artistic creation … an abstract entity." An *expression* is "the specific intellectual or artistic form that a work takes each time it is 'realized'"; "the intellectual or artistic realization of a work in the form of alpha-numeric, musical, or choreographic notation, sound, image, object, movement, etc., or any combination of such forms." A *manifestation* is "the physical embodiment of an expression of a work ... [the set of] all the physical objects that bear the same characteristics, in respect to both intellectual content and physical form." An item is "a single exemplar [or instance] of a manifestation ... a concrete entity ... in many instances a single physical object."

One note I'll make here is that this use of "physical" in the definition of "manifestation" is rather odd, since a set or class of physical items isn't physical—its members might be, but the class itself is an abstraction, just as expressions and works in FRBR are abstractions. The main point is that, in FRBR-speak, it is the FRBR entity-type called "Item" (and not the one called "Work") that most closely corresponds with the CCO entity-type "Work." In CCO, works are concrete, physical objects. In FRBR, the only things that are concrete, physical objects are items. The other Group 1 entities in FRBR are all abstractions.

So let's try to make *this* discussion a little less abstract, and a little more concrete! According to FRBR, this is how works, expressions, manifestations, and items are related to one another: works are *realized* through expressions, which are *embodied* in manifestations, which are *exemplified* by items. What does this mean in practice? Here is a literary example. Imagine that I have in my hand a single copy of Ecco's 2003 edition of Edith Grossman's English translation of *Don Quixote*. That copy would exemplify or instantiate a distinct edition (or manifestation), which in turn would embody a distinct text (or translation, or version, or expression), which in turn would realize a distinct intellectual or artistic creation (or work). One way of looking at this might be to think about a hierarchy of sets and supersets and supersupersets of copies. In this view, the work that we call *Don Quixote* is ultimately the set of all the copies of all the editions of all its texts.

The point of FRBR's making these kinds of relationship explicit is to improve the design of catalogs and thus to improve catalog users' experiences. Before FRBR, most library catalog records would represent manifestations, and people searching on the titles of works would be faced with results lists that look something like this [Slide #18][1]—which

---

1   https://litwinbooks.com/books/information-studies-and-other-provocations/

is a display of the top eight results, sorted in no immediately discernible order, that one gets if one searches for *Don Quixote* in the title field of the CARLWeb interface to Los Angeles Public Library's current catalog (see http://www.lapl.org/catalog/). None of these eight records happens to point to an edition of the novel by Cervantes.

In contrast, this [Slide #19][2] is what one gets when one tries the same search on OCLC Research's FictionFinder (see http://fictionfinder.oclc.org/), a "post-FRBR" catalog that neatly groups its results, initially by work, ranked in order of the number of manifestations in each workset, and only then [Slide #20][3] by manifestation, this time ranked in order of the number of libraries holding physical copies.

Here is a simple musical example to compare with the literary example of *Don Quixote*: my copy of the vinyl record released by Columbia Records in 1976 that encodes a 1975 recording of Abba performing a work (*Dancing queen*) created by songwriters Andersson, Ulvaeus, and Anderson.

But what happens if we try to think about works of visual art, rather than musical works or literary works, using this scheme of Works, Expressions, Manifestations, and Items ("WEMI")? What happens if, for instance, we try to fit Magritte's *La condition humaine* (1935) into this scheme? Truth is, it doesn't really work very well. We might even wish to ask ourselves, "Why bother?" The fundamental difference is that the painting, the *object*, like many other cultural objects, is unique. It's not like a book or a vinyl record, of which multiple instances or "copies" exist. It's not as if we really need to go to the trouble of counting the instances of manifestations of expressions of this work: there's only one instance of this *work*, period. If we continue to think about manifestations, expressions, and works as sets, then we will presumably conclude that the work that we call Magritte's *La condition humaine* (1935) has one member expression, which has one member manifestation, which has one member item. And it's important to recognize that it's not simply that this singularity is *actually* the case. It's that, in the case of painting as an art form, it's *necessarily* the case.

So something interesting is going on here. It seems as if FRBR's "WEMI" scheme is applicable to *certain* kinds of cultural objects—specifically,

---

2   https://litwinbooks.com/books/information-studies-and-other-provocations/

3   Ibid.

the ones that CCO explicitly excludes from its definition of cultural objects—but not others.

Works in ontology of art

People working in cultural informatics aren't the only ones thinking about these kinds of issue. In fact, philosophers have been thinking about them over a much longer period, and questions like "What is a work?" are central to the subfield of philosophy of art known as ontology of art. Other related questions considered in ontology of art include: What is the nature of the various sorts of relationship that exist between works of art and things of other sorts? And, in what does the identity of a work of art (of a given sort) consist? (For instance, are translations of novels, "cover" versions of songs, and "director's cuts" of movies new works, or just different expressions of the same work?)

Why should we in cultural informatics take any interest in the results of work in the ontology of art? The reason is the same as the reason for taking account of the work in library science, most recently exemplified by FRBR but stretching back to Cutter, that emphasizes the importance of identifying the kinds of groups (or sets, or classes) to which objects belong, and providing catalog users with the means to browse or navigate among those classes so that they can find the objects they want.

So let's take a quick look at some of the findings, firstly of ontology of literature, and then of ontology of art in general. Most contemporary philosophers treat literary works, such as *Don Quixote*, as types, where the word "type" is used in a special sense derived from Peirce, in which any given type is instantiated (or, more strictly speaking, instantiatable) by multiple tokens. The idea is that, just as there exist multiple separate occurrences of the same word, and multiple separate utterances of the same sentence, there can exist multiple separate instances (or "copies") of the same work.

But what criteria do philosophers use to decide whether two tokens are tokens of the same type? Different people have come up with different ideas to take care of various problem cases in different ways, and I'm not going to go further into these today, except to specifically note one idea dating back to Charles Stevenson in the 1950s, which is relevant because his conception of what he called the "megatype" is similar to FRBR's conception of "work," and in fact serves as a bridge connecting (i) the ideas underlying FRBR's WEMI hierarchy, and (ii) the ideas underlying vocabulary control as it is applied in library science. Just as a concept can be viewed as a set of words that share the same meaning, and a proposition can be viewed as a set of sentences that share the same meaning, so a work can be viewed as a set of texts or translations that share the same meaning.

In ontology of art in general, there is continuous debate between proponents of what are called uniform theories and proponents of non-uniform theories. Uniform theories are those that explain the nature of all artworks, in whatever art form, in the same way. Among the proponents of uniform theories, there are unitarians and dualists. Unitarians argue that the Peircean distinction between types and tokens is not actually characteristic of any of the arts, not even the literary arts. I've provisionally characterized CCO as an application of a unitarian theory, since CCO similarly does not allow for the representation of type/token relationships (at least, not at the entity-type level). Dualists argue that the Peircean type/token distinction is in fact characteristic of all the arts, even the visual arts, in which at first glance it might not appear particularly useful to distinguish between the work we call *La condition humaine* and the particular object hanging on the wall that instantiates that work. I've provisionally placed FRBR in the dualist category, since FRBR similarly does not allow for simpler treatment of works of visual art.

Proponents of non-uniform theories, including Stephen Davies—arguably the leading figure in contemporary ontology of art—argue that the type/token distinction is characteristic of some arts, but not others. According to this view, some art forms are characterized by the creation of what might be called singular works—paintings, hewn sculptures, Polaroids, many buildings—that do not have multiple instances. Other art forms are characterized by the creation of what might be called "type-works," that can have multiple instances. The thing to note is that here we're not just talking about literary works and musical works, but also several common kinds of works of visual art—cast sculptures, prints, and photographs from negatives, for instance.

Conclusion

What this all leads us to, in conclusion, is some questions for discussion: two and a half questions, to be exact. The two main questions are: 1. Should CCO be modified in the light of FRBR?, and 2. Should FRBR be modified in the light of CCO? In FRBR, we have the explicit facility to represent the relationships between type-works and their instances. In CCO, this facility is buried below the level of the underlying conceptual model. Does that matter? Then, in CCO, we have the explicit facility to represent the relationships between objects and their images. In FRBR, this facility is buried below the level of the underlying conceptual model. Does that matter?

Then, finally, if images—that is, photographs from negatives, slides, and digital images—are themselves type-works in the sense that they can be instantiated by multiple copies, is it possible that the distinction in CCO between works and images at the entity-type level is less useful than a simple distinction between different sub-types of "Work"? In fact, isn't it precisely their "type-workness"—their instantiatability—that makes images distinctive? Could this recognition form the basis of a FRBRized CCO?

References

Baca, Murtha, et al. 2006. *Cataloging cultural objects: A guide to describing cultural works and their images*. Chicago, IL: American Library Association.

Davies, Stephen. 2006. Varieties of art. In *The philosophy of art*, 81–108. Oxford: Blackwell.

Howell, Robert. 2002. Ontology and the nature of the literary work. *Journal of Aesthetics and Art Criticism* 60: 67–79.

IFLA Study Group on the Functional Requirements for Bibliographic Records. 1998. *Functional requirements for bibliographic records*. München: K. G. Saur.

Stevenson, Charles L. 1957. On "What is a poem?" *Philosophical Review* 66: 329–62.

Thomasson, Amie L. 2003. The ontology of art. In *The Blackwell guide to aesthetics*, ed. Peter Kivy, 78–92. Oxford: Blackwell.

Wolterstorff, Nicholas. 1992. Ontology of artworks. In *A companion to aesthetics*, ed. David Cooper, 310–14. Oxford: Blackwell.

14

The ontology of documents, revisited

June 12, 2019

This talk was given as a keynote at DOCAM 2019: Of Documents and Data: The 2019 Annual Meeting of the Document Academy (Toulon, France, June 12–14, 2019), and was published in slightly different form in Proceedings from the Document Academy *6, no. 1 (2019), article 1.*

The title of the talk is gesturing towards the fact that I'm far from the first to give a talk on this topic. The philosopher Barry Smith has been talking about the ontology of documents since at least 2005, and part of my goal today is to shine the DOCAM lamp on his work.

The talk is divided into three sections.

First of all, building from Michael Buckland's well-known paper "What is a document?," I'm going to present a brief survey of definitions of "document" from the last century or so. My conclusion from this will be that those definitions which most accurately reflect the ways in which the term "document" is used in practice are typically *compound* definitions, consisting of two or three elements. Each part refers to a different mode or function of documents: document-as-carrier or medium, document-as-text or message, and document-as-content or meaning. This is because documents are complex objects, not simple ones.

The second section of the talk introduces the idea of *category theory*, a branch of the philosophical subfield of ontology, whose contributors work towards the identification of the most fundamental categories of things that exist (or could possibly exist) in the world. One celebrated contributor to category theory is the philosopher E. J. Lowe, and I'm going to look at his so-called four-category ontology with a view to locating documents' place in it. As we'll see, this isn't as easy as it might initially appear to be, but my tentative conclusion is that documents are universals, not particulars. (And I just want to note from the outset that I'm going to be using that term "universal" in the narrow philosophical sense, referring to a metaphysical category, not a linguistic or cultural one. Neither is this an argument that the *concept of "document"* is a universal in the philosophical sense. That much I'm assuming to be obvious. Rather, it is an argument that *Moby-Dick* and every one of the trillions of documents that are produced daily are each universals.)

Thirdly, I'm going to switch from consideration of Lowe's work in ontology to look at that of philosopher Barry Smith, who has written specifically about the ontology of documents. At first it might seem as if Smith is working with a narrower definition of "document" than we are used to in library and information science, but I argue that ultimately we may have much to learn by taking Smith's approach, one takeaway being that what Smith calls document acts are analogous to speech acts and should be viewed as events or occurrents as opposed to objects or continuants, but another, more importantly, being that all documents, not just the ones that are involved in the kinds of acts that Smith identifies as *declarations*, are *creative* in the special sense that they are generative of quasi-abstract entities of the kind that collectively comprise social reality.

The goal of all of this though is not to draw definite conclusions, but to contribute to a solidification of connections between LIS and literatures that might not previously have loomed large on our collective radar, and to spark conversations about this material, so I'll be more than happy if I manage to do that, and I hope you'll be somewhat satisfied too.

Part I

Obviously the initial touchstone when it comes to any discussion of definitions of "document" is Michael Buckland's seminal and highly-cited 1997 paper. This will be so familiar to everyone more than 20 years later that I hesitate to give more than the most cursory review, but I do think it's worth reminding ourselves what Buckland's goal was with this article and what he consequently chose to leave out.

Buckland explicitly poses the question "What is a document?" in the context of a *historical* discussion of the limits of *documentation*, as that activity was pursued and developed in the first half of the twentieth century. He asserts (p. 804) that such discussion is still "relevant to the clarification of the nature and scope of information systems," given the way documentation has developed in the second half of the twentieth century, but (apart from brief consideration of "contemporary" definitions drawing from semiotics) restricts his survey of definitions of "document" to those emerging from the documentation movement prior to the mid-1960s.

So Buckland begins by considering the oeuvre of Paul Otlet, the Belgian visionary well-known to all of us, who with Henri La Fontaine founded the Institut international de bibliographie in 1895, which in 1931 became the Institut and in 1937 the Fédération internationale de documentation, and who wrote the *Traité de documentation*, published in 1934. For Otlet, says Buckland, the category of "document" includes not just graphic and written records (i.e., representations of ideas or of objects) but also the objects themselves—"if you are informed by observation of them" (Buckland, p. 805). For example: "natural objects, artifacts, objects bearing traces of human activity (such as archaeological finds), explanatory models, educational games, and works of art" (Buckland, p. 805)—that is, objects "not intended as communication" (p. 807). Comparing Otlet's ideas to some of those promoted by modern-day cultural anthropologists and museologists, Buckland further quotes Otlet: "Collections of objects brought together for purposes of preservation, science and education are essentially documentary in character (Museums and Cabinets, collections of models, specimens and samples). These collections are created from items occurring in nature rather than being delineated or described in words; they are three dimensional documents." (Otlet 1920, translated in Otlet 1990, cited by Buckland, p. 807).

Here are some further definitions of document cited by Buckland, all except the last focusing on the supposed materiality of documents:

> 1935: Schürmeyer—"any **material** basis for extending our knowledge which is available for study or comparison"
> (Schürmeyer translated by Buckland, p. 805).
>
> 1937: Institut international de coopération intellectuelle / Union française des organismes de documentation—"Any source of information, in **material** form, capable of being used for reference or study or as an authority. Examples: manuscripts, printed matter, illustrations, diagrams, museum specimens, etc."
> (cited by Buckland, p. 805).
>
> 1942: Donker-Duyvis—"the **repository** of an expressed thought" (Donker-Duyvis 1942, translated Voorhoeve 1964, cited by Buckland, p. 806).
>
> 1951: Briet—"evidence in support of a fact"; i.e., "any physical or symbolic **sign**, preserved or recorded, intended to represent, to reconstruct, or to demonstrate a physical or conceptual phenomenon"
> (Briet translated by Buckland, p. 806).

Table 14.1. Definitions of "document," 1900–1965.

The last is Suzanne Briet, of course—the French librarian who co-founded the Union française des organismes de documentation in 1931 and published *Qu'est-ce que la documentation?* in 1951, and who is celebrated in library schools around the world for her recognition that a photo of a star, a stone in a museum, an antelope in a zoo—all have "become physical evidence being used by those who study" them (p. 806) and therefore can be considered to be documents.

> "tout indice concret ou symbolique, conservé ou enregistré, aux fins de représenter, de reconstituer ou de prouver un phénomène ou physique ou intellectuel" (1951, p. 7).
>
> "any concrete or symbolic indexical sign, preserved or recorded toward the ends of representing, of reconstituting, or of proving a physical or intellectual phenomenon" (2006, p. 10).
>
> "Is a star a document? Is a pebble rolled by a torrent a document? Is a living animal a document? No. But the photographs and the catalogues of stars, the stones in a museum of mineralogy, and the animals that are cataloged and shown in a zoo, are documents." (2006, p. 10).

Table 14.2. Briet's definition of "document."

Non-documents	Documents
Star in sky	Photograph of star Catalog (record) of star
Stone in river	Stone in museum
Animal in wild	Animal in zoo

Table 14.3. Briet's definition of "document," continued.

Especially since the publication of Ron Day's masterful translation and analysis of *Qu'est-ce que la documentation?* in 2006, much has been written about Briet's supposedly structuralist and proto-semiotic approach to the definition of "document." (See Tables 14.2–14.3. My own take on it is shown in Table 14.4.)

Object	Function	Origin
photograph catalog record	representing	*made as* a document
specimen	reconstituting	*made into* a document
living being	proving	*read as* a document

Table 14.4. Three kinds of document?

Buckland infers from Briet four "rules for determining when an object has become a document":

- the object must be material (this despite the translation of Briet: "any physical or *symbolic* sign … ," emphasis added)
- it must have been someone's intention that the object is to be treated as evidence
- the object must have been processed in some way
- the object must be perceived as a document

Buckland then cites Day as specifying that it is "indexicality—the quality of having been placed in an organized, meaningful relationship with other evidence—that gives an object its documentary status" (p. 806).

In contrast to the emphasis on the materiality of documents that pervades his prior discussion, Buckland's conclusions include (p. 808) the identification of an "evolving" notion of "document" that has "increasingly emphasized whatever function[s] as a document rather than traditional physical forms of documents." Buckland sees (p. 804) a move from a traditional concern with "text and text-like records (e.g., names, numbers, and alphanumeric codes)" to "any phenomena that someone may wish to observe: Events, processes, images, and objects as well as texts," and remarks (p. 808) that "The shift to digital technology would seem to make this distinction even more important."

Buckland never intended to provide comprehensive coverage, even of the time period to which he limited himself. A few of the definitions that didn't make it into his survey are listed in Table 14.5.

1907: Institut international de bibliographie (trans. Weitenkampf 1908)—"anything which represents or expresses, by the aid of any **signs** whatever (writing, image, diagram, symbols), an object, a fact or an impression."

1943: American Library Association / Thompson—"Any written, printed, or otherwise recorded item or **physical** object that may serve as evidence of a transaction."

1956: Ranganathan—"Record—made on more less flat surface or on surface admitting of being spread flat when required, made of paper or other **material**, fit for easy handling, transport across space and preservation through time—of **thought** created by mind and expressed in language or symbols or in any other mode, and/or of natural or social phenomena made directly by instrument without being passed through human mind and woven into thought created and expressed by it."

Table 14.5.   More definitions of "document," 1900–1965.

Buckland did of course cite the famous Indian librarian, but the work he chose was from a slightly later date. Some further definitions from American sources are listed in Table 14.6.

> 1956: Mack & Taylor—"A single piece of written or printed **matter** which furnishes evidence or information upon any subject."
>
> 1957: Perry & Kent—"An arbitrary unit of recorded knowledge which furnishes information upon a subject. A graphic record or group of such records which are **physically** bound together or otherwise contained or attached so that it may be recognized as a single object. Examples of documents are books, reports, letters, films, photographs, and tape recordings."
>
> 1960: Wagner—"Any recorded information **regardless of its physical form** or characteristics, and includes, but is not limited to, the following: (1) all written material, whether handwritten, printed, or typed; (2) all painted, drawn or engraved material; (3) all sound or voice recordings; (4) all printed photographs and exposed or printed film, still and motion picture; and (5) all reproductions of the foregoing, by whatever process reproduced."

Table 14.6. Even more definitions of "document," 1900–1965.

Document-as-medium

Over the last century, various suppliers of definitions of "document" have chosen to emphasize the supposed physical, material, or concrete nature of documents. The first of Buckland's (1997) four "rules for determining when an object has become a document," inferred from analysis of Briet's (1951) discussion, points to materiality as a necessary condition. (Buckland's translation of Briet's definition—which begins "any physical *or symbolic* sign …" (emphasis added)—might seem to contradict this inference, but other authorities cited by Buckland, including Schürmeyer 1935 and IIIC / UFOD 1937, certainly lie in the explicitly materialist camp.) We might call definitions of this kind definitions of document-as-medium, since the idea they promote is of documents as media, vehicles, or channels, for the storage and/or carrying of messages.

Document-as-message

At the same time, other definitions (including Briet's) have been constructed so as to emphasize a different kind of essence—not documents' materiality, but instead their informative, evidentiary, or signifying quality. We might call definitions of this kind definitions of document-as-message, since they represent documents as aggregations of signs (i.e., messages or texts), for the expression and/or transmission of meanings.

Document-as-meaning

Thirdly, yet other definitions focus neither on documents' materiality nor on their signhood—i.e., not on documents as *bearers of* meaning, physical or otherwise—but on their status as *meanings in themselves*. These are definitions of document-as-meaning.

Compound definitions are those that simultaneously assign to documents two or three of the essential qualities of materiality, signhood, and meaninghood (where those latter terms stand for "being a sign" and "being meaning," respectively). For example, Wersig & Neveling (1976) define "document" as "A unit consisting of a data medium, the data recorded on it, and the meaning assigned to the data."

Table 14.7 presents, in chronological order, the highlights from a list of more than 25 definitions extracted from glossaries, dictionaries, standards, and other literature dating from 1966 through 2019.

> 1970: NATO Advisory Group for Aerospace Research and Development / Stolk—"a record of data, or a concept, **in any form** from which information can be derived, e.g. a page containing data, a graphic representation, a tape recording, or a book."
>
> 1971; 1977: Harrod (3rd & 4th eds.)—"A **work** recorded in language or symbols, or by other means."
>
> 1974: Society of American Archivists / Evans et al.—"Recorded information **regardless of medium** or characteristics."
>
> 1976: BS 5408—"A **combination** of a **medium** and the information recorded on or in it, which can be used for consultation, study or evidence."
>
> 1976: Buchanan—"Generic term for the information-bearing **media** handled by librarians—books, serials, sound recordings, films, illustrations etc."
>
> 1976: Unesco / Wersig & Neveling—"A **unit** consisting of a data **medium**, the data recorded on it and the **meaning** assigned to the data."
>
> 1983: ISO 5127-1—"recorded information which can be treated as a unit in a documentation process."
>
> 1983; 2013: American Library Association / Young (2nd ed.); Levine-Clark & Carter ("4th" ed.) —"A **physical** entity of any substance on which is recorded all or part of a **work** or multiple works. Documents include books and booklike materials, printed sheets, graphics,

> manuscripts, sound recordings, video recordings, motion pictures, and machine-readable data files."
>
> 1984; 1988: International Council on Archives / Walne [1st & 2nd eds.]—"A **combination** of a **medium** and the information recorded on or in it, which may be used as evidence or for consultation."
>
> 1987; 1990; 1995; 2000; 2005: Harrod (6th–10th eds.)—"A record which conveys information; originally an inscribed or written record, but now considered to include **any form** of information—graphic, acoustic, alphanumeric, etc. (e.g. maps, manuscripts, tape, videotapes, computer software)."
>
> 2000: Wellisch—"A **medium** on or in which a **message** is encoded; thus, the **combination** of medium and message. The term applies not only to objects written or printed on paper or on microforms (for example, books, periodicals, maps, diagrams, tables, and illustrations) but also to non-print media (for example, artistic works, audio and video recordings, films, machine-readable records, and multimedia) and, by extension, to naturally occurring or humanly made objects intended to convey information (for example, zoo animals, plants in botanical gardens, museum collections of hand tools, etc.)."
>
> 2001: ISO 5127—"recorded information or **material** object which can be treated as a unit in a documentation process."
>
> 2003: Feather & Sturges (2nd ed.)—"A record that contains information content. In common usage it still normally means a piece of paper with words or graphics on it. In library and information work, the term is however used to mean any information-carrying **medium**, regardless of format. Thus books, manuscripts, videotapes and computer files and databases are all regarded as documents."
>
> 2004: Reitz—"A generic term for a **physical** entity consisting of any substance on which is recorded all or a portion of one or more **works** for the purpose of conveying or preserving knowledge. In the words of the communication theorist Marshall McLuhan, a document is the '**medium**' in which a '**message**' (information) is communicated. Document formats include manuscripts, print publications (books, pamphlets, periodicals, reports, maps, prints, etc.), microforms, nonprint media, electronic resources, etc.… . Also, any form printed on paper, once it has been filled in, especially one that has legal significance or is supplied by a government agency, for example, an application for copyright protection… ."

Table 14.7. Yet more definitions of "document," 1966–2019.

No particular *synchronic* trend is apparent in this data, but what *is* apparent is (a) the wide variety of definitions, and of combinations of category memberships, and (b) the fact that such combinations, that is, compound definitions, are more common than single ones. I take this

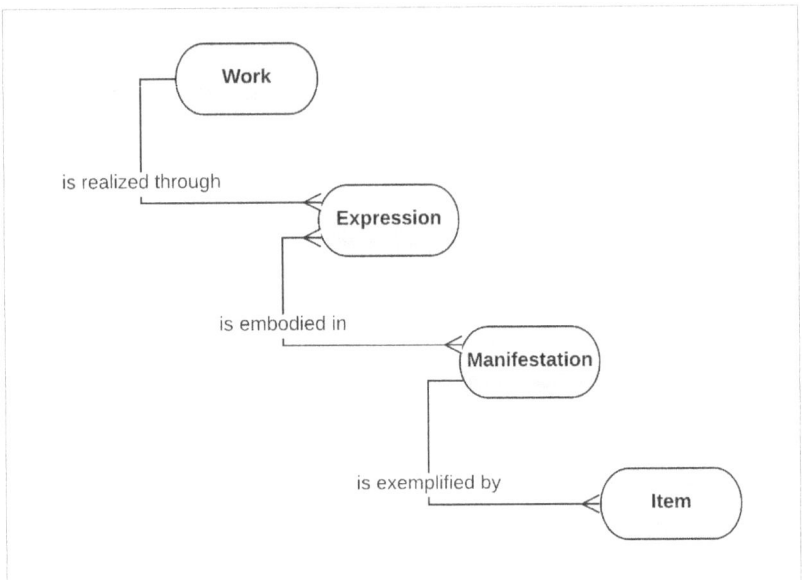

Figure 14.1. FRBR's Group 1 entities and primary relationships.

data as evidence for concluding that documents are (or, at least, are typically considered to be) complex objects rather than simple ones.

The three-part compound definition corresponds partially to the four-entity data model (see Figure 14.1) that lies at the heart of IFLA's Functional Requirements for Bibliographic Records (FRBR; 1998). This model distinguishes between works, expressions of those works, manifestations of those expressions, and items (i.e., copies of those manifestations). Items are the only physical entities recognized in this model; each item can be viewed as the medium for (or carrier of) a given expression or aggregation of expressions, which in turn can be viewed as the message(s) representing a given work or aggregation of works. On the face of it, at least two separate conceptions of "document" can be derived from the WEMI model: one that treats documents simply as items, i.e., as physical media; and a second that conceives of documents as complex entities that exist simultaneously as material, signifying, and meaningful things, i.e., as messages (expressions) and meanings (works) as well as as media (items).

As a possible way of deciding between these two alternatives, we might consider that, in the course of a discussion of the scope of FRBR (p. 8 of the final report, 1998), the word "document(s)" is used eight times as a synonym for "information resource":

"... [U]sers may make use of bibliographic records for a variety of purposes ... : to determine what information resources exist ... ; to verify the existence and/or availability of a particular **document** ... ; to identify a source ... from which a **document** can be obtained ... ; to select a **document** or group of **documents** that will serve the information needs of the user; ... .

"... [T]he functional requirements for bibliographic records are defined in relation to the following generic tasks that are performed by users when ... making use of ... library catalogues:

- using the data to <u>find</u> materials that correspond to the user's stated search criteria (e.g., in the context of a search for all **documents** on a given subject ...);

- using the data retrieved to <u>identify</u> an entity (e.g., to confirm that the **document** described in a record corresponds to the **document** sought by the user ...);

- using the data to <u>select</u> an entity that is appropriate to the user's needs ... ;

- using the data in order to acquire or <u>obtain</u> access to the entity described (e.g., ... to access online an electronic **document** ...)."

Even though "document" is not subsequently used in the rest of the final FRBR report, the clear implication is that, in the FRBR world-view, documents are the sorts of things that are sought, found, selected, and acquired, as a result of judgments made by catalog users as to the relevance of those things, given users' needs and wants. Such judgments are made on the basis of assessments of documents' formats and contents—i.e., on the basis of evaluation of the qualities of documents as media, as messages, and as (aggregations of) meanings. On this reading, documents are not to be conceived primarily as physical items that *have* the properties of instantiating given manifestations, given expressions, and given works; rather, any given document *is*, simultaneously, a medium, a message, and a meaning.

Part II

So much for an empirical survey of the various kinds of definitions of "document" that have been suggested over the years. The results raise a question which demands an ontological approach: in other words, it requires some input from the philosophical subfield of ontology, the study of the nature of being.

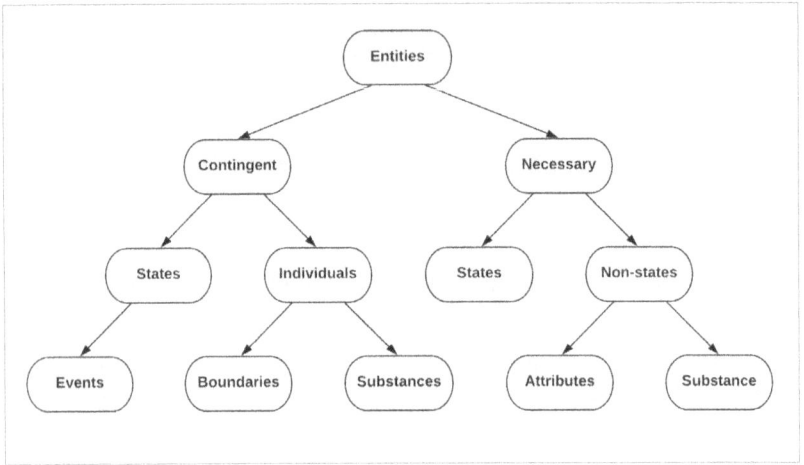

Figure 14.2. Chisholm's top-level ontology.

One of the tasks of ontology that has been deemed more or less important since at least the time of Aristotle is the identification of the "highest," "topmost," or most general categories or kinds of things that exist in the world. Some ontologists have established systems of top-level categories that are hierarchical in structure, with one category containing all things at the very top, divided into a small number of sub-categories, each of which is subdivided into a small number of sub-sub-categories, and so on. Typically in such structures, the sub-categories at any given level are both exhaustive and exclusive, so that any individual thing is a member of one and only one sub-category at that level. Figure 14.2, for example, depicts the top-level structure proposed by the American philosopher Roderick Chisholm (1916–1999) in his *A Realistic Theory of Categories* from 1996.

One of the most well-known contemporary top-level ontologies is that devised by the British philosopher Jonathan Lowe, who wrote as E. J. Lowe and who was Professor of Philosophy for many years at Durham University in England before he died in 2014. Lowe's system, which he promoted as a means of understanding the foundations of natural science, rests on three basic binary distinctions. Lowe distinguishes between universals and particulars, between substances and properties, and between abstracta and concreta, in arriving at the structure depicted in Figure 14.3. The diagram as presented here is lifted straight from one of Lowe's earlier publications. He would subsequently make some changes in his use of terminology, and a few slight corrections

The ontology of documents, revisited

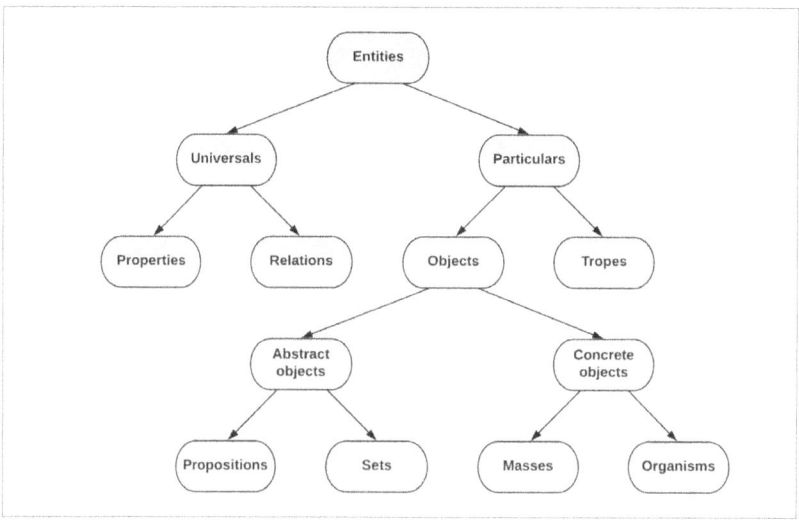

Figure 14.3. Lowe's top-level ontology.

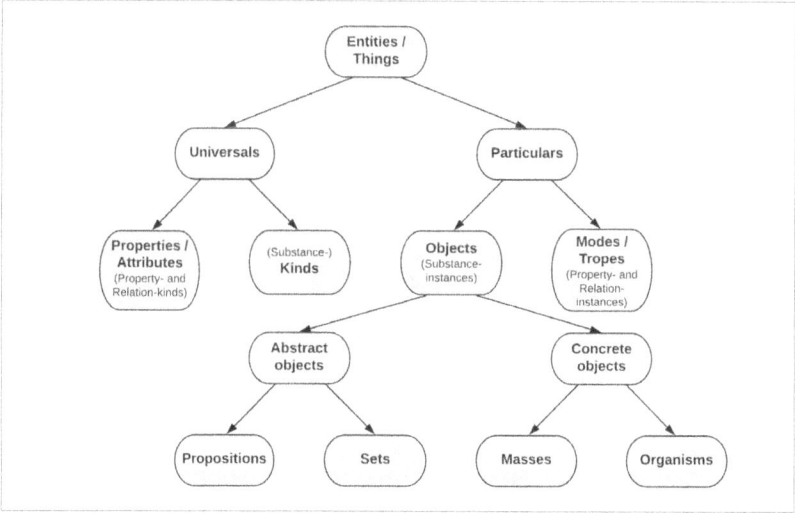

Figure 14.4. Lowe's top-level ontology (amended).

to this diagram are needed here and there, as in Figure 14.4: Properties would be merged with Relations to form a category of Attributes; the place of Relations would be taken by Kinds; and Tropes would be replaced by Modes).

Questions about whether or not these distinctions may be sustained, and if they can, how that may be done, have been among the most hotly debated in metaphysics for more than two thousand years and it's certainly not my goal to attempt to survey answers to those questions today. What I'm going to do instead is very briefly to characterize the distinctions that Lowe makes.

Firstly, universals vs. particulars. "Even in this matter," Lowe says (2003, p. 8), "there is controversy." Lowe conceives of universals as things that are repeatable, that is, as things that may be "borne" or possessed by many different particulars, at different times and places; whereas particulars are each "wholly confined to a unique space-time location and cannot 'recur' elsewhere and elsewhen" (p. 8). In other words, universals are instantiable (by particulars), and particulars are not. Examples of universals include properties such as the property of being red, and kinds such as the kind denoted by the word "apple." Examples of particulars include the apple I ate yesterday and the redness of that apple.

Lowe's distinction between substances and properties is among particulars. It is the distinction between objects and modes (or tropes). An object is "an entity which bears properties but which is not itself borne by anything else" (p. 8), like the apple I ate yesterday; a mode or trope is a particular that is borne as a property by no more than one object (p. 9), like the redness of that apple.

We might say objects "instantiate" kinds, "exemplify" attributes, and are "characterized" by modes. Similarly, attributes "characterize" kinds, and are "instantiated" by modes. Another way to think of attributes is as property-kinds, in parallel with the substance-kinds that are instantiated by objects. Objects are substance-instances, characterized by modes as property-instances. It has sometimes been suggested that the so-called "four-category ontology" (Lowe, 2006) depicted in the so-called "ontological square" (see Figure 14.5) was first proposed by Aristotle, and on this basis Lowe and others in his camp are known as proponents of neo-Aristotelian metaphysics. (The version of the ontological square shown in Figure 14.6, by the way, is lifted from a 1997 article by Barry Smith, whom we'll hear more about in Part III.)

The third basic distinction that Lowe draws in his top-level hierarchy is among objects (that is, among substance-instances), and it's between abstract objects and concrete objects. Concrete objects are those that exist in space-time (that is, are "datable and locatable") or at least exist in time, whereas abstract objects are those that do not. Examples

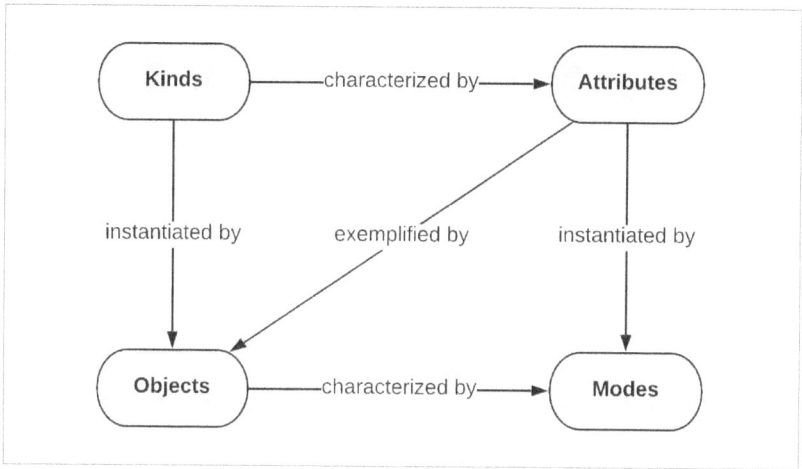

Figure 14.5. Lowe's four-category ontology.

	do not require bearers	inhere in substances as their bearers
multiply located	IV: Universals in the category of substance e.g., man, ox	III: Universals in the category of accident e.g., redness, wisdom
simply located	I: Individual substances e.g., this man, this ox	II: Individual accidents e.g., this redness, this wisdom

Figure 14.6. Smith's four-category ontology.

of concrete objects include individual apples; examples of abstract objects (according to Lowe) include numbers, sets, and propositions. A different criterion that may not coincide exactly in its picking out of abstract objects is the capability of an object to enter into causal relations: an abstract object is one that is incapable of such interaction.

Controversy abounds in relation to the category of abstract object. For example, Lowe identifies propositions as a canonical sub-category of abstract object. But in what sense are propositions conceivable as particulars (that is, non-instantiable) rather than as universals instantiated by sentences (expressions of propositions) and in turn by utterances of those sentences in physical (spoken or written) form? Similarly, in what sense are works—often conceived as aggregations of propositions—comprehensible if not as universals instantiated by copies of those works in physical form?

Another bone of possible contention has to do with the category of concrete object. Two sub-categories of concrete object highlighted by Lowe (p. 5) are masses, or material bodies, and living organisms.

"Entities belonging to these two categories have quite different existence- and identity-conditions, because a living organism, being the kind of thing that is by its very nature capable of undergoing growth and metabolic processes, can survive a change of its constituent matter in a way that a mere mass of matter cannot. A mere mass, being nothing but an aggregate of material particles, cannot survive the loss or exchange of any of those particles, any more than a set can undergo a change of its members. As a consequence, it is impossible to identify a living organism with the mass of matter which constitutes it at any given stage of its existence, for it is constituted by different masses at different stages."

Lowe does not clearly establish what other sub-categories of concrete object there are. The category of artifacts is one obvious candidate, but Lowe has little to say about artifacts in general or sub-categories of artifact more specifically, which means we're forced to speculate a little about where in his scheme certain entities might fit. In a 2014 paper entitled "How real are artefacts and artefact kinds?" Lowe distinguishes between utensils and machines as sub-categories of artifacts, arguing that machines and machine kinds, like natural kinds, are fully and mind-independently real, whereas utensils and utensil kinds—things like "tables, chairs, tents, cooking pots, knives, and hammers" (p. 24)—are not. In the conclusion to this paper, he says "I should stress that I am not urging that machines are the *only* real artefacts. I am content to allow, for instance, that *works of art* may well qualify as real artefacts too." (p. 26, emphasis in original). At the beginning of the paper, however, he had already stipulated that he was "setting aside here putative examples of *abstract* artefacts, such as musical scores, conceived as *types* rather than tokens." (p. 18, emphasis in original) thus leaving tantalizingly open the question as to whether works of art should be counted as particulars at all.

The important question for the would-be ontologist of *documents*, then, is the question of where in such a system of categories documents fit.

Are documents universals or particulars? substances or properties? and so on? It's a question that's not as easily answered as it might at first seem. We might have an inkling of the difficulties now that we've conducted our survey of definitions of "document," and especially now that we've distinguished between the ideas of document-as-medium, document-as-message, and document-as-meaning.

In particular, if we cleave to a *compound* definition, we might expect to have to do some extra work in situating documents among what are typically conceived as exclusive categories. And if it turns out that the concept of "document" is too "complex" for easy placement in a top-level ontology, so be it; the ontology must be revised to accommodate our concept of the thing, not vice versa.

One way to proceed is to start at the top of Lowe's hierarchy, and attempt to justify our choice of placement of "document" on successive branches.

Beginning at Level 0, as it were, the first question is, Are documents things or not?

The answer is, Yes. Since the intention is that *all* things fall in the top category of "things," documents should be treated as things. So far so good.

At the next level down, Level 1, the question is, Are documents universals or particulars?

Almost immediately, we run into a problem. On the one hand, if we consider the document-as-medium option, it seems to be fairly clear that documents are particulars (that is, they are non-instantiable). On the other hand, if we take any of the other views (simple or compound) on the nature of documents as suggested by the survey, we implicitly commit to a conception of documents as instantiable, just as (some, but not necessarily Lowe, would argue) works and propositions are.

Let's continue, for the time being, on the assumption that the document-as-medium option is the more attractive. In that case, documents are particulars. At the next level down, then, Level 2, the question becomes, are documents objects (substance-instances) or modes/tropes (property-instances)? The simple answer is that, since documents are the bearers of properties, and are not borne by anything else, they are clearly objects, not modes. Next!

At the next level down, Level 3, the question is, are documents abstract or concrete?

Even for the document-as-medium conception, there is uncertainty here created by the absence of artifacts among the sub-categories of Lowe's concrete object. But this is probably a limitation of the presentation of Lowe's hierarchy and a reason to revise that presentation rather than a reason to place documents-as-media in any category other than concrete object. So far so simple.

If we make a retreat from our choice of document-as-medium, and consider how to handle documents-as-messages and documents-as-meanings, as well as documents-as-combinations, we need to go back to Level 1, and ask again, Are documents universals or particulars? In these cases, the conception is of documents as instantiable—that is, documents as texts or works that exist as types rather than as tokens. In the absence of a motivation to apply any theory that differentiates between the type-token distinction and the universal-particular distinction, our decision should be to consider documents as universals.

Moving down to Level 2, the question becomes, are documents substance-kinds or property-kinds (attributes)? Since documents are characterizable, the simple answer is substance-kinds.

So we have a situation where on the one hand, documents "live" in a new sub-category of concrete objects, possibly called artifacts, where the challenge will be to identify the qualities that distinguish documentary artifacts from non-documentary artifacts (if there are such things as the latter); and on the other hand, "document" is placed in the category of "Kinds." There is actually a third possibility not suggested by our navigation through Lowe's hierarchy, but which is nevertheless suggested by Lowe's characterization of the category of abstract objects as including not just the sub-categories of numbers and sets, but also propositions. If works are considered to be aggregations of propositions, then it might seem that works should also be placed here; from work, it's a short step to document-as-meaning, and thus to thinking of documents as abstract objects.

Ideally we would use different words to refer to these different concepts. But we don't. We use a single word, "document," interchangeably in different contexts to mean different things. Perhaps this is no bad thing. It keeps us on our toes. But I want to suggest that much of the time, many people use the word "document" to mean something that's a universal not a particular—something that's not *necessarily* material. And I think that's important for our understanding of documents, and for our ideas as to where document theory could or even should be going.

In essence, my argument is an empirical one about the use of language. What do we talk about when we talk about documents? Much of the time, the properties of documents that we're most interested in are properties of documents-as-meaning, or if you like, documents-as-works, documents-as-universals, documents-as-types that are multiply instantiated by physical tokens. Of course it's important to recognize the existence of and to understand the nature of the type/token relationship, but that doesn't necessarily mean that the sole or even the primary focus of document theory should be on the materiality of document tokens. Instead, or at least in addition, understanding the universality of document types should be high on our agenda.

We've reached the end of Part II. In the third and final part of the talk, I'd like briefly to discuss what I take to be the most substantive contribution to the ontology of documents of the last few years.

Part III

The philosopher Barry Smith published a short conference paper called "The ontology of documents" in 2011, following up on a presentation on a similar topic from 2005. In these and several related papers on his so-called "theory of document acts," Smith has developed an account of the status of documents in the context of the picture of social reality painted by fellow philosopher John Searle over a period of several decades.

This work is not really about categories per se, but is ontological in the sense that it explains how documents—or more precisely *document acts* like signing a document, filling it in, delivering it, or archiving it—have the effect of bringing new entities into existence, that is, how document acts have ontological consequences.

Sign it	Deliver it (de facto, de jure)
Stamp it	Declare it active/inactive
Witness it	Display it
Fill it in	Register it
Revise it	Archive it
Nullify it	

Table 14.8. What you can do *to* a document.

Use it to …
… grant or withhold permission
… verify identity
… set down rules
… create a new entity
… amend or destroy an entity

Table 14.9. What you can do *with* a document.

Smith builds on John Searle's ideas about speech acts—the things we do with words. Searle explains how certain kinds of speech acts—the ones he calls "declarations" —can bring about changes in the ontology of social reality, and Smith similarly describes how certain kinds of document acts—generally speaking, the things we do *with* rather than to documents—bring into existence not just *physical* entities like document tokens, and document-related artifacts like filing systems, but also document-related social practices and *quasi-abstract* entities ("at one and the same time *subject to historical changes* yet *not made of physical parts*," Smith, 2011, p. 2, emphasis in original), especially in the realms of commerce, law, and government. These quasi-abstract entities are things like organizations, contracts, laws, money, rights, obligations, identities, claims, privileges, corporations, capital, permissions, debts, trusts … that is, they are entities that form vitally important parts of social reality.

Smith argues that we need to pay more attention to document acts than Searle does. His primary reason for doing so is to address issues relating to the "anchorage" of digital documents to the people who created them, by implementing systems for the certification of authenticity that are on a par with signatures and fingerprinting for physical documents.

But in the course of setting this up, Smith also makes important contributions to our understanding of the basic ontological categories to which documents belong.

Firstly, Smith points out (as others have done before and since) how Searle's categorization of speech acts may be applied to documents. Thus we may distinguish among documents that are representative, directive, commissive, expressive, and declarative. Representatives "commit the [writer] … to the truth of … expressed proposition[s]";

directives "attempt ... to get the [reader] to do something"; commissives "commit the [writer] ... to some future course of action"; expressives "express the [writer's] psychological state ... about a state of affairs"; and declarations "bring about correspondence between ... propositional content and reality." (Searle 1975, pp. 354-361).

Smith is most concerned with declarations, those which are most clearly generative of new entities. Smith uses the term "creative" rather than generative, with the somewhat counter-intuitive result that he classes books (fiction and non-fiction), journal articles, maps, artworks as "non-creative"; on the other hand, certificates, contracts, receipts, banknotes, licenses, agreements, filled-in forms, passports, diplomas, medical records, meeting minutes, etc., all have "creative power" in social reality.

Secondly, Smith follows Goodman in distinguishing those documents that are autographic, and those that are allographic. For Goodman (*Languages of Art*), a work of art is autographic "if and only if the distinction between original and forgery of it is significant; or better, if and only if even the most exact duplication of it does not thereby count as genuine." (Goodman, 1976, p. 113). Painting, sculpture, and architecture are autographic; music, photography, and literature are allographic.

	Non-creative	Creative
Allographic	novel textbook newspaper recipe map business card	advertising flier timetable guarantee tax form (filled-in) minutes of a meeting
Autographic	painting statue building	license birth certificate degree certificate deed contract will receipt banknote

Table 14.10. Allographic vs. autographic, non-creative vs. creative.

The autographic/allographic distinction seems to correspond at least roughly to the distinction between documents that exist as both types and tokens, and those that do not tokenize a type.

Briet's photograph of a star? Allographic. The stone in a museum, and the antelope in a zoo? Autographic. Many of the "creative" document-types listed above? Autographic. Whether the type/token distinction itself corresponds to the universal/particular distinction is a complex matter that might be better left for another day, although clearly any conclusions will be significant for our decision-making when it comes to situating documents in a top-level hierarchy of categories like Lowe's.

Thirdly, and perhaps also significantly for that decision-making, Smith seems to conceive of document acts, including document production acts, like Searle's speech acts, as events or occurrents, notwithstanding that the physical records that are among the products of such acts are definitively classed by Smith as continuants (eliding the type/token distinction). Scope for further sub-categorization of concrete objects?

A more general question raised by Smith's analysis is, What might be the more productive route for Document Academy-style document theory to follow? On the one hand, we might imagine a future document theory that commits wholeheartedly to the distinction drawn by Smith between creative and non-creative documents, carving out a subfield that focuses on the former and on kinds of issues identified by Smith as critical for a digital social reality whose effective and efficient organization depends so much on reliable authentication of autographic creative documents. In this way we may contribute to the kind of "scientific understanding" that Smith says is necessary for arriving at an "intelligent appreciation of the changes in social reality that are being effected through the trillions of documents being created daily in the digital realm." (Smith 2014).

On the other hand, might it be productive to extend the notion of declarative documents' creative or generative power so that all documents, including those that Smith identifies as non-creative but that are traditionally the main concern of document theory, are considered to be creative in some respect and/or to some degree? Smith enumerates some of the kinds of things one can do *to* a document, such as sign it, fill it in, register it, and archive it. It is surely a short step to take to consider that some other such document acts include finding it, identifying it, selecting it, and obtaining access to it (just to choose those suggested by the FRBR final report), as well as organizing it, classifying it, and indexing it, and reading it, interpreting it, citing it, and using it, in many and various ways. Similarly, the products of such acts include quasi-abstract entities of many and varied kinds, including metadata, bibliographies, catalogs, result-sets, recommendations, rankings, metrics, and networks, to name just a few.

And there I'll stop, with a reminder of my three conclusions:

- documents are complex things, not simple ones;
- documents are universals, not particulars; and
- all documents are creative, not just declarative ones.

References

Briet, Suzanne. 2006. *What is documentation? English translation of the classic French text*, translated and edited by Ronald E. Day and Laurent Martinet with Hermina G. B. Anghelescu. Lanham, MD: Scarecrow Press.

Buckland, Michael K. 1997. What is a document? *Journal of the American Society for Information Science* 48, no. 9: 804–09.

Chisholm, Roderick M. 1996. *A realistic theory of categories: An essay on ontology.* Cambridge: Cambridge University Press.

Goodman, Nelson. 1976. *Languages of art: An approach to a theory of symbols*, 2nd ed. Indianapolis, IN: Bobbs-Merrill.

IFLA Study Group on the Functional Requirements for Bibliographic Records. *Functional requirements for bibliographic records: Final report.* Munich: K. G. Saur, 1998.

Lowe, E. J. 2003. Recent advances in metaphysics. *Facta Philosophica* 5: 3–24.

———. 2006. *The four-category ontology: A metaphysical foundation for natural science.* Oxford: Oxford University Press.

———. 2014. How real are artefacts and artefact kinds? In *Artefact kinds: Ontology and the human-made world*, edited by Maarten Franssen, Peter Kroes, Thomas A. C. Reydon, and Pieter E. Vermaas, 17–26. Cham, Switzerland: Springer.

Searle, John R. 1975. A taxonomy of illocutionary acts. In *Language, mind, and knowledge*, edited by Keith Gunderson, 344–69. Minneapolis, MN: University of Minnesota Press.

———. 2010. *Making the social world: The structure of human civilization.* Oxford: Oxford University Press.

Smith, Barry. 1997. On substances, accidents, and universals: In defence of a constituent ontology. *Philosophical Papers* 26, no. 1: 105–27.

———. 2005. How to do things with paper: The ontology of documents and the technologies of identification. Presentation to Ontolog (October 13). http://ontolog.cim3.net/wiki/ConferenceCall_2005_10_13.html.

———. 2011. The ontology of documents. In *Proceedings of the Conference on Ontology and Analytical Metaphysics* (February 24–25, 2011), 1–6. Tokyo: Keio University Press. https://philpapers.org/rec/SMITOO-20.

———. 2014. Document acts. In *Institutions, emotions, and group agents: Contributions to social ontology*, edited by Anita Konzelmann-Ziv and Hans Bernhard Schmid, 19–31. Dordrecht: Springer.

15
The ontology of subjects of works

November 5, 2006

This talk was given at ASIS&T 2006: 69th Annual Meeting of the American Society for Information Science and Technology (Austin, TX, November 3–8, 2006) as part of a panel session on "Theoretical topics in FRBR." The panel chair was Allen Renear, and speakers were Jonathan Furner, Jerome McDonough, and Allen Renear.

I'm going to talk fairly briefly today about a couple of questions raised (or, I should say, raisable) in philosophy of logic and ontology. At this stage, I don't claim to have anything resembling definitive answers to these questions. My limited aim is just to indicate that those answers, if and when they come, will be not only of purely academic interest, but will have a bearing on very practical matters such as the design of library catalogs, and specifically that it's worthwhile and useful to take a philosophical approach when thinking about theoretical aspects of the Functional Requirements for Bibliographic Records (FRBR).

FRBR's Group 3

The particular aspect I'm concerned about is FRBR's treatment of subjects—i.e., those things that works are said to be about. The treatment of subjects in the FRBR model is the concern of a separate working group (WG) called the FRSAR (Functional Requirements for Subject Authority Records) WG, established in April 2005 and chaired by Marcia

Lei Zeng, whose tasks include the review of the so-called Group 3 entities or entity-types, defined in the original FRBR final report of 1998 and listed here (Table 15.1), and those entities' associated attributes and relationships.

Entity-type	Definition	Examples
Concept	"an abstract notion or idea"	economics; romanticism; supply-side economics
Object	"a material thing"	Buckingham Palace; the Lusitania; Apollo 11
Event	"an action or occurrence"	the Battle of Hastings; the Age of Enlightenment; the Nineteenth Century
Place	"a location"	Howard Beach; the Alacran Reef; Bristol

Table 15.1. FRBR's Group 3 entity-types.

A few things to note here:

- The entities that are instances of Object, Event, and Place, are similar in that they are all individual named things—concrete particulars, if you like.
- The examples given here of instances of Concept don't include what we might call *kinds* of Object, Event, and Place—such possible subjects as *palaces* in general, *battles* in general, and *beaches* in general. But the intention is that such subjects should be considered as Concepts.
- That there exist important relationships between instances of these entities is indicated by the examples given of *economics* and *supply-side economics* as separate concepts.

And, just a side note: Things are already confusing because of the abstract terminology. In particular, we've already used "instance" in two senses—once to describe *Buckingham Palace* as an instance of the entity-type Object, and once to describe it as an instance of the kind *palaces*. We mustn't forget, also, that instances of any of the other FRBR entity-types (Work, Expression, Manifestation, and Item in Group 1;

Person and Corporate body in Group 2) can serve as the subjects of a given work.

Some of the questions raised by Delsey in his 2005 paper (in *Cataloging & Classification Quarterly*) are as follows:

- Do these entity-types collectively exhaust the sorts of things that works can be said to be about?
- Are they individually appropriate and meaningful for bibliographic purposes?
- In FRBR, the only attribute associated with Group 3 entities is Term. Is that sufficient and appropriate for the characterization of these entities?
- Is the has-as-subject relationship between entity-types sufficient and appropriate?
- How are the paradigmatic (necessary) and syntagmatic (contingent) relationships between specific instances of entity-types to be handled?

Some proposals in response to these questions have recently been offered. In the FRAR (Functional Requirements for Authority Records) model of 2003, the additional entity-types of Name and Identifier were defined. Delsey himself suggests Time as a separate entity-type. Buizza and Guerrini have made a case for a new entity-type Subject whose instances would be related in various ways to multiple instances of other entity-types, thus expressing the syntagmatic relationships between the elements of a pre-coordinate or faceted subject string. Again in the FRAR model, the additional attributes Type of concept, Type of object, and Type of name are defined to allow expression of the facets to which entities belong. And the FRSAR WG has made several concrete proposals on how hierarchical relationships of various kinds between entity-instances should be defined. Delsey calls these issues "substantial" and "complex." Members of the FRSAR WG are working hard, and various interesting proposals have been made in presentations and drafts following the publication of Delsey's 2005 paper.

Philosophical analysis of aboutness

Meanwhile, in what might fairly be considered a surprise move, I'm going to take a step back to the 1930s, and some honest-to-goodness ordinary language philosophy. This was roughly the time when philosophers such as Gilbert Ryle began to express an interest in this question: "What do we really mean when we say that a given proposition or statement (*p*) is about a given thing (*z*) or has a given topic or subject (*z*)?" On reflection, we might decide that this question can actually be broken down into two separate sub-questions, one that falls in the domain of philosophy of logic, the other in the domain of ontology (i.e., the philosophy of the nature of being).

In the first place, we might ask, "What is the logical nature of the relationship between a proposition *p* and the thing that *p* is said to be about?" Looking ahead a little, if we think of works (or, if you like, documents) as aggregates of propositions, then we might consider that our answers to this question will have a bearing on our understanding of the nature of subject cataloging (i.e., the act by which we express our conception of the relationship between *p* and *z*), as well as on our understanding of the nature of relevance (i.e., one of the important kinds of relationship that exist between works and people) and our understanding of the retrieval models that underlie the design of information retrieval systems. Some of these models are in fact explicitly based on ideas drawn from philosophical logic.

In the second place, we may ask, "What is the ontological nature of the thing that a given proposition *p* is said to be about?" In other words, what sort of thing is *z*, the subject of *p*? Our answers to this question will clearly have impact on our understanding of the nature of subjects, and on our understanding of the conceptual models that underlie the design of library catalogs. So let's take a quick look at each of these questions in turn.

Firstly, the question of the nature of the relationship between a proposition and its subject. The example I'm using here is a proposition of a simple subject–predicate form, *x is A*, attributing the property *A* to the object *x*: *Cataloging is exciting!* (In the phrase "subject–predicate," the word "subject" means subject in the grammatical sense, by the way.) Since the 1930s, various philosophers have answered this question in various ways. Ryle was the first to get the ball rolling, claiming that a proposition like this is literally about its grammatical subject—the concept (if not the word) *cataloging*—at the same time as literally being about its predicate—the concept (if not the phrase) *is exciting*. Thalheimer was the first to make the response—one that might seem kind of obvious in hindsight—that propositions are about the things denoted by their grammatical subjects and predicates—i.e., the actual activity of cataloging, and the actual property of being exciting, or indeed the actual class of exciting things (things that share the property of being exciting).

In the 1960s, Nelson Goodman started to think about this question and recognized that propositions are very often conceived to be about things that aren't explicitly mentioned in the proposition. For example, we might decide that the proposition *Cataloging is exciting* is about library science because cataloging is part of library science, or even that it's about subject cataloging because subject cataloging is part of cataloging. Goodman was concerned to identify the precise conditions under which we can appropriately say that a proposition is about something not mentioned in it. He realized that if we can't specify those conditions then we'll be led to say that every proposition is somehow about everything. He concluded that aboutness is relative, in the sense that propositions are about things only relative to certain other propositions. In fact, Ryle had half-recognized something similar when he wondered aloud in his original paper whether propositions are actually about whatever the discourse or context in which a sentence expressing that proposition is uttered is about. Putnam, drawing on information theory, went on to suggest that aboutness is a matter of degree—that propositions are about things to the extent that they provide a certain amount of information about them.

These sorts of argument are very interesting from the point of view of information retrieval (IR). Very similar arguments have in fact been developed in the IR literature, but it's a point of historical interest that little cross-citation occurs between the two literatures. Cooper cites Goodman in his famous paper on relevance, but that's about it. One wonders what might have happened had the workshop mentioned by Goodman in his 1961 paper actually taken place. (Goodman had written there that "A memorandum concerning the bearing of the present paper upon problems of information retrieval is planned for The Transformations Project on Information Retrieval, at the University of Pennsylvania, sponsored by the National Science Foundation.")

What sorts of things are subjects?

The second of our two questions, then, is the explicitly ontological one: What sort of thing is the subject of a proposition? Or, if you like, what sorts of things are those whose existence we commit ourselves

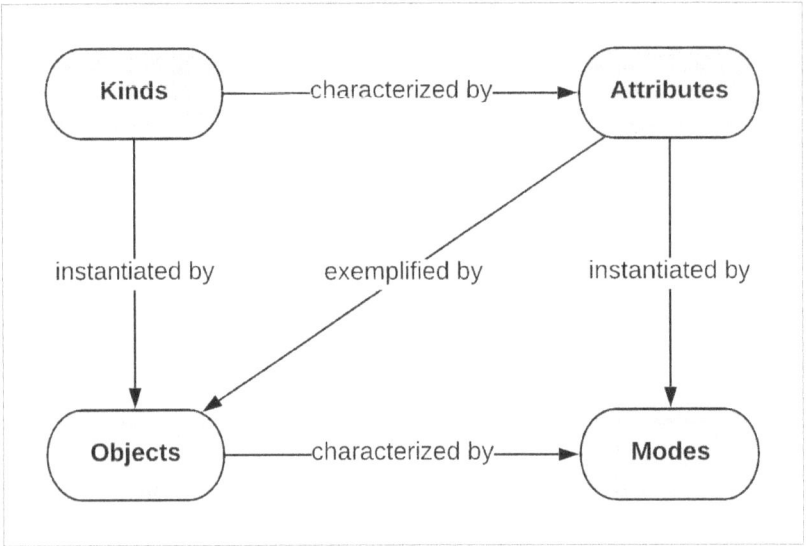

Figure 15.1. Lowe's four-category ontology.

to when we say something like "The proposition *Cataloging is exciting* is about cataloging"? Or, if we construe (which I think we can) works as aggregates of propositions, when we say something like "*Two kinds of power* is about cataloging"—which is the sort of thing, of course, that library catalogs say all the time?

Ontology is the philosophical study of the sorts of thing—the fundamental categories of thing—that exist in the world. It has a long and very rich history. Lots of different proposals have been put forward of the basic categories, but one common distinction that is made is the one between concrete particulars—i.e., individual things that are "datable and locatable"—and abstract universals—i.e., things that are "repeatable." Some people deny the existence of particulars; some deny the existence of universals. Some people recognize several different categories of universal. Some propose that there are such things as abstract particulars—individual properties such as the blackness of my jacket.

Here (Figure 15.1) is an example of a four-category ontology recently developed by E. J. Lowe. (It's also one which some people have attributed to Aristotle, and which people like Barry Smith, who does a lot of work on ontology of information systems, seem broadly to accept.) Lowe distinguishes both between particulars and universals, and between objects and properties. So, as well as identifying particular objects

referent	sense	legisign	sinsign
	megatype	type	token
object	**concept**	**word-type**	**word-token**
situation	proposition	sentence	utterance
	work	manifestation	item

Figure 15.2. A four-level semiotic ontology.

such as my jacket, and universal properties such as being black or blackness, he also recognizes particular properties such as the blackness of my jacket, and universal objects or kinds such as "jacket," of which my jacket is an instance. Only objects are concrete: all the rest are abstract.

Cross-cutting that kind of ontology is another kind which focuses on the ontological status of linguistic or semiotic phenomena. Here (Figure 15.2) the basic idea is to distinguish between (i) the thing in the world that a term refers to, (ii) the idea of that thing that we have in our minds, (iii) the term that we use to denote that thing or that idea, and (iv) any particular utterance or inscription of that term. Peirce was the first to make the distinction between type and token. (He originally called them legisign and sinsign.) There are some very interesting analogies to be drawn between the hierarchies of concept–word-type–word-token, proposition–sentence–utterance, and work–manifestation–item. I think there are a number of important implications for FRBR of doing that, but today I'm just going to suggest one.

Given all these proposals of basic categories, what are our options for determining the ontological status of subjects?

Separatism: I suppose we might decide that the category of subject is something different from any one of the categories we've already met. That doesn't sound promising.

Pluralism: The answer embedded in FRBR is to take the pluralist approach and say, Well, clearly some things that are subjects are particulars and we're going to call them Objects, Events, and Places, and some are universals and we're going to call them Concepts.

Unitarianism 1: An option of another kind would be to decide that everything that is a subject is actually a *set*—maybe a set of works or aggregates of propositions—and then the knotty question would arise of where sets fall in our ontology.

Unitarianism 2: Again, we might wish to argue that all subjects are in fact *kinds*, rather than sets, of work or proposition.

Here is another, unitarianist, idea. Maybe when we say that a work is about cataloging or about Buckingham Palace, what we really mean is that it's about the concept of cataloging, or the concept of Buckingham Palace. And all subjects are concepts. Does that make any sense? Does it help in any way? Let's think about this for a second.

Maybe this will provide some clarification. My use of "concept" here relates to its use in the semiotic ontology, where the sense or meaning of a term is distinguished from its referent or object. Sometimes people use "concept" to mean "kind" in Lowe's sense of a kind of object such as "jacket" or "palace." In FRBR, the entity-type Concept seems to include both kinds in Lowe's sense and other non-particular things. Another incidental point of clarification is to distinguish between the use of "type" in the semiotic sense, and the common use of type more loosely as a synonym of "kind" in Lowe's sense.

That last distinction is important because it allows us to keep the type/token dichotomy separate from the kind/instance dichotomy that's central to Lowe's ontology and that is expressed by one of the sorts of hierarchical relationship commonly defined in subject authority files.

Some proposals

So—to some concrete proposals made on the basis of this discussion:

- Eliminate the entity-types Object, Event, and Place. Keep Concept as an entity-type in the sense of the meaning of a term. Introduce Subject in Buizza and Guerrini's sense as a statement or proposition to which instances of Concept are related in various ways.

- Create a new attribute of Concept—maybe call it Type. All it tells you is whether the given Concept is a particular (object) or a universal (kind).

- Express all the paradigmatic relationships you need between instances of Concept.

- And, finally, treat subjects as analogous to works. Create two new entity-types Term-type and Term-token to mirror, in Group 3, the WMI (Work–Manifestation–Item) hierarchy of Group 1 entity-types. (I'm not a fan of Expression, so I like to ignore it.) This would also have the effect of demonstrating that FRBR takes seriously the idea that the subject of a work is not somehow a property that inheres in the work and is only to be uncovered by a cataloger, but is something whose contingent relationship to the work is created in a certain context at a certain time. In an important sense, works do not "have" subjects—it's items that "have" term-tokens. This echoes the idea prevalent in IR theory that documents, queries, and terms are ontologically equivalent.

References

Delsey, Tom. 2005. Modeling subject access: Extending the FRBR and FRANAR conceptual models. *Cataloging & Classification Quarterly* 39, no. 3/4: 49–61.

Goodman, Nelson. 1961. About. *Mind* 70, no. 277: 1–24.

Lowe, E. J. 2003. Recent advances in metaphysics. *Facta Philosophica* 5: 3–24.

Putnam, Hilary. 1958. Formalization of the concept "about." *Philosophy of Science* 25, no. 2: 125–30.

Ryle, Gilbert. 1933. "About." *Analysis* 1, no. 1: 10–11.

Thalheimer, Ross. 1936. More about "about." *Analysis* 3, no. 3: 46–48.

Wetzel, Linda. 2006. Types and tokens. In *The Stanford Encyclopedia of Philosophy*, ed. Edward N. Zalta. Stanford, CA: Center for the Study of Language and Information, Stanford University. Retrieved November 1, 2006, from http://plato.stanford.edu/entries/types-tokens/.

16
"Records in Context" in context: A brief history of archival data modeling

July 31, 2015

This talk was given at I-CHORA 7: 7th International Conference on the History of Records and Archives (Amsterdam, The Netherlands, July 29–31, 2015). A paper with the same title as the talk was published in **Engaging with records and archives: Histories and theories**, *edited by Fiorella Foscarini, Heather MacNeil, Bonnie Mak, and Gillian Oliver (London: Facet, 2016), 41–62.*

Part I

In this talk, I'm going to attempt to identify some historical factors that combine to explain current differences in the data modeling practices of the ALM (archives, libraries, and museums) community. Why would anyone want to do this? Well, there's something going on in the world of archival description and it's important. The International Council on Archives (ICA) has an Experts Group on Archival Description (EGAD), and this group is building a new archival data model to replace the old one. It's intended that the new one will be more in line with those developed in the library and (in particular) museum communities.

It struck me that a historical analysis might help us weigh up the pros and cons of doing this. Or, maybe I should say, I *assumed* that it would.

The idea was, well, if we can understand the historical conditions for the distinctive direction taken by developers of archival standards since 1987, and compare them with library and museum developments, then that will help us to account for differences in the data models that have been produced in each domain, and perhaps also help us to understand the need for a new archival model.

There's also an ethical subtext to all of this, which arises from asking the question, *Should* data models be *more* or *less* like one another than they currently are? I'm characterizing this as an ethical question because your answer might depend on how much you value uniformity versus diversity, which could be a complicating factor in your feelings about different data models.

You might be wondering, All right, but what's a data model when it's at home? and I'll get to that in a minute. Meanwhile, I want to point out some reasons why I *shouldn't* have tried to write this paper. The thing is, the history of this stuff doesn't really go back much further than about 1980, which makes it what's sometimes called *recent* history, where the word '"recent" is almost being used as a pejorative term. So the typical criticisms are, it's way too soon to start thinking about the events in question from a historical point of view, and I'm way too close to the events in question to be able to think about them in the non-politicized way that good history requires.

Also, there's the issue that I didn't actually go into any "traditional" archives to get this done, but at least I didn't carry out any interviews either, so I guess I dodged *that* bullet.

Now, my response to all these potential criticisms is that it wouldn't matter how non-recent the events in question were, I still wouldn't magically have access to the facts of the matter, I still wouldn't turn into someone who somehow is perfectly neutral. So, my view is that recent history is just like regular history, it can be done well, it can be done badly, but it isn't inherently bad.

Anyway, back to the assumption I mentioned earlier. Archival data modeling is a practice whose nature, purpose, and value are shaped by the specific historical and cultural conditions under which it is carried out. There are various kinds of these conditions, and various kinds of narratives corresponding to these kinds of conditions that might be written. Three kinds are an *individualist* / *agent*-oriented kind, a *functionalist* / *artifact*-oriented kind, and a *structuralist* / *domain*-oriented kind. I know I'm simplifying massively here, but I'm a classificationist and that's what classificationists do.

Here's an example of a narrative of the first of these kinds. The specific individuals and/or groups who have been involved in the production of the different data models, and their respective sets of interests, are different (in relevant ways). If you combine that empirical observation with another that you might have developed over a longer period of time, that different individuals/groups are likely to take different actions in similar situations, then that could be your explanation for any differences that you observe among data models.

And I'm sure you can imagine similar sorts of arguments that, instead of being agent-oriented, are artifact-oriented or domain-oriented. Needless to say, most historical explanations involve factors of more than one type. But then again, the second and third types of explanation do sound pretty good.

Part II

So actually that's the end of Part I, which was a general kind of preamble, and now we're into Part II, which itself starts with a more specific preamble. Let's take a look at some of the terminology used in data modeling. A *conceptual model* is a representation of reality, a simplification that reduces complexity. It reduces the world to a specification of the classes (types) of things that are (considered to be) the most important in a given domain, e.g., agents, actions, artifacts, ideas, places, periods, properties, relations.

A *data model*₁ adds flesh to the bare bones of a conceptual model. It identifies the kinds of data (i.e., data about the things classified in the conceptual model) that may be collected, stored, accessed, and used. An *entity–relationship model* is a species of conceptual/data model₁,

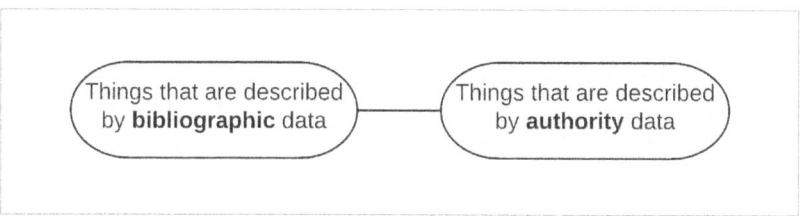

Figure 16.1.   The most basic data model ever.

in which each class of things is modeled as an entity or as a relationship. A *data model*$_2$ can be any of the above.

So here (Figure 16.1) is a graphical representation of the most basic data model ever—two entities (Things that are described by bibliographic data, and Things that are described by authority data), one many-to-many relationship. It's for libraries.

Here (Figure 16.2) is a more general one, that would do for archives too: Things that are described by resource data, and Things that are described by authority data.

And here (Figure 16.3) is one that's specific to archives—Archival resources, and Persons—but it obviously doesn't cover all kinds of things that are describable by authority records.

Here (Figure 16.4) we're getting a bit closer to something that's actually useful: Archival resources—Fonds, Series, Files, Items—and Archival authorities—Corporate bodies, Persons, Families, Repositories, Functions.

And if we slap *this* (Figure 16.5: Model of the levels of arrangement of a fonds) on top, then we're really getting somewhere.

Anyway, I'd like to change the mood a little at this point and take you down memory lane, all the way back to 1987! A pretty momentous year, as I'm sure you'll agree. (Among other things, it was the year I graduated

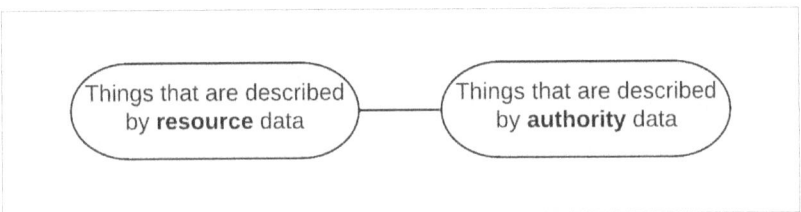

Figure 16.2. The most basic data model ever (amended).

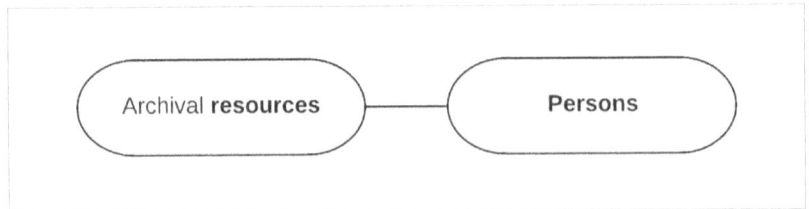

Figure 16.3. The most basic data model ever (amended again).

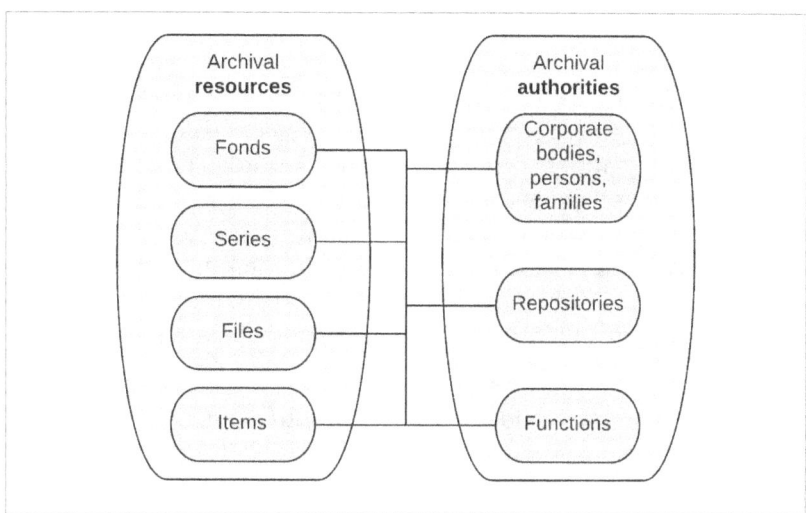

Figure 16.4. An archival data model.

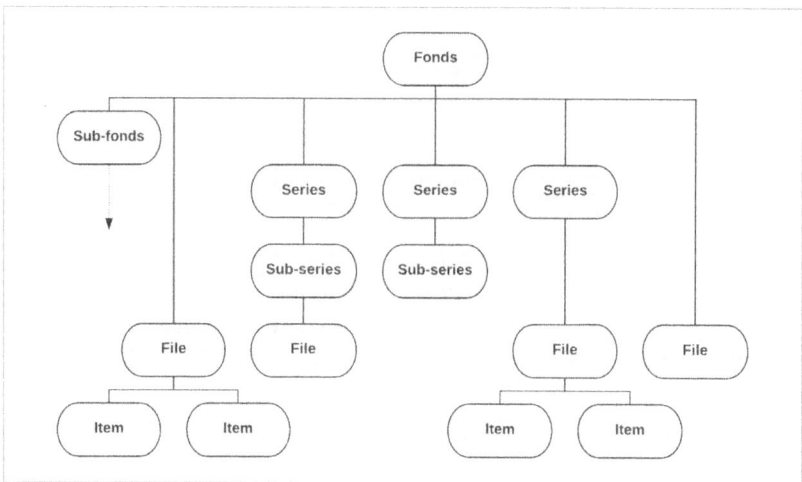

Figure 16.5. A model of the levels of arrangement of a fonds.

with two things, a philosophy degree, and not one single idea about what to do next.) It was also the year when the ALM community started to think seriously about data modeling. The International Council on Museums (ICOM) had a special committee on documentation, CIDOC, which itself had a working group on Data Standards, and at their meeting that year, they started to talk about devising a data model that would identify and standardize "those data fields most essential for adequate documentation of collection objects."

About a year later, the ICA in collaboration with the National Archives of Canada held an Invitational Meeting of Experts on Descriptive Standards (IMEDS). Check out what David Bearman said about it at the time. "To me, the agreement around the table that a number of entities other than holdings—entities such as repositories, records-creating organizations, retention schedules, facilities, and users—might be promising areas for development of description standards was an exciting outcome of the meeting. Clearly archivists are ready to think about the possibility of sharing authority records of various sorts in order to realize the potential benefits of information exchange at the international level."

And then the librarians were the last to get in on the act—a whole two years later IFLA held a seminar on Bibliographic Records that kick-started the process that would eventually lead to the FRBR model.

So right now we have three data model standards: the Conceptual Reference Model (CRM) maintained by ICOM-CIDOC; the model that underlies ICA's International Standard Archival Description (ISAD) and related standards, and FRBR itself. I'll come back to these in a minute, but for now I'll just say that it doesn't take much study to reveal that these are three very different animals, but it's not so clear how they got to be so different.

First, I'm going to take a slightly more detailed look at the context in which the IMEDS meeting took place, starting with the situation in Canada. "It was fitting that this meeting was held in Canada because, during the 1980s, the Canadian archival professional community had devoted a great deal of attention to the issue of such standards and had created a national infrastructure to develop them." (Stibbe 1993). In 1986, the Bureau of Canadian Archivists (BCA) had issued a report called *Toward descriptive standards* which made 35 recommendations for the development of descriptive standards for archival materials, and this was followed the next year by *Developing descriptive standards: A call to action*.

Moving to the US: If you wanted to, you could argue that 1977 was Year Zero when it comes to archival data modeling, but you know, whatever. (That was when the Society for American Archivists, SAA, established the National Information Systems Task Force, NISTF, which recommended "that archivists agree on categories of descriptive information and employ common data elements to convey this information" [Gibbs Thibodeau 1993].) The first edition of Steven L. Hensen's *Archives, Personal Papers, and Manuscripts* (APPM) was published in

1983; the USMARC format for Archival and Manuscripts Control (AMC) was made available in 1984; and in 1987, the SAA published Bearman's *Towards national information systems for archives & manuscript repositories: The National Information Systems Task Force (NISTF) papers, 1981–84*.

Meanwhile, in the UK, the British Library and the Society of Archivists had collaborated on a survey of archival automation in 1983, and a first draft of the *Manual of Archival Description* (MAD) appeared in 1986.

We're very lucky, as it happens, to have a rather useful artifact available to us, which is a compilation of the papers that were presented at IMEDS. It wasn't published until five years later, but that doesn't bother us in 2015 of course. The reference is *Toward international descriptive standards for archives: Papers presented at the ICA Invitational Meeting of Experts on Descriptive Standards* (National Archives of Canada, Ottawa, October 4–7, 1988), München: K. G. Saur, 1993. From these papers, all written in 1988 or earlier, we can infer several things about the situation in 1987. One is that not many people had at that time given any thought to archival data modeling. Both Weber and Bearman identify data structure, content, and value standards, but no data model standards. "The archival profession traditionally has balked at rigorously examining archival description … . Archivists do not have clearly articulated, precise statements about descriptive requirements. Quite frankly, the profession's understanding of the role of archival description is unclear. We do not know what the purpose of our descriptive systems is other than the broadly defined goal of improving access to materials." (Weber 1993).

On the other hand, we can see the first small steps taken in the direction of data modeling. Michael Cook, for instance, was eloquent about his understanding of the relation of computer science to archival science. "The arrival of computers has revealed that much traditional archival practice has been based upon theories and assumptions common to computer work… . In the light of computer practice, we can for the first time see what we were always trying to do; and for the first time, we have a strong motive for doing it effectively… . For example, sets of archival descriptions are files in a database. The information within the database is an assembly of data elements, each with a special characteristic: these are the values associated with fields within the record. The way in which the various fields are linked within records is a data structure." (Cook 1993).

OK, a second major inference we can draw is about the perception that archival data are qualitatively very different from the sorts of data you get in libraries and museums. Essentially this was the mainstream view. "Toward the end of the 1970s, descriptive standards in librarianship … began to become much more codified… . At least some archivists began to feel pressure to conform to these standards. The first response of these was principally rejection. The challenge and the response revealed that there was little common ground in professional language and terminology, in common practice, or in the understanding of professional aims." (Cook 1993).

Lisa Weber had quite a bit to say on this point, emphasizing that archival description was about providing access to collections. "Cataloging is the library function most analogous to archival description, although the two processes are not the same. Archival description encompasses a lengthy process of providing access to collections or groups of materials… . Creating library-like catalog records for archival materials is only one activity in the process and usually not the most important one. Comparatively, library cataloging is generally at the item level, takes less time per item, and is the primary means of providing access to published materials." (Weber 1993).

"Even assuming that some library standards can accommodate archival needs, clear distinctions exist between library and archival materials. Common sense suggests that archival descriptive systems will need to answer different kinds of questions beyond the ones intended to be answered by the four objectives of the library catalog… . For example, if provenance is often more important than authorship in the context of archival materials, how can archival descriptive systems improve access to the corporate entity that created the records? Does an archival descriptive system need to provide access to the functions of a creating agency or body? … The answers to these questions should determine the categories of data that archivists include in an archival description. To determine the answers, we must study users to determine how they discover the archival materials that they seek." (Weber 1993).

"One of the most valuable lessons U.S. archivists learned from developing the data element dictionary and the USMARC AMC format was the recognition that archivists collect and distribute different categories of information. These categories include data about provenance or context, content, physical aspects of the materials, access to the materials, and actions, or what archivists do to the materials. The ability to separate these categories is helping to articulate just what we do and to see new options and possibilities in how we do things." (Weber 1993).

Not only were archival data about different things, they were arranged in different ways, specifically in the hierarchical arrangement that is so familiar. Lisa Weber called this "the principle of levels." "Both the British and Canadian archival communities are examining archival description from 'first principles'; that is, they are establishing principles of archival description from which archival descriptive standards follow. One result is the central principle of levels of records and the subsequent identification of categories of information for each specific level." (Weber 1993). "British and Canadian archivists are approaching standards development from the perspective of levels of arrangement and description. Though American archivists are concentrating on less hierarchically confined levels of access, all archivists must be concerned about these issues." (Weber 1993).

Michael Cook also talked about this principle. "Data management by automated systems is quite amenable to the idea of linked files arranged in hierarchical levels of dependence. … [T]he principal objection to using library standards in archival management is that library cataloguing systems do not accommodate the concept of level (especially where changes of level require different models of description)." (Cook 1993).

So to summarize, what we have in archival science in the mid-1980s are the following three unique perspectives on the kinds of things, and the kinds of data about things, that are important to archivists: A general orientation towards the *collection*; a focus on the *logical scope of description* as a basis for structuring entity-types; and an identification of *fonds*, *series*, *file*, and *item* as the core entity-types of interest. If you like, you could characterize this as a unique ontology, but essentially these three perspectives combine to form the data model that is implicit in archival science.

I say implicit because there is no single document in existence that adds the archival resource–authority data model (Figure 16.4) to the model of the levels of arrangement of a fonds (Figure 16.5), so that both are set in the context of four different ways of categorizing archival descriptions (Figure 16.6) and in relation to the universe of archival content and encoding/structure standards (Figure 16.7).

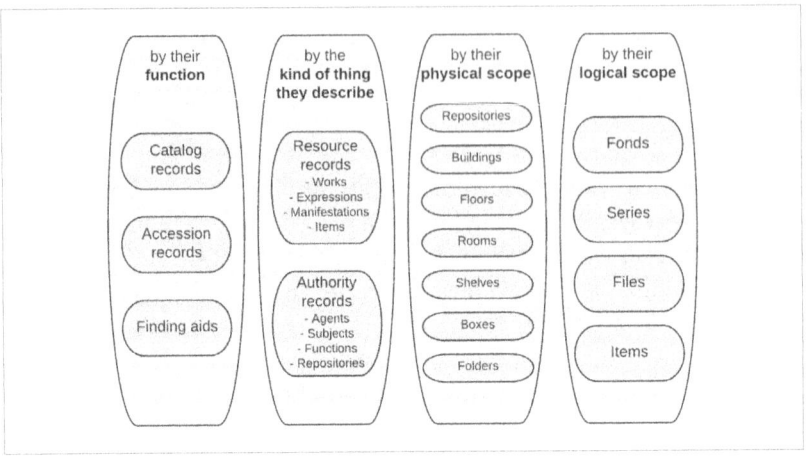

Figure 16.6. Four different ways of categorizing archival descriptions (every one of them excellent in its own way).

	Archival resource records	Archival authority records: Creators	Archival authority records: Repositories	Archival authority records: Functions
International content standards	ISAD(G)	ISAAR(CPF)	ISDIAH	ISDF
U.S. national content standards	DACS2	DACS2	DACS3?	DACS3?
International encoding / structure standards	EAD	EAC-CPF	EAG	EAC-F?

Figure 16.7. Archival content and encoding/structure standards.

I'd like to ask you now to keep that implicit model in mind as best you can, and mentally compare it with the two other data models, the librarians' FRBR model, and the museologists' CRM. So here (Figures 16.8–10) are three canonical diagrams from the Final Report on FRBR from 1998. And here (Figure 16.11), this is interesting, I didn't steal this from anywhere, I made it up. It's an ultra-simplification of CIDOC's CRM, with not just Object, but also Event taking center-stage. If you're not satisfied with that (and why would you be?), take a look at the website where you can view the latest version of the CRM: http://www.cidoc-crm.org/docs/cidoc_crm_version_6.1.pdf (February 2015). It's 219 pages long!

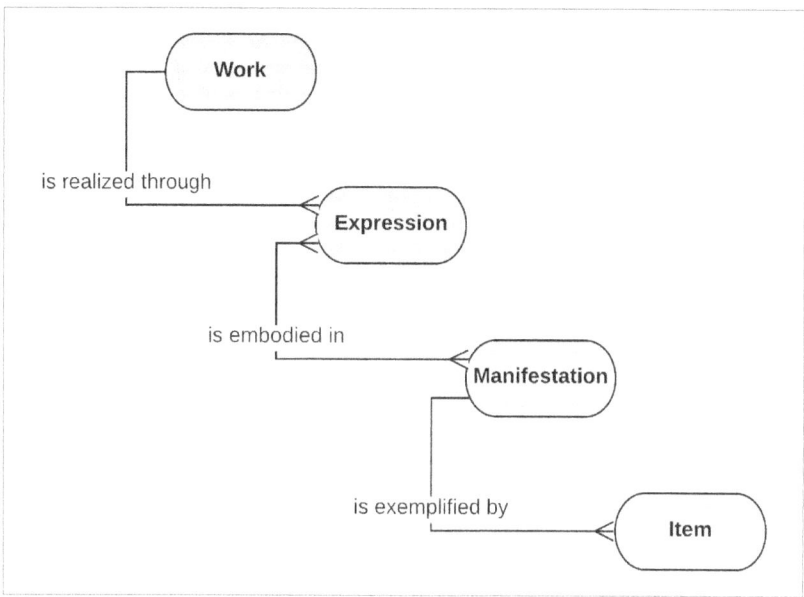

Figure 16.8. FRBR's Group 1 entities and primary relationships.

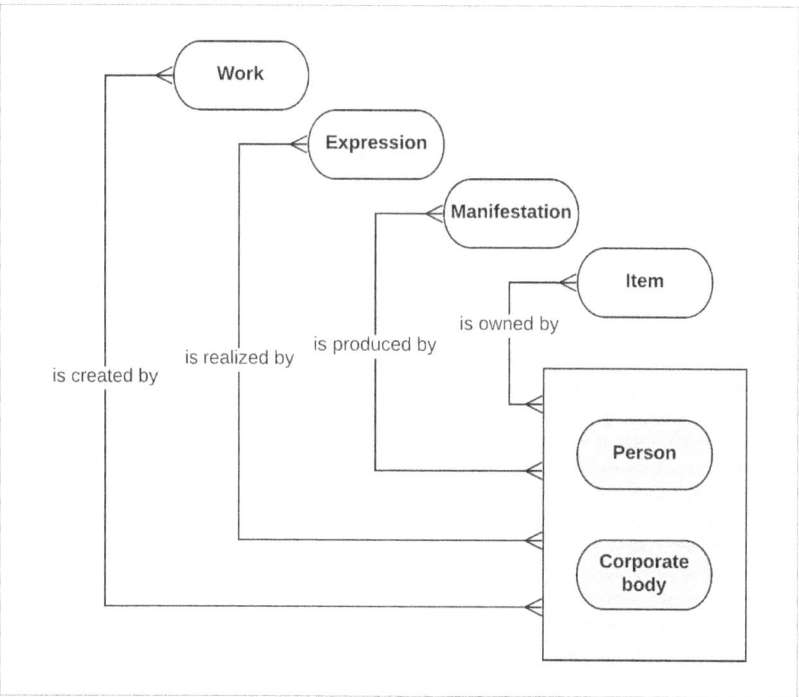

Figure 16.9. FRBR's Group 2 entities and "responsibility" relationships.

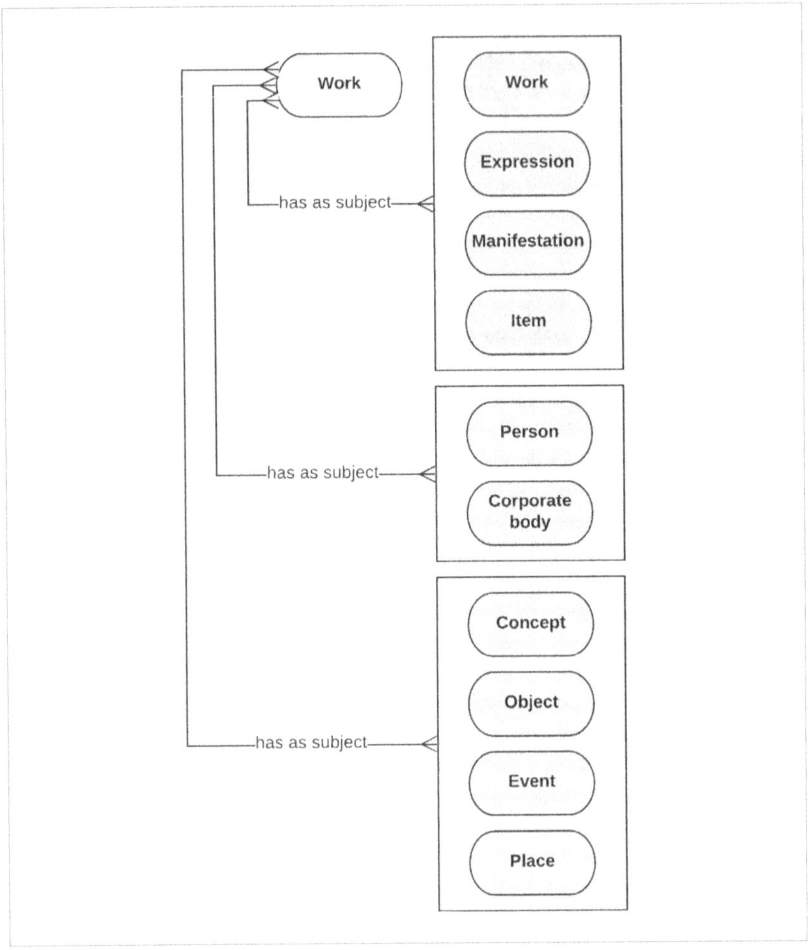

Figure 16.10. FRBR's Group 3 entities and "subject" relationships.

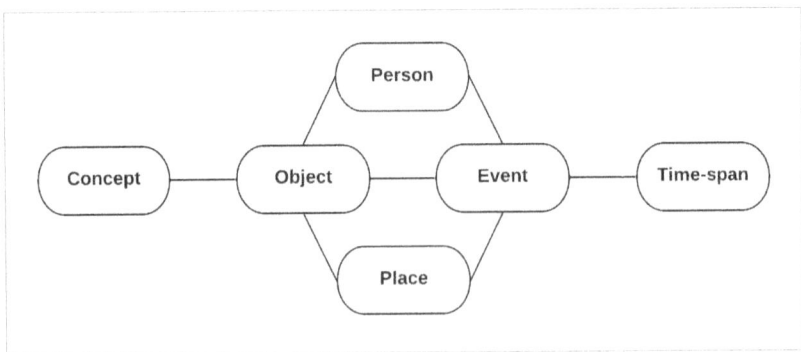

Figure 16.11. Ultra-simplified CIDOC CRM.

Sector	General orientation	Basis for structuring entity-types	Core entity-types	Relation to encoding-standard development
Archives	collection	logical scope of description	fonds, ..., items	around the same time
Libraries	object	role played by resource	works, ..., items	later
Museums	event	relative location in space-time	relationships between events	earlier

Table 16.1. Properties of ALM data models.

See Table 16.1 for a summary of the key differences between existing data models in archives, libraries, and museums.

Part III

We're at Part III already!

One upshot of the fact that the archival data model has never been codified in any official document is that, in 2012, ICA decided to rectify this by charging an Experts Group on Archival Description "to develop a conceptual model for archival description" with "clearly defined entities and ... relationships." The goal is for such a model—which has come to be called "Records in Context"—to be in close alignment with CRM and FRBR.

In the light of the preceding discussion, here's a question we might wish to ask ourselves: Will harmonization with CRM require wholesale replacement of a well-established family of standards, developed over a two-decade period, in which data elements for the description of records and their contexts are already clearly defined?

Or, there's this one, too. Does our analysis reveal that there are clear, predictable, persistent, pervasive differences in the opinions of leadership groups; in the types of resources handled, and the techniques used to handle them; and/or in the dominant theoretical traditions in each domain? If so, then what is to be gained by changing any existing data model to one that is better aligned with others?

Or, there's these. Which of the following conditions are different now? Is there any less of a focus on collections, logical scope of description, or fond, series, file, item? Is there any more of a focus on events or objects, relative location in space-time or role played by resource, relationships between events or work, expression, manifestation, item? If the answer to any is "yes," then absolutely, I can see why we should be going full steam ahead with the realignment with CRM.

But I don't think "yes" is the right answer.

So this is my slightly polemical conclusion: Don't do it.

In 1987, Lisa Weber made an interesting distinction between pseudo-standards, "practices that appear to be standards but are not," and de facto standards, "standards that arise through common practice without any formal agreement." The current archival data model may well be a de facto standard, but will EGAD's be a pseudo-standard?

David Bearman also made an interesting point: "New description standards should not be totally revolutionary, because they need to connect to existing practice, not only to convince people to follow them but also to link past descriptions to future descriptions. New standards could simply be a codification of existing practice; indeed, the simplest way to make behavior conform to a standard is to declare a current practice as the standard. If current practice embodies a range of approaches, a standard can be defined to encompass them all." (Bearman 1993).

And so did Michael Cook: "Because of the MDA's interest in archival materials associated with museum collections, it is quite likely … that in Britain, the development of national databases will occur through collaboration between archives and museum services rather than between archives and libraries. This divergence of tradition may well have serious consequences for the long-term development of the profession." (Cook 1993).

The last thing I wanted to say is this. Obviously I could have used other methods. Oral history, for example, or discourse analysis. And as much as I think history can tell us a lot, it's evaluation, against time-honored criteria, that will fill in the blanks.

On evaluation, we can leave the final word to David Bearman, written in 1988, but still no less valid today. "… We must always subject our standards to the test of use. Whoever the users are for whom the standards were designed, we must study their use of the descriptions and the implementations we offer, and be ready to evolve these standards and implementations in response to needs… . No standards deserve to be implemented as a strategy to improve access unless they can be shown to work… . Only empirical evidence should be accepted as an argument for standards if the standards are intended to promote access through automated systems. In all aspects of the standardization process, we must stoutly resist introducing requirements that have no warrant in archival practices and that will return few, if any, benefits." (Bearman 1993).

References

Bearman, David. 1988. Archives description practices. *Archival Informatics Newsletter* 2, no. 3: 54–57.

Bearman, David. 1993. Strategy for development and implementation of archival description standards. In International Council on Archives, Invitational Meeting of Experts on Descriptive Standards, *Toward international descriptive standards for archives: Papers presented at the ICA Invitational Meeting of Experts on Descriptive Standards* (National Archives of Canada, Ottawa, October 4–7, 1988), 161–171. München: K. G. Saur, 1993.

Cook, Michael. 1993. The relationship between automation and descriptive standards. In International Council on Archives, Invitational Meeting of Experts on Descriptive Standards, *Toward international descriptive standards for archives: Papers presented at the ICA Invitational Meeting of Experts on Descriptive Standards* (National Archives of Canada, Ottawa, October 4–7, 1988), 119–132. München: K. G. Saur, 1993.

Gibbs Thibodeau, Sharon. 1993. Archival descriptive standards in the United States. In International Council on Archives, Invitational Meeting of Experts on Descriptive Standards, *Toward international descriptive standards for archives: Papers presented at the ICA Invitational Meeting of Experts on Descriptive Standards* (National Archives of Canada, Ottawa, October 4–7, 1988), 91–94. München: K. G. Saur, 1993.

IFLA Study Group on the Functional Requirements for Bibliographic Records. 1998. *Functional requirements for bibliographic records: Final report.* München: K. G. Saur.

Pitti, Daniel, Bogdan-Florin Popovici, Bill Stockting, and Florence Clavaud. 2014. Experts Group on Archival Description: Interim report. In *Girona 2014: Arxius I Indústries Culturals: Proceedings of the 2nd Annual Conference of Archives.*

Stibbe, Hugo L. P. 1993. Foreword. In International Council on Archives, Invitational Meeting of Experts on Descriptive Standards, *Toward international descriptive standards for archives: Papers presented at the ICA Invitational Meeting of Experts on Descriptive Standards* (National Archives of Canada, Ottawa, October 4–7, 1988), iii–iv. München: K. G. Saur, 1993.

Weber, Lisa B. 1993. Archival descriptive standards: Concepts, principles, and methodologies. In International Council on Archives, Invitational Meeting of Experts on Descriptive Standards, *Toward international descriptive standards for archives: Papers presented at the ICA Invitational Meeting of Experts on Descriptive Standards* (National Archives of Canada, Ottawa, October 4–7, 1988), 105–118. München: K. G. Saur, 1993.

D
Classification

17

The Universal Decimal Classification and its historical relationship to the DDC

November 7, 2006

This talk was given at ASIS&T 2006: 69th Annual Meeting of the American Society for Information Science and Technology (Austin, TX, November 3–8, 2006) as part of a panel session on "Paul Otlet, documentation, and classification." The panel chair was Boyd Rayward, and speakers were Jonathan Furner, Kathryn La Barre, and Boyd Rayward.

Paul Otlet had many great ideas. The Universal Decimal Classification (UDC) was arguably the lasting concrete outcome of his ambitious attempt to implement "universal bibliographic control," i.e., to create and maintain a complete catalog of all published documents—journal articles as well as monographs. Convinced of the value of open access to knowledge as a prerequisite for world peace, and of international cooperation and standardization as the most effective means of achieving their goals for the "documentation movement," Otlet and his friend Henri La Fontaine set up the Institut International de Bibliographie (IIB) at a conference of bibliographers in Brussels in 1895. The first edition of the classification scheme used for their catalog was published in French as the *Manuel du Répertoire Universel Bibliographique* under the aegis of the IIB in 1907. Belgian government funding for maintenance of the RUB and its *Manuel* ceased in the 1920s, and the production of later editions in twenty-three languages of what came to be known as the Classification Décimale Universelle (and ultimately as the UDC) was supervised by a committee of the IIB headquartered in Le Hague, Netherlands. The IIB became the International Federation for Documentation and Information (FID) before filing for bankruptcy in 2000. From 1992, the UDC has been maintained by a separate international consortium currently consisting of standards bodies from Russia, Spain, and the United Kingdom, and is widely used in various versions around the world, mainly in special and technical libraries, and predominantly in Eastern Europe.

I'd like to take the opportunity today to make a single point about the historiography of classification. From one point of view, the history of bibliographic classification could be written straightforwardly as an account of the *professionalization* of a particular set of *practices* intended to serve library users' needs, and the *rationalization* of a particular set of *principles* that serve to guide practitioners. The ideal of establishing "universal bibliographic control" through the global standardization of techniques for describing, organizing, and providing access to the world's recorded knowledge served as the motivation for much of the technical work of library and information scientists through the twentieth century, and continues to drive the development of metadata standards (for digital and multimedia as well as printed resources) in the twenty-first. Universal classification schemes—i.e., schemes intended for general application to library materials of all kinds across all subject areas—have come to serve as core components of a global infrastructure that has been strongly facilitative of cross-national flows of information and ideas. Correspondingly, the history of the rise to dominance, since their origins in a forty-year period spanning the nineteenth and twentieth centuries, of the three most widely used universal schemes—the Dewey Decimal Classification (DDC), Library of Congress Classification (LCC), and Universal Decimal Classification (UDC)—is commonly told from a teleological perspective, with little questioning of the benefits that the transnationalizing infrastructure to which they contribute is assumed to bring.

A complementary view of the universal schemes treats them as the *objects of* (rather than as *supports for*) transnationalization, and focuses on explaining the conditions under which *some* schemes have proven their utility far beyond the boundaries of the contexts in which they were produced, while other schemes have remained purely local in application or have failed even to maintain a lasting local prominence despite their apparent technical advantages. This approach emphasizes the impact not only of aspects of the social, cultural, political, economic, and technological contexts in which classification schemes are developed and promoted, but also of the motivations and intentions of the schemes' developers and promoters. The figures of Melvil Dewey, an efficiency-conscious entrepreneur, and the more idealistic Paul Otlet still loom large in the parallel histories of the "big three" schemes, which are marked by several incidents involving negotiations among proponents of rival schemes that subsequently proved to be crucial turning points.

Dewey's initial decision to adopt an innovative notation amounted to a huge advance on existing schemes: decimal fractions expressed in the form of Arabic numerals were easily understood by speakers of different languages, and infinitely hospitable to new subtopics, and the advantages of this notation were immediately understood by Otlet and La Fontaine when they began their search for a means of ordering their universal bibliography. Dewey's agreement with Otlet and La Fontaine in the 1890s that allowed the two Belgians to base their "Brussels expansion" on the DDC so long as they refrained from publishing a version in English was as significant as his subsequent refusal to allow the Library of Congress similarly to model the LCC on the DDC, and his assistant Dorcas Fellows' refusal in the 1920s to countenance any future convergence between the DDC and the UDC, thereby setting the two schemes off on quite separate trails. Later decisions that have proved equally important include Dewey's own lack of commitment in his final years to producing different versions of the DDC for application in different kinds and sizes of library (leaving doors open for other schemes); DDC editor Benjamin Custer's implementation in the 1960s and 1970s of modern techniques for faceting and synthesis (raising the bar for rivals); and the terminal decline of the UDC's parent organization, the International Federation for Documentation and Information (forcing the modernization and rationalization of procedures for coordinating the UDC's many translations).

Much excellent commentary on the historical relationship between the UDC and the DDC may be found in the references listed here.

References

Comaromi, John Phillip. 1976. *The eighteen editions of the Dewey Decimal Classification*. Albany, NY: Forest Press.

McIlwaine, Ia C. 1997. The Universal Decimal Classification: Some factors concerning its origins, development, and influence. *Journal of the American Society for Information Science* 48: 331–339.

Miksa, Francis L. 1998. *The DDC, the universe of knowledge, and the post-modern library*. Albany, NY: Forest Press.

Rayward, W. Boyd. 1994. Visions of Xanadu: Paul Otlet (1868–1944) and hypertext. *Journal of the American Society for Information Science* 45: 235–250.

18

The treatment of topics relating to people of mixed race in bibliographic classification schemes: A critical race-theoretic approach

July 14, 2004

This talk was given at ISKO 2004: 8th International Conference of the International Society for Knowledge Organization (London, England, July 13–16, 2004). A paper with the same title as the talk, co-authored with Anthony W. Dunbar, was published in **Knowledge organization and the global information society: Proceedings of the Eighth International al ISKO Conference,** *edited by Ia C. McIlwaine (Würzburg, Germany: Ergon), 115–120.*

The structure of my talk today is as follows [Slide 2]. I'll begin by presenting our original motivation for embarking on our study and stating the research question that grew from there, before moving on to a specification of the variety of available approaches on which we would draw, and a brief indication of the kinds of conclusions we came to. As we were doing the work of thinking about these aspects, however, it became increasingly clear that our focus on the treatment of topics relating to racially mixed people was limiting in the sense that that treatment was reflective of some much broader issues that themselves seemed to be under-investigated. I considered that it might be more interesting to leave that detailed analysis for another occasion and to introduce the broader research question instead, with the intention of stimulating further discussion. In that sense, the content of this talk should be taken as the result of a very preliminary exploration of the chosen topic rather than that of any completed project, and I would very much welcome your feedback.

Our original motivation

So here essentially was the motivation. The data in Table 18.1, above, form an extract from Table 5 in the 21st edition of the Dewey Decimal Classification, published in 1996. Table 5 is the table for "Racial, Ethnic, National Groups," which made its first appearance in the 18th edition of 1971. The notations listed here (like those in the rest of the table and in fact in all of the DDC's tables) are intended for use in number building, as extensions to base numbers.

–03 Basic races
–034 Caucasoids
–035 Mongoloids
–036 Negroids
–04 Mixtures of basic races
–042 Caucasoids and Mongoloids
–043 Mongoloids and Negroids
–044 Negroids and Caucasoids
–046 Caucasoids, Mongoloids, Negroids

Table 18.1.   DDC Table 5 (1971–2003, 18th–21st eds.).

We might infer from the vocabulary and structure of this portion of the classification scheme that the distinctions made here are based on assumptions of four kinds:

- that people may be grouped according to some shared racial characteristic (or combination of such characteristics);
- that some of the resulting populations or "races" are more "basic" than others;
- that the races listed at –03 are all the basic ones; and
- that it is possible for a person to share or "mix" the racial characteristics of more than one race.

The vocabulary used here might strike you as old-fashioned or pretentious at best, offensive at worse. We might prefer now to think of these categories as being labeled Whites, Blacks, and Asians. In any case, any criticism we might have of the terminology is rendered irrelevant by several changes that were implemented in the 22nd edition of DDC, published last year [in 2003]. Table 5 is now simply called "Ethnic and national groups," in order (as the press release states) "to reflect the de-emphasis on race in current scholarship." Class –03 disappears, because it is perceived to be (quote) "without meaning in context." In fact, with the new edition, it seems as if the populations that are typically referred to as races are no longer available as subject matter for writers. We are told that "A work that emphasizes race should be classed with the ethnic group that most closely matches the concept of race described in the work," as if races are defined on the same basis as ethnic groups are. Finally, class –04 is not only renumbered but recast in very different terminology, as "Persons of mixed ancestry with ethnic origins from more than one continent," without using the word "race" at all.

Our original research question

When first reading about, and then seeing these changes at first hand, our first inclination was to engage in an analysis of their implications for classifying material about *racially mixed people*. Topics relating to racially mixed people have become of increasing interest to authors and readers over the last half-century, and the number of books published on such topics is increasing exponentially. Conceptions of the nature of "mixture" are interesting from an ontological point of view, and we thought it would be particularly interesting to carry out an analysis of the logical rationale for reconceptualizing class −04, and of the potential and actual effects of that reconceptualization.

Some potentially useful approaches

We identified quite a number of approaches as being potentially useful in guiding us in analysis of this kind. Within LIS, we identified the following work as being particularly helpful: Hjørland on *domain analysis* (which provides for critical analysis of the "social and ideological embeddedness" of classification schemes); Foskett, Berman, Olson, and Bowker and Star on *critical classification* (which views schemes as social constructions reflecting the biases of their contexts); Frohmann on *discourse analysis* (which sees schemes as interpretable texts); and Tennis on *subject ontogeny* (which promotes historical accounts of the "social life" of a domain's terminology).

The fields outside of LIS that we have drawn from most, fairly predictably, include the *philosophy of race* (e.g., Taylor), focusing on the ontological status of racial and ethnic categories; the *sociology of race* (e.g., Omi and Winant), focusing on the formation of racial groups; and *ethnic studies* (e.g., Root), focusing on personal multiethnic identity. The *public policy* literature on racial categorization is also interesting in the context of recent changes in the decennial census in the US and UK. And then there is *critical race theory* (CRT; e.g., Delgado). CRT emerged from critical legal studies in the 1980s as an approach to the study of the persistent, endemic, systemic racism that is attributed to legal institutions. It draws not only from the fields already mentioned, but also radical feminism (in its making explicit the systemic nature of discrimination) and the civil rights movement (in its activist motivation). We suggest that, if the field of knowledge organization is to retain its relevance and vitality in an age in which the true diversity and complexity of racial attributes are increasingly apparent, it is of crucial importance to evaluate the potential usefulness of CRT as a tool for the analysis of bibliographic classification schemes. The identification of CRT as such a tool is the primary contribution of the paper published in the proceedings.

An instructive alternative to Dewey

For comparison, this (Table 18.2) is how racial categories are handled in the US census, or at least how they were handled in the most recent US national census of 2000. Respondents were asked to select from a list of options including the six basic categories that you see in bold here. The identification of Latino people as members of an ethnic group and not of a race or of mixed race is interesting—in fact is of particular interest given our current focus on racially mixed people—but is not an issue we have time to consider further today. The 2000 census was notable for its allowing respondents to select more than one race in answer to the race question. Given the individual's capability to select as few as one or as many as six basic categories, that means census analysts have 63 racial categories to track (where, for instance, someone checking just "Asian" falls in a separate category from someone checking both "Asian" and "White"). Alternatively, the 57 combinations of two or more races could be collapsed into a seventh "Mixed Race" category that is mutually exclusive from the other six.

Ethnicity
− Hispanic or Latino
− Not Hispanic or Latino
Race
− American Indian or Alaska Native [+ write-in box for tribe(s)]
− Asian [6 specified categories + write-in box for Other]
− Black or African American
− Native Hawaiian or Other Pacific Islander [3 specified categories + write-in box for Other]
− White
− Some Other Race [+ write-in box]

Table 18.2.   Ethnic and racial categories for self-identification in US census, 2000.

1 American Indian or Alaska Native
2 Asian
3 Black or African American
4 Native Hawaiian or Other Pacific Islander
5 White
6 Some Other Race

7 Racially Mixed
   712 American Indian or Alaska Native / Asian
   7256 Asian / White / Some Other Race
   etc.

Table 18.3. A simple classification scheme for documents about topics relating to racial populations.

Taking our lead from the census categories, we might imagine a simple classification scheme for the organization of resources about racial populations looking something like this (see Table 18.3). It would be hopelessly US-centric, but we might also imagine simple ways in which its scope could be extended globally. Here, five races are listed; a category for topics relating to "Some Other Race" is added; and a seventh category for topics related to racially mixed people is sub-divided into as many of the 57 possible combinations as are deemed necessary. We might wish to set up such a simple scheme as a kind of straw man to introduce discussion of several of the challenges facing the classification scheme designer at this point.

Some challenges

Challenges that are generic to bibliographic classification

The first generic challenge is to satisfy what we might call the *exhaustivity principle*, which specifies that the scheme should be designed so that all documents may be assigned to existing classes, with minimal assignment to any category for items called "Other." We may ask: Do our five basic categories truly exhaust the races existing in the country in question, or indeed the world? Similarly, the *specificity principle* specifies that it should be possible using our scheme for documents to be classed specifically, with minimal assignment to classes that are broader than the subjects of those documents. Again, we might ask of our simple scheme: Is it possible for the basic classes that we have identified to be divided into narrower subclasses, allowing for more specific classification? If so, what are the criteria that may be used to guide the direction and frequency of such division?

The answer to this kind of question that is implicitly supplied by our scheme and the census is that, yes, the basic classes may be subdivided—in the case of the census, in at least two ways. One kind of subdivision is that carried out in order to cater for people who are members of two or more populations—people who are "racially mixed." The other kind, implemented in the census but not in our simple scheme as it currently stands, is that carried out in order to cater for people who specify their membership of a narrower population whose members are all also members of one of the broader populations. An interesting, possibly problematic, tendency is for these narrower populations to be defined on the basis of *ethnic* rather than *racial* characteristics—that's something I'll say something a little more about in a moment.

A third generic challenge is to satisfy the *nonlinearity principle*, which specifies that classes should not be arranged in any order that connotes a ranking or hierarchy that does not correspond with reality. It's often considered that alphabetical order satisfies such a principle. A question that might arise in connection with our simple scheme is whether the "Racially mixed" should be separate from the primary alphabetical order, or indeed whether its subclasses should appear at a lower level of the hierarchy than the other main classes. In what sense, for instance, is the class of mixed White and Asian people at a lower level, in reality, than the class of White people? The difficulty is the implication that the mixed categories are somehow less important than the basic categories, that the "basic" races are in some sense more pure than any "mixtures."

Challenges that are specific to racial categorization

Turning now to some of the more specific challenges faced in the current context, the first we might identify is the commonly-stated and well-understood result of centuries of work in physical anthropology, which is that racial populations are not natural kinds. In other words, races cannot be defined in biological or genetic terms, but rather are *social constructs* based primarily on perceptions of bodily appearance. We routinely identify a given person as White not on the basis of any knowledge of his or her genetic structure, but on the basis of the way he or she looks. Such assignment is essentially subjective, but the meaning assigned to a given bodily appearance may be a matter of intersubjective convention.

Many social constructionists are also realists, however, or (if you like) *radical constructionists*, in the sense that they see no reason to conclude from this characterization of race that races do not exist. In the jargon, races, though ontologically subjective, are epistemically objective. They are human artifacts, but artifacts nonetheless, and are very real, especially for those people who self-identify with them or are allocated social goods on the basis of their membership of them.

A second specific challenge is the very complex *intersectionality* of personal attributes. A person's race is not the only social population of which he or she is a member—clearly there are an infinite number of such populations, defined on the basis of one's ethnicity, class, gender, sexual orientation, and so on, and it is difficult to imagine what it would mean to identify any one of these characteristics of division as generally more important than any other, outside specific situations.

A third challenge is the *continuity* of racial populations. In the real world, racial populations are not discrete classes with clearly marked boundaries. Nor is it clearly the case that those classes may be placed on a single spectrum with two poles, for example white and black. To illustrate the significance of this latter point, consider a two-dimensional space, where each dimension is graded on a scale of 0 through 7. We might imagine that such a space may be used in the classification of people on the basis of their sexual orientation, where the *x*-axis represents the degree of the given person's attraction to other people of the same sex, and the *y*-axis represents the degree of attraction to people of the opposite sex. So homosexuals would be placed at bottom right, heterosexuals at top left, bisexuals at top right, and asexuals at bottom left. Such a space might allow for more specific classification of people by sexual orientation, but would be difficult to reduce to a one-dimensional linear scheme. Would *n*-dimensional spaces be useful for the classification of people by race? How many dimensions would we need? What would be the meaning of each dimension? Would a faceted scheme be a reasonable way of allowing for the representation of multiple dimensions? What kind of balance could we achieve between specificity and simplicity? These are all questions that any designer of a classification of racial populations is forced to address.

Schemes like the DDC—essentially enumerative schemes with some supplementary faceting—typically handle the kinds of challenge that we've been talking about in simple, routine, standard ways, not always because these ways are the best ways in terms either of correspondence with reality or effectiveness of retrieval, but because they're simple to implement and understand. For instance, given the fact of the ontological subjectivity of certain classes, bibliographic classification schemes typically make a selection from the full range of alternative options, of a single one of those options. Given the extreme intersectionality of attributes, enumerative schemes prioritize those attributes in a certain way (for example, gender first, race second). Given the continuity of classes, bibliographic schemes simply ignore it and treat classes as discrete and mutually exclusive. This is what we do in our simple scheme; this is what the census does; and this is what the DDC does.

Perhaps the most significant challenge for designers of schemes relating to racial populations, however, is one that we haven't really addressed yet. This is the challenge of satisfying the *self-identity principle*, which specifies that a scheme should support its users in the retrieval of documents about topics relating to the populations with which they self-identify. This principle is as important for people of mixed race as it is for others. In her statement of a "Bill of Rights for Racially Mixed People," Maria Root emphasizes the rights that a person of mixed race has to identify herself differently in different situations, to identify with more than one group of people, not to have to keep the races separate within herself, and to use the vocabulary that she prefers in communicating about being multiracial. Translating some of these rights to the context of document retrieval, we might imagine a situation in which a particular searcher, let's say a Métis from Canada, may choose to identify with, and seek resources about, (i) racially mixed people *generally*—in which case, in our simple scheme, she would look in class 7—or (ii) the Métis *in particular*—in which case she would look in class 715—or (iii) both First Nation people *and* White people—in which case she would look in classes 1 and 5—or (iv) either First Nation *or* White—in which case she would look either in class 1 or 5. We might ask:

Why should this person be forced to look in three separate main classes, perhaps widely separated on the shelves or in the catalog, simply in order to find resources about people she perceives to be like herself? And why should she be expected to be satisfied with a search in class 1, for instance, which would not retrieve relevant material classed in 715?

In our analysis of the revised Table 5, we identified many potential instances in which recall and precision failures are predictable. The details are complex and are best presented on paper, so we're saving those, hopefully, for publication. Fortunately, the impact of recall failures (at least) can be reduced through the implementation of a variety of devices such as "see also" references to other useful classes. Further enhancement of recall can be achieved with the development of retrieval systems that take advantage of the implicitly faceted structure of the DDC by allowing searches on individual components of class numbers, so the future prospects for increasingly effective searches on Table 5 notation look promising.

Modern race theory

I said earlier that we quickly found our focus on the treatment of topics relating to racially mixed people to be limiting, and that the issues that we addressed turned out to be indicative of some much broader issues that themselves seemed to be under-investigated. Essentially, the primary issue seems to be the eradication of most mentions of "race" from Table 5. As we saw earlier, Table 5 is now simply called "Ethnic and national groups," in order "to reflect the de-emphasis on race in current scholarship." Class –03, with its "basic races," has been dropped because it is perceived to be "without meaning in context." In the final few minutes, I do want to suggest one way in which the validity of this decision to de-racialize Table 5 might be brought into question. To do that requires a very quick overview of the development of race theory in modern times, moving from the classical race theory that originated in the 18th century, through the liberal perspective that emerged in the 19th century, to the critical race theory of the late 20th century.

Classical race theory

François Bernier was one of the first to express the notion that all the people in the world could be divided into four or five basic groups on the basis of physiological differences. Linnaeus of course is famous for his taxonomy of biological species, in which Homo Sapiens is divided into four varieties, defined primarily by geography but associated with certain specific characteristics.

The German naturalist J. F. Blumenbach seems to be the person responsible for the first classification of the world's people specifically on the basis of bodily appearance. He was also the first to rank his groups, specifically on the basis of their physical beauty. In later versions of classical race theory, this ranking would be extended to embrace the idea that moral, cognitive, and cultural characteristics are determined by physical traits, so that Asians and Blacks, for instance, were considered not simply less beautiful than whites, but less intelligent, less hard-working, and so on.

These, then, are the basic assumptions of classical race theory as it had emerged by the end of the eighteenth century:

- races are discrete and global;
- each race has a unique set of physiological traits;
- each cluster of physiological traits is associated with an equally distinct set of moral, cognitive, and cultural characteristics;
- races are rankable according to the value assigned to those characteristics;
- these characteristics are heritable as a kind of racial essence.

Liberal race theory

Each one of these assumptions has, of course, been called into question, with the result that most versions of contemporary liberal race theory may be characterized by their commitment to some kind of *eliminativism*—either a metaphysical eliminativism that denies the existence of races, or an ethical eliminativism that argues for the abolition of racial categories and/or abstention from racial discourse. This mode of thinking appears to be the source of the recent decisions made by the DDC.

Critical race theory

Critical race theory, on the other hand, is characterized by a *realism* with respect to races, one that allows for the existence of races as human artifacts defined by convention. In this mode of thinking, the races are simply those specific populations that result from the operation of the processes of racial formation—the processes identified by Omi and Winant as racial projects that both assign meaning to human bodies and bloodlines, and distribute social goods along the lines suggested by the resulting systems of meaning.

For the critical race theorist, a belief in the realism of races is a necessary prerequisite for mounting an effective challenge to the racism that is considered to be persistent, endemic, and systemic in contemporary Western society. The kind of color-blindness that is encouraged by the liberal race-theoretic approach, and that is reflected in the latest version of the DDC's Table 5, is perceived to have the effect merely of sustaining the status quo in which discrimination and economic and social inequities in favor of whites are institutionally maintained.

Two possible interpretations

In conclusion, then, we can identify two opposing evaluations of the changes to DDC. On the one hand, we might be convinced that those changes reflect quite an ingenious way of addressing the problems in the old Table 5 that were presumably seen by the editors—problems to do with the validity of engaging in racial discourse, reifying racial categories, using outdated terminology, etc. On this reading, there are a few technical issues to do with optimizing the effectiveness of retrieval that still await resolution, but on the whole this reading would be generally positive.

On the other hand, we might recognize that *racial identity* is incapable of expression through or reduction to *ethnic identity*, by definition, since racial identity results from interpretation of bodily appearance, whereas ethnic identity results from interpretation of culture, language, and religion etc. Similarly, *multi-racial ancestry* is not reducible conceptually to *multi-continental ancestry*, since races are not defined geographically. Any attempt to elide these conceptual distinctions, as in the latest Table 5, will necessarily fail.

Summary

The minimal aim of today's talk has been to highlight the historical significance of some of the changes made in the recent edition of the Dewey Decimal Classification—changes that might otherwise have passed without substantial comment—and to identify some of the issues that these changes raise. We intend in the near future to complete a full subject ontogeny (in Tennis's words) of "race" in the Dewey system, using discourse and domain analysis to track the ways in which the scheme has dealt with race since its inception in 1876, to analyze the context in which such changes occurred, and on which they have had reciprocal impact.

References

Berman, Sanford. 1971. *Prejudices and antipathies: A tract on the LC subject heads concerning people*. Metuchen, NJ: Scarecrow.

Bernier, François. [1684] 2000. A new division of the earth. In *The idea of race*, ed. Robert Bernasconi and Tommy L. Lott, 1–4. Indianapolis, IN: Hackett.

Blumenbach, Johann Friedrich. [1795] 2000. On the natural variety of mankind. In *The idea of race*, ed. Robert Bernasconi and Tommy L. Lott, 27–37. Indianapolis, IN: Hackett.

Bowker, Geoffrey C., and Susan Leigh Star. 1999. *Sorting things out: Classification and its consequences*. Cambridge, MA: MIT Press.

Delgado, Richard, ed. 1995. *Critical race theory: The cutting edge*. Philadelphia, PA: Temple University Press.

Foskett, A. C. 1971. Misogynists all: A study of critical classification. *Library Resources & Technical Services* 15, no. 2: 117–21.

Frohmann, Bernd. 1994. Discourse analysis as a research method in library and information science. *Library & Information Science Research* 16, no. 2: 119–38.

Hjørland, Birger. 2002. Domain analysis in information science: Eleven approaches—traditional as well as innovative. *Journal of Documentation* 58, no. 4: 422–62.

Linnaeus, Carolus. 1758. *Systema naturae*. 10th ed. Stockholm.

Olson, Hope A. 1998. Mapping beyond Dewey's boundaries: Constructing classificatory space for marginalized knowledge domains. *Library Trends* 47, no. 2: 233–54.

Omi, Michael, and Howard Winant. 1994. *Racial formation in the United States*. 2nd ed. New York: Routledge.

Root, Maria P. P. 1996. A bill of rights for racially mixed people. In *The multiracial experience: Racial borders as the new frontier*, ed. Maria P. P. Root, 3–14. Thousand Oaks, CA: Sage.

Taylor, Paul C. 2004. *Race: A philosophical introduction*. Cambridge: Polity.

Tennis, Joseph T. 2002. Subject ontogeny: Subject access through time and the dimensionality of classification. In *Challenges in knowledge representation and organization for the 21st century: Integration of knowledge across boundaries: Proceedings of the Seventh International ISKO Conference, 10-13 July 2002, Granada, Spain*, ed. María J. López-Huertas, 54–59. Würzburg, Germany: Ergon.

19

The Classification Research Group, 1952–2000: A citation analysis

July 11, 2000

This talk was given at ISKO 2000: 6th International Conference of the International Society for Knowledge Organization (Toronto, Canada, July 10–13, 2000).

Last week, I settled down to a nice evening in with Dialog's RANK command. I wanted to search in ISI's Social Sciences Citation Index for records of documents written by any of the 32 current editors of *Knowledge Organization*. I also wanted to limit my retrieval set to those records whose sources are categorized by ISI under the subject heading "Information science & library science." At the time of my search, the coverage of the database was 1972 – June 2000, so no documents published before that date would be recorded: neither would any documents appearing in sources not indexed by ISI—monographs or reports, for example, or "low-impact" journals.

So I searched on 32 queries, each of which looked like this:

S AU=[*name*]? AND SC=INFORMATION SCIENCE & LIBRARY SCIENCE

When I combined all the 32 retrieval sets, I obtained a final set of 408 records. Next, I applied Dialog's RANK command to this combined set in order to determine the authors whom *Knowledge Organization* editors cite most often. The function of the command RANK CA was to create a ranking, by frequency of citation, of those authors that are cited by the authors in my initial set.

Table 19.1 shows the top 10 authors who have been most highly cited by *Knowledge Organization* editors. Interesting, huh? OK, I did the same for cited documents too, and lots of even more interesting things emerged. It's a real shame we don't have time for them today. Anyhow, if you want to find out what happened, well, hopefully you'll be able to see extended results if or when I get to publish a full report.

Rank	Name	Country	Freq. of citations
1	Ranganathan, S. R.	India	31
2	Lancaster, F. W.	USA	24
	Svenonius, E.	USA	24
4	Pejtersen, A. M.	Denmark	19
5	Comaromi, J. P.	USA	17
6	Markey, K.	USA	15
	Soergel, D.	USA	15
	Vickery, B. C.	UK	15
9	Cutter, C. A.	USA	14
	Dahlberg, I	Germany	14
	Wilson, P.	USA	14

Table 19.1. Authors most highly cited by *KO* editors.

Now, we know that citation analysis is routinely criticized precisely on the grounds of the lack of validity of assumptions made by its practitioners about the correlation between degree of citedness and the level of quality of the cited work. But, if we can assume, firstly, that our original set of 32 citing authors is a representative sample of the "invisible college" whose members drive contemporary classification research, and secondly, that the authors cited by this initial set are those whose work has influenced or informed the work of the citing authors, then this list may be considered as an indication of the core authors in the field—those to whom newcomers might be directed in their early studies, or to whom established scholars might profitably return. Ranganathan, appropriately, is at the head of the list.

Ranganathan's position in the canon of twentieth-century classification theorists is assured. Of present interest, however, are the occurrences in this list of the names of eight core members of the British Classification Research Group: Derek W. Austin (1921–), Eric J. Coates (1916–), Jason E. L. Farradane (1906–1989), Douglas J. Foskett (1918–), Barbara R. F. Kyle (1913–1966), Jack Mills (1918–), Bernard I. Palmer (1910–1979), and Brian C. Vickery (1918–).

Rank	Name	Country	Freq. of citations
6	Vickery, B. C.	UK	15
12	Austin, D.	UK	13
27	Foskett, D. J.	UK	9
33	Coates, E. J.	UK	8
	Mills, J.	UK	8
57	Farradane, J. E. L.	UK	5
77	Palmer, B. I.	UK	4
117	Kyle, B.	UK	3
193	Classification Research Group	UK	2

Table 19.2. Citations made by KO editors to the "CRG core."

Five of the eight are cited eight times or more. But hang on: we're talking about eight citations? Isn't it the relative infrequency of such citations that might be considered surprising? Especially when you hear what people have had to say about the impact of the CRG.

Ia McIlwaine has written: "[I]ts influence has been pervasive … it is clear that the CRG has made a profound contribution to thinking about classification … and has laid the foundations … for a complete reform in the way that people think about the organization of knowledge." Eric Hunter has agreed that the CRG has had "a far-reaching effect … the members of this group advanced dramatically the frontiers of knowledge in classification…" Phyllis Richmond's review of Vickery's work for the CRG was simply entitled "Precedent-setting contributions to modern classification."

The pre-history of the CRG—the chain of events leading up to its formal inauguration by Vickery and Wells in 1952—is well-documented, usually beginning with the war-time meeting of Palmer and Ranganathan in India. Certainly, the early work of the CRG was drenched in Ranganathanian theory. The main concern was with facet analysis as an approach to developing classification schemes, which is commonly considered to be the primary contribution of Ranganathan himself to library science. But it could be argued that it was the members of the CRG, individually and in concert, who were most responsible both for developing this theory to the "standard" state that we take for granted today, and for fully exploring its practical potential by constructing numerous and various real-life schemes, many of which have enjoyed widespread and successful use over more than a quarter-century. Richmond advises that we "should give credit where credit is due. The Classification Research Group itself is unique … [filling] a gap between theory and practice."

Stage	Dates	Prime mover	Principal area of interest
1	1943–1951	Palmer	Faceted classification
2	1952–1961	Vickery	Special classification
3	1962–1968	Foskett	Universal classification
4	1969–1974	Austin	PRECIS
5	1975–2000	Mills	BC2

Table 19.3. History of the CRG.

My perception is that the work of the CRG remains undervalued in North America. My view is that there is much in the group's work of the 1950s, 1960s, and 1970s that is of far more than historical interest, but that the relative significance of this work and its actual impact on current classification theory and practice, is barely reflected in contemporary citation patterns. This is a view to which no manner of citation analysis can in itself lend conclusive support. We can easily determine which authors have been cited more often than others, but it is not so easy to demonstrate the frequency of absence of citations in contexts where they might otherwise have been expected to occur.

But there are some things that we can do with a purely descriptive, quantitative analysis of the type I'm about to describe. We can provide confirmatory evidence; inform historical interpretation; identify neglected materials; and stimulate renewal of interest.

The first step in this citation study was the creation of an initial subset of records from SSCI, records that name one of the people in the "CRG core" as cited author. There were three difficulties at this stage.

The first was that of optimizing recall. But since ISI implements no authority control of authors' names, each of the members of the CRG is represented on different occasions by different forms of his or her name. Farradane, for instance, is represented sometimes as FARRADANE J, sometimes as FARRADANE JEL, etc. We had to take care to exhaust all the possibilities we could think of.

The second problem was that of optimizing precision. But as a further consequence of SSCI's lack of authority control, there are many cases of the same name being used to refer on different occasions to different people. MILLS J and PALMER B, for example, are both used to refer to several people other than the ones in which we were interested. In the printed indexes, we were able to disambiguate manually, but in the online searches, we could only approximate to this process by deliberately limiting retrieval to the "Information science & library science" area of subject coverage.

We found it especially difficult to identify cited documents attributed to the Classification Research Group as a corporate body. Many variations beyond what might be expected were found, and there seemed to be no alternative but to attempt to ensure that our manual exploration of possible variation was as systematic and comprehensive as possible.

The third problem was the one whose solution required by far the most manual effort. It arose once more out of SSCI's lack of authority control, but this time the control lacking is of the titles of cited documents rather than of the names of cited authors. Any individual cited document may be represented in the SSCI database on different occasions by a variety of different values. This means that, for example, we should not be led to accept, from the output 3 FARRADANE J, 1966, REPORT RESEARCH IN 1 that there are recorded in the online database only three citations to the work of March 1966 by Farradane, Datta, and Poulton published by the City University entitled *Report on research on information retrieval by relational indexing: part 1: methodology.*

FARRADANE J, 1966, MAR CIT U REP 1

FARRADANE J, 1966, METHODOLOGY 1

FARRADANE J, 1966, P50, REPORT RESEARCH INFO

FARRADANE J, 1966, REPORT INFORMATION R

FARRADANE J, 1966, REPORT RES INFORMA 1

FARRADANE J, 1966, REPORT RES INFORMATI

FARRADANE J, 1966, RES INFORMATION RE 1

FARRADANE JEL, 1965, REPORT RES INFORMATI

FARRADANE JEL, 1966, P39, INFORMATION RETRIE 1

FARRADANE JEL, 1966, REPORT RES INFORMA 1

FARRADANE JEL, 1966, REPORT RES INFORMATI

FARRADANE JEL, 1966, REPORT RESEARCH IN 1

FARRADANE JEL, 1966, REPORT RESEARCH INFO

Table 19.4. Variant forms of representation of one cited document.

In fact, further exploration will reveal 16 other citations, scattered among the forms listed in Table 19.4. We regarded it as essential that we should attempt to merge multiple citations to the same cited documents. This proved to be a thankless task: both portions of the data-set, pre-1972 and post-1972, were largely handled manually—the manual effort taking rather more time and energy than might at first be imagined. What we ended up doing was creating a comprehensive bibliography of the works of each member of the CRG core and assigning a unique identifying code to each of these works. We then tagged each citation retrieved from SSCI with the appropriate code, with the result, for instance, that all the citations to the work by Farradane et al. mentioned above would be tagged with the same ID.

So on to the analysis stage, and the tip of the iceberg of the results are as follows.

First, we consider the cited documents, and ask the question: Which documents authored by the CRG core have been cited most often? Table 19.5 shows the top 10 most frequently cited documents. The older a document is, the more time it's had to receive citations, so Table 19.6 lists the documents with the highest rate of annual citation, which you get if you divide the total number of citations received by the number of years that have elapsed since date of publication.

Rank	Document	Freq. of citation
1	Austin, 1974, *PRECIS: A manual* …	84
2	Vickery, 1948, in *Journal of Documentation*	69
3	Austin, 1974, in *Journal of Documentation*	46
4	Coates, 1960, *Subject catalogues* …	39
5	Vickery, 1961, *On retrieval system theory*	37
6	Vickery, 1960, *Faceted classification* …	36
7	Vickery, 1975, *Classification and indexing* …	34
8	Vickery, 1965, *On retrieval system theory*	32
9	Austin, 1984, *PRECIS: A manual* …	30
	Vickery, 1959, *Classification and indexing* …	30

Table 19.5. Most frequently cited CRG documents.

Rank	Document	Annual citation
1	Austin, 1974, *PRECIS: A manual* …	3.23
2	Vickery & Vickery, 1993, in *Journal of Documentation*	2.43
3	Vickery & Vickery, 1987, *Information science* …	2.23
4	Austin, 1984, *PRECIS: A manual* …	1.88
5	Austin, 1974, in *Journal of Documentation*	1.77
6	Vickery, 1997, in *Journal of Documentation*, no. 2	1.67
	Vickery, 1997, in *Journal of Documentation*, no. 5	1.67
8	Vickery, 1948, in *Journal of Documentation*	1.53
9	Vickery, 1975, *Classification and indexing* …	1.36
10	Farradane, 1980, in *Journal of Information Science*, no. 6	1.00
	Foskett, 1972, in *Information Storage and Retrieval*	1.00

Table 19.6. CRG documents with highest rate of annual citation.

Also, you might have noticed that several of the most highly-cited documents are books, which have been published in multiple editions, so the ranking in Table 19.7 is what you get if you merge the figures for multiple editions of the same monographic work.

Rank	Book	Freq. of citation
1	Vickery, 1958/1959/1975, *Classification and indexing in science*	82
2	Vickery, 1961/1965, *On retrieval system theory*	69
3	Coates, 1960/1988, *Subject catalogues* …	41
4	Foskett, 1963/1974, *Classification and indexing in the social sciences*	39
5	Vickery & Vickery, 1987/1992, *Information science* …	34

Table 19.7. Most frequently cited CRG book titles (editions combined).

And this (Table 19.8) is what you get if you do the same for the actual classification schemes and indexing languages that the CRG produced.

Rank	Scheme	Freq. of citation
1	Austin, 1969/1974/1984, *PRECIS: A manual* …	125
2	Mills & Broughton, 1977–, *Bliss Bibliographic Classification*	35
3	Foskett & Foskett, 1974, *The London Education Classification* …	8
	Coates, Lloyd, & Simandl, 1978, *BSO* …	8
5	Coates, 1960, *The British Catalogue of Music classification*	5

Table 19.8. Most frequently cited CRG schemes (editions combined).

Then this (Table 19.9) is what happens if you restrict your consideration to journal papers, reports, or edited collections about classification. So you're controlling both for document type and subject matter. You could argue that it's this list, this ranking, that is most important for the student of classification theory.

Rank	Paper/report	Freq. of citation
1	Austin, 1974, in *Journal of Documentation*	46
2	Vickery, 1960, *Faceted classification* …	36
3	Farradane, 1950, in *Journal of Documentation*	28
4	Farradane, Datta, & Poulton, 1966, *Report on research* …	24
5	Farradane, 1967, in *Information Storage and Retrieval*	23
6	Farradane, 1980, in *Journal of Information Science*, no. 6	20
7	Farradane, 1952, in *Journal of Documentation*	19
	Farradane, 1980, in *Journal of Information Science*, no. 5	19
	Farradane & Gulatzan, 1977, in *International Classification*	19
10	Vickery, 1966, *Faceted classification schemes*	17

Table 19.9. Most frequently cited CRG papers/reports on classification.

Alternatively, you could take a look at this list (Table 19.10), which is of papers about classification that were most highly cited in the pre-1972 period. Just further down this ranking occur many papers by Barbara Kyle, papers that have been almost entirely forgotten since her death and that may well repay further renewed attention.

Rank	Paper/report	Freq. of citation
1	Farradane, 1950, in *Journal of Documentation*	13
	Vickery, 1960, *Faceted classification ...*	13
3	Kyle, 1964, in *Journal of Documentation*	12
	Vickery, 1966, *Faceted classification schemes*	12
5	Farradane, 1952, in *Journal of Documentation*	10
6	Vickery, 1960, in *Journal of Documentation*	9
7	Farradane, 1963, in *Information Storage and Retrieval*	8
8	Austin, 1969, in *Journal of Librarianship*	6
	Farradane, 1955, in *Journal of Documentation*	6
	Kyle, 1957, in *Journal of Documentation*	6

Table 19.10. Most frequently cited (1956–1972) CRG papers/reports on classification.

OK, so much for cited documents. In the second place, we can shift the focus to the cited authors themselves, asking the question: Which members of the CRG core have been cited most often?

Well, unsurprisingly, it's Vickery who has consistently maintained his position as the most highly-cited member of the CRG. Only in one year of the 35 considered was he cited on fewer occasions than one of his colleagues.

Rank	Name	Freq. of citations	Percentage of total citations
1	Vickery	259	39%
2	Foskett	111	17%
3	Farradane	79	12%
4	Kyle	57	9%
5	Coates	49	7%
6	Mills	45	7%
7	Palmer	25	4%
8	CRG	22	3%
9	Austin	15	2%

Table 19.11. Most frequently cited CRG authors (1956–1972).

The main difference in the two rankings, pre-1972 and post-1972, is that Kyle did much better in the earlier period, and I'll say a bit more about that in a minute.

Rank	Name	Freq. of citations	Percentage of total citations
1	Vickery	384	32%
2	Austin	202	17%
3	Foskett	201	17%
4	Farradane	169	14%
5	Mills	94	8%
6	Coates	74	6%
7	Palmer	37	3%
8	CRG	27	2%
9	Kyle	15	1%

Table 19.12. Most frequently cited CRG authors (1972–2000).

Thirdly, we turn to the citing documents, and take a look at the years in which they were published. In which years were the CRG core cited most often? Well, as you can imagine I do have a whole complex table of results but I just want to mention a few of the major trends here.

The overall rate of citation to the CRG core was highest in the two-decade period between 1963 and 1982. The overall rate has been in continuous decline since the mid-1980s, and this decline is reflected in most members' individual citation patterns. Austin, in particular, has suffered badly in the last decade.

Kyle's rate of citation has been in marked decline from a much earlier date, that of her untimely death in 1966. We might wonder whether, if she had lived to publish further, her earlier, seminal work on classification schemes for the social sciences would have continued to have the influence that it undoubtedly deserved. This work, however, is now almost completely forgotten: Kyle has been cited on a total of three occasions in the last 14 years, and just once in the last eight.

Individual members have accounted for larger or smaller percentages of the total number of citations to the CRG at different times. We could argue that the level of influence of these individuals may be tracked by these changes in percentage. Kyle, for instance, was most "influential" in these terms in the period 1956–1962, when (although the absolute number of citations to her work was still rather low) among the group she was second only to Vickery. Foskett and Mills saw citation peaks in the mid-1960s; Austin in the late 1970s; Farradane in both the late 1960s and the early 1980s; and Vickery in the 1990s.

Fourthly, we examine the sources of citing documents. In which serials have the CRG core been cited most often?

The two British journals *Journal of Documentation* and *Aslib Proceedings* dominate the table for the period 1956–1972, between them accounting for a quarter of all citations to the CRG core. The combined total for the American journals *American Documentation*, *JASIS* and *LR&TS* accounts for just 6% of all citations.

In the period 1972–2000, the *Journal of Documentation* maintains its position, but *Aslib Proceedings* is well down the list: the main challengers now are *JASIS* and *Knowledge Organization* itself (when its score is added to that for its original title, *International Classification*).

Rank	Serial	Freq. of citation
1	Journal of Documentation	87
2	Aslib Proceedings	83
3	Library Resources & Technical Services	49
4	Information Storage and Retrieval	40
	Nachrichten für Dokumentation	40
6	Annual Review of Information Science & Technology	37
	Nauchno-Tekhnicheskaya Informatsiya Seriya 2	37
8	American Documentation	29
	Unesco Bulletin for Libraries	29
	Special Libraries	29

Table 19.13. Sources of most citations to the CRG (1956–1972).

Rank	Serial	Freq. of citation
1	Journal of Documentation	109
2	Journal of the American Society for Information Science	78
3	International Classification	61
4	Journal of Information Science	54
5	Information Processing & Management	47
6	Annual Review of Information Science & Technology	45
7	Library Resources & Technical Services	38
8	Libri	34
9	Journal of Librarianship	32
10	Aslib Proceedings	30

Table 19.14. Sources of most citations to the CRG (1972–2000).

Fifthly, we consider the citing authors. Who has cited the CRG core most often?

Unsurprisingly, high in the list of citing authors are the members of the CRG core themselves. But of course it's the other names that are of more interest. Only four of the top 22 citers are North American: Richmond, Quimby, Fairthorne, and Shera.

Rank	Citing author	Freq. of citation
1	Vickery, B. C.	34
2	Richmond, P. A.	28
3	Farradane J.	18
	Soergel, D.	18
5	Quimby, G.	13
	Sukhmaneva, E. G.	13
7	Foskett, D. J.	12
8	Neufeld, M. L.	11
9	Kyle, B.	10
10	Perreault, J. M.	10

Table 19.15. Authors of most citations to the CRG (1956–1972).

Richmond is there again, near the head of the post-1972 list, eased off the top only by the string-indexing specialist Craven. Less than a third of the top 20 citers are North American.

Finally, we turn our attention briefly to co-cited authors. Who is most often also cited by those who cite the CRG core?

We only did this for the post-1972 period, simply because the electronic facilities make it so much easier. It is interesting to compare this list with the one I showed you at the beginning, of the authors most commonly cited by *Knowledge Organization* editors. The occurrence in this list of the names of Saracevic, Salton, Belkin, Cooper, Swanson, Wilson, Bookstein, Bates, and Robertson give it far more of the flavor of a roll call of the greats in the general field of information science—rather than classification theory per se.

Rank	Citing author	Freq. of citation
1	Craven, T. C.	18
2	Foskett, D. J.	13
3	Richmond, P. A.	11
4	Fugmann, R.	10
	Vickery, B. C.	10
6	Biswas, S. C.	9
7	Svenonius, E.	8
8	Austin, D.	7
	Bakewell, K. G. B.	7
	Beck H.	7
	Chan, L. M.	7
	Farradane, J.	7
	Harter, S. P.	7
	Hjørland, B.	7
	Jones, K. P.	7
	Satija, M. P.	7

Table 19.16. Authors of most citations to the CRG (1972–2000).

Rank	Co-cited author	Freq. of citation
1	Lancaster, F. W.	150
2	Brookes, B. C.	119
3	Ranganathan, S. R.	101
4	Saracevic, T.	100
5	Salton, G.	98
6	Belkin, N. J.	81
7	Bradford, S. C.	61
	Svenonius, E.	61
9	Cooper, W. S.	60
	Dahlberg, I.	60

Table 19.17. Other authors most cited by those who cite the CRG core (1972–2000).

The principal intention, then, of this paper—a descriptive, quantitative analysis of citations to the CRG—is simply to contribute to attempts to re-ignite interest in the group itself and its unparalleled body of work. Although CRG meetings are still held at regular intervals, its younger members are few. At a time when facet analysis is increasingly attracting attention both within and beyond the traditional classification-research community as the most promising approach to the problems of organizing electronic documents, we may reflect with a sense of irony on the fact that Austin, Coates, Foskett, et al., are all long retired from professional work. If the CRG is not subsequently to be viewed as a distinctively twentieth-century institution, some form of renewal is surely to be encouraged.

A content analysis of the CRG's oeuvre, including an assessment of the continuing utility of individual ideas and principles established by its members, was beyond the scope of this study. We did not even attempt to analyze the content-based or context-based nature of citations to the CRG, as others have done, for instance, for citations to Ranganathan. But it is sincerely intended that at least the limits of the purely quantitative approach presented here have been thrown into appropriate relief, and that it will be helpful in the writing of a comprehensive work of a more qualitative nature—perhaps in time for 2002, the year of the group's 50th anniversary.

20

Knowledge organization, *Knowledge Organization*, and the Classification Research Group: A citation study

November 6, 2001

This talk was given at ASIS&T 2001: 64th Annual Meeting of the American Society for Information Science and Technology: Information in a networked world: Harnessing the flow (Washington, DC, November 2–8, 2001) as part of a panel session on "The history and continuing influence of the Classification Research Group." The panel chair was Jonathan Furner, and speakers were Jonathan Furner, Alexander Justice, Ia McIlwaine, and Shawne Miksa.

In this talk, I report the results of a quantitative study of the influence of the Classification Research Group that I've been conducting in some irregularly-snatched spare moments over the last couple of years.

The point of departure for this study is the things that people have had to say about the impact of the CRG. Ia McIlwaine has written: "[I]ts influence has been pervasive … it is clear that the CRG has made a profound contribution to thinking about classification … and has laid the foundations … for a complete reform in the way that people think about the organization of knowledge." Eric Hunter has agreed that the CRG has had "a far-reaching effect … the members of this group advanced dramatically the frontiers of knowledge in classification ..." Phyllis Richmond's review of Vickery's work for the CRG was simply entitled "Precedent-setting contributions to modern classification."

In short, many experts have agreed that the CRG has been, and continues to be, uniquely influential on the development of both the theory and the practice of knowledge organization. My aim is not to confirm or reject that claim. My approach is rather to assume the truth of that claim, and to attempt instead to examine the claim that citation analysis is a reliable method of quantifying level of influence, treating the CRG as the object of a kind of case study. I'd like to demonstrate what can be achieved using just a few, very simple quantitative techniques; but also perhaps to show what the limitations of those techniques are.

In outline then, here's my plan for today. I'm going to briefly introduce firstly the CRG, and secondly some basic principles of citation analysis. Then I'm going to describe the methods and results of two separate approaches that I took in conducting the study. I'm going to focus on the second of these approaches, since I talked about the first in a paper that I gave last year at the Sixth International ISKO Conference in Toronto [see Chapter 19], and I don't want to repeat myself too much if I can help it. I'll end with a few remarks about the conclusions that I think we can draw from my results.

For the purposes of the study, I have deliberately chosen to restrict analysis to eight members of the CRG that I have identified as the "core." Of course, the intention is not to push into the background the work of other members such as Derek Langridge, Jean Aitchison, and Ia McIlwaine, but simply to focus on the people that I think most would agree were among the prime movers of the group in its heyday. These are, in alphabetical order, Austin, Coates, Farradane, Foskett, Kyle, Mills, Palmer, and Vickery. Four of these are alive today, including Vickery who left the CRG in the 1960s.

The pre-history of the CRG—the chain of events leading up to its formal inauguration by Vickery and Wells in 1952—is well-documented, usually beginning with the war-time meeting of Palmer and Ranganathan in India. Certainly, the early work of the CRG was drenched in Ranganathanian theory. The main concern was with facet analysis as an approach to developing classification schemes, which is commonly considered to be the primary contribution of Ranganathan himself to library science. But it could be argued that it was the members of the CRG, individually and in concert, who were most responsible both for developing this theory to the "standard" state that we take for granted today, and for fully exploring its practical potential by constructing numerous and various real-life schemes, many of which have enjoyed widespread and successful use over more than a quarter-century. Richmond advises that we "should give credit where credit is due. The Classification Research Group itself is unique ... [filling] a gap between theory and practice."

Now, as I mentioned, one of my aims is to demonstrate the usage and utility of simple quantitative techniques in describing the influence of the CRG on contemporary scholarship in knowledge organization.

The techniques I have in mind are those of citation analysis. The idea here is that, firstly, we may identify a set of citing documents, such as those shown on the right in Figure 20.1, each of which contain a certain number of references to other, citable documents. (The sets of citing and citable documents may well overlap to a considerable extent.) Secondly, we may identify the set of observed citations that relate the sets of citing and citable documents. Each citation may thus be considered as a document–document pair.

And given that any document may itself be viewed as a set of attribute–value pairs, any citation may be viewed as a pair of sets of

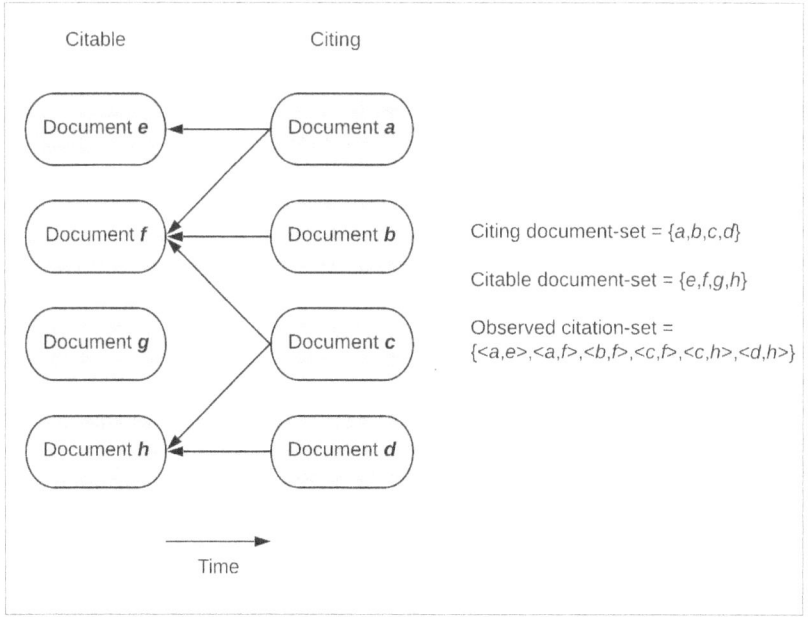

Figure 20.1. Citation analysis: Definitions.

attribute–value pairs, as in the example given here, which represents the citation made by Jack Andersen, in his recent journal article, to Egan and Shera's classic paper on social epistemology.

({<citing_author, Andersen_J>,
<citing_title, Written_knowledge … >,
<citing_journal, Knowledge_Organization>,
… }
{<cited_author, Egan_M>,
<cited_author, Shera_JH>,
<cited_title, Foundations_of_a_theory … >,
<cited_journal, Library_Quarterly>,
… })

Perhaps the single most useful tool at the citation analyst's disposal is Dialog's RANK command, which allows the searcher automatically to classify an initial set of documents or citations on the basis of some given property or attribute–value pair, such as citing author or publication year, and then equally speedily to rank the resulting classes in order of the number of members in each.

So, for example, we might choose to use Dialog's SEARCH or S command to create an initial set of documents authored by Ranganathan, and then to use RANK or R simultaneously to partition that initial set into subsets on the basis of the content of each document's CA or Cited Author field, and to rank those subsets in order of their size. The result is a ranked list of the authors most cited by Ranganathan. Several more such examples are coming up.

I think on one dark day I must have become addicted to the RANK command, and since then I suppose I've been trying to pass of the resulting obsession as some sort of harmless hobby. To no avail.

So we should note that there are several discrete steps in this procedure. Firstly, we need to define (and if the spirit takes us, to analyze) the citing document-set (or CD-set). Secondly, we need to identify and analyze the observed citation-set (or OC-set). It's this last step, the analysis of the OC-set, that justifies carrying out the prior ones.

So let's just take a quick look at what's involved in the first of those steps, the definition of the citing document set. Here there are a few decisions that need to be made.

For instance, do we choose to limit membership in the CD-set to documents that are indexed by the Institute for Scientific Information? This would certainly make things much easier, since that organization has already carried out much of the dirty work of citation analysis in compiling its citation indexes. But it would also mean that only those documents contained in high-impact serials could be considered candidates for the CD-set, since ISI does not index monographs.

Similarly, there are other restrictions that may be placed on the composition of the CD-set, that relate to subject matter (for example, classified in ISI's "Information science & library science" category), date of indexing (for example, indexed between 1972 and 2001), and document type (for example, categorized by ISI as "Article").

Some difficulties involved in defining the citing-document set lie simply in coming up with a persuasive justification of the decisions that you make. But there are other, more intractable difficulties that tend to arise further along in the process of analysis, particularly when it comes to interpreting the results of RANK commands. These problems derive from the lack of consistent authority control displayed by ISI's indexing.

For one thing, it is important to be able to collocate the synonymic terms that are used by different indexers to refer to the same authors or the same titles, otherwise raw RANK results may easily give the impression that those authors or titles are ranked lower than they actually are. Similarly, it is no less important to be able to disambiguate among the homonymic terms that are used by different indexers to refer to different authors.

To take an extreme example of title synonymy, we might assume from this listing—3 FARRADANE J, 1966, REPORT RESEARCH IN 1—that SSCI records only three occurrences of a citation to the work of March 1966 by Farradane, Datta, and Poulton published by the City University entitled *Report on research on information retrieval by relational indexing: Part 1: Methodology*.

In fact, further exploration will reveal 16 other citations, scattered among various forms. I regarded it as essential that I should attempt to merge multiple citations to the same cited documents. This proved to be a thankless task: both portions of the data set, pre-1972 and post-1972, were largely handled manually—the manual effort taking rather more time and energy than might at first be imagined.

So much for the practical problems that were faced. Now I want to describe the two separate approaches that I took, the first rather briefly, and the second in a little more detail.

In the first approach, my aim was to characterize the universal set of citations to the CRG core whose sources have been indexed in SSCI since 1956. I placed no other restrictions on the definition of either the citing document-set or the observed citation-set.

Through application of Dialog's RANK command and additional manual analysis, I was able to produce definitive lists of various kinds (see Chapter 19): lists of cited documents, written by the CRG "core," categorized by form in various ways, and ranked in order of citedness (that is, the frequency with which they have been cited); lists of cited authors, also ranked in order of citedness, in the two periods, 1956–1972 and 1972–2000; and lists of publication years of citing documents, ranked in order of productivity.

Specifically, we can answer the question, "Who has cited the CRG core most often?" by applying RANK to citing authors. Unsurprisingly, high in the list of citing authors are the members of the CRG core themselves (see Chapter 19). But of course it's the other names that are of more interest. Only four of the top 22 citers in the pre-1972 list are North American: Richmond, Quimby, Fairthorne, and Shera. Richmond is there again, near the head of the post-1972 list. Less than a third of the top 20 post-1972 citers are North American.

And finally, using this approach, we may ask, "Who is most often also cited by those who cite the CRG core?" I only did this for the post-1972 period, simply because the electronic facilities make it so much easier (see Chapter 19). The occurrence in this list of the names of Saracevic, Salton, Belkin, Cooper, and then, a little further down, Swanson, Wilson, Bookstein, Bates, and Robertson, give it far more of the flavor of a roll call of the greats in the general field of information science—rather than classification theory per se.

Right, now to consider the second approach to a quantitative evaluation of the level of influence of the CRG. This time, rather than addressing the question as one that asks, "Who has cited (and, by implication, been influenced by) the CRG?" I'm approaching it from a different direction, by asking "Who is cited by the authors of contemporary work in knowledge organization?" Given the level of influence that is invariably claimed for the CRG, we might expect that its members would ride high in lists of those authors that are "most cited" by contemporary KO researchers.

In this approach, I actually defined two citing document-sets, so that the results from each could be compared and, if necessary, contrasted.

CD-set A was a complete set of documents (431) appearing since 1972 in serials classified by ISI in their "Information science & library science" category and authored by at least one current member of the editorial board of the journal *Knowledge Organization*, while Set B was a complete set of the full-length articles (387) published since 1993 in *Knowledge Organization* or since 1974 in its forerunner *International Classification*.

I was able to analyze the two citing document-sets in a variety of ways using my beloved RANK, producing, for example, lists of authors ranked in order of so-called productivity and journals ranked in order of "core-ness" or centrality. So in Table 20.1, just for prurient interest, is a list of the "top 10" most productive *KO* editors.

Rank	Author	Freq. of documents	Freq. of full-length articles
1	Satija, M. P.	68	12
2	Svenonius, E.	52	12
3	Soergel, D.	35	13
4	Beghtol, C.	20	9
	McIlwaine, I. C.	20	5
6	Williamson, N. J.	17	6
7	Gopinath, M. A.	16	8
	Hudon, M.	16	1
9	Olson, H. A.	15	7
	Pollitt, A. S.	15	5
	Green, R.	15	8

Table 20.1. Author productivity: CD-set A.

And here (in Table 20.2) is a list of authors who have published most articles in *KO* itself.

Rank	Author	Freq. of full-length articles
1	Dahlberg, I.	14
2	Fugmann, R.	14
3	Riggs, F. W.	8
	Judge, A. J. N.	8
5	Rada, R.	7
6	Satija, M. P.	6
7	Iyer, H.	5
8	Beghtol, C.	4
	Beloozerov, V.	4
	Dahlberg, W.	4
	Johansen, T.	4
	Somers, H. L.	4
	Sukiasyan, E. R.	4

Table 20.2. Author productivity: CD-set B.

And we can do things like list (in Table 20.3) the journals that *KO* editors are most likely to get their papers published in. No prizes for predicting what's number one there.

Rank	Journal	Freq. of documents
1	Knowledge Organization	161
2	Library Quarterly	27
3	Information Processing & Management	22
4	Journal of the American Society for Information Science	20
5	Canadian Journal of Information Science	19
6	Journal of Documentation	17
7	Proceedings of the ASIS Annual Meeting	17

8	Library Resources & Technical Services	15
9	Library Journal	13
10	Library Science with a Slant to Documentation	11

Table 20.3. Journal core-ness: CD-set A.

Okay, so much for those results which have little to do with our main object of interest, the CRG. Before turning to an analysis of the observed citation sets, here (in Table 20.4) is a summary of the composition of the two citing document-sets and corresponding OC-sets.

Set	Freq. of documents	Freq. of references	Mean references/document
A	431	4744	11.0
B	387	5938	15.3

Table 20.4. CD-set and OC-set summary.

Once again, we may apply the RANK command in various ways to these sets of citations. We may produce lists of the journals that are most likely to be the targets of references contained in either of the two CD-sets, or lists of the most cited documents, or lists of the most cited authors. And that's what we have here, beginning with journals in Table 20.5.

Rank	Journal	Freq. of citations
1	Knowledge Organization	153
2	Journal of the American Society for Information Science	77
3	Journal of Documentation	71
4	Information Processing & Management	55
5	Nachrichten für Dokumentation	35
6	Library Quarterly	21
7	International Forum on Information and Documentation	20
8	Library Resources & Technical Services	19
9	Library Science with a Slant to Documentation	19
10	Nauchno-Tekhnicheskaya Informatisiya	19

Table 20.5. Journal citedness: OC-set B.

And these are the documents most cited, firstly (Table 20.6) in documents written by current editors of the journal KO, and secondly (Table 20.7) in documents published in the journal KO. Here the figures on the right are the number of citations received by each document, the figures on the left are the ranks, and the figures in the second column are the ranks of the documents when Set B is used as the original citing-document set. A dash indicates that a document is ranked outside the top 10, by the way.

Rank	Rank (B)	Document	Freq. of citations
1	5	Dewey, 1876,* Dewey decimal classification …	16
2	1	Ranganathan, 1933,* Colon classification …	15
	2	Ranganathan, 1937,* Prolegomena …	15
4	4	Lancaster, 1972,* Vocabulary control …	11
5	–	Cutter, 1876,* Rules …	9
	–	Soergel, 1985, Organizing information …	9
	–	Hutchins, 1975, Languages of indexing …	9
8	–	Cooper, 1971, in Information Storage and Retrieval	8
	–	Maron, 1977, in Journal of the ASIS	8
10	8	Aitchison et al., 1972,* Thesaurus construction …	7
	–	Foskett, A. C., 1969,* The subject approach …	7
	–	Pejtersen, 1980, in Theory and application …	7
	–	Wilson, P., 1973, in Information Storage and Retrieval	7

Table 20.6. Document citedness: OC-set A.

The derivation of these data was particularly labor-intensive. If I had just presented the raw RANK results, without manual collocation of title synonyms, they would look very different. I also decided to collocate citations to different editions of the same work. The works that have been cited in multiple editions are indicated with an asterisk, and the date given in those cases is the date of the work's first edition.

In this list, it's interesting to note the presence of some of the most widely used schemes and texts, but also a few research papers by the likes of Cooper, Maron, Pejtersen, and Wilson. There are documents authored by people associated with the CRG, but none by any member of the CRG core.

Similarly, this (in Table 20.7) is the list for Set B, with ranks for Set A in parentheses. There is notable overlap with the list for Set A. An interesting difference is the appearance of two documents by Dahlberg, founder of the *KO* journal, neither of which received a single citation in Set A. A member of the CRG core makes an appearance in ninth place.

Rank	Rank (A)	Document	Freq. of citations
1	2	Ranganathan, 1933,* *Colon classification* …	34
2	2	Ranganathan, 1937,* *Prolegomena* …	26
	–	Dahlberg, 1974, *Grundlagen* …	23
4	4	Lancaster, 1972,* *Vocabulary control* …	19
5	1	Dewey, 1876,* *Dewey decimal classification* …	18
6	–	Soergel, 1974, *Indexing languages* …	17
7	–	Dahlberg, 1978, in *International Classification*	16
8	10	Aitchison et al., 1972,* *Thesaurus construction* …	13
9	–	Austin, 1974,* *PRECIS: A manual* …	12
	–	Kuhn, 1962,* *The structure of scientific revolutions*	12

Table 20.7. Document citedness: OC-set B.

Finally we reach the lists of most interest, the authors most cited, firstly, (Table 20.8) in documents written by current editors of the journal *KO*, and, secondly, (Table 20.9) in documents published in the journal *KO*. Again the figures on the right are the numbers of citations received by each author, the figures on the left are the ranks, the figures in parentheses are the ranks of the authors when the other set is used as the original citing-document set. A dash indicates that an author is ranked outside the top 50.

Rank	Rank (B)	Author	Freq. of citations
1	2	Ranganathan, S. R.	39
2	3	Lancaster, F. W.	28
3	6	Svenonius, E.	21
4	41	Comaromi, J. P.	19
5	10	Vickery, B. C.	18
6	–	Pejtersen, A. M.	17
7	–	Cutter, C. A.	16
8	1	Dahlberg, I.	15
	4	Soergel, D.	15
10	25	Langridge, D. W.	14
	19	Markey Drabenstott, K.	14
	–	Satija, M. P.	14
	–	Wilson, P.	14

Table 20.8. Author citedness: OC-set A.

Similarly, this (Table 20.9) is the list for Set B, with ranks for Set A in parentheses. This is intended to highlight the difference in results you get when you take slightly different decisions as to what set of documents most appropriately represents the body of public knowledge produced by a particular scholarly community, in this case, those scholars involved in contemporary research in knowledge organization. The differences are instructive and repay further analysis.

Rank	Rank (B)	Author	Freq. of citations
1	8	Dahlberg, I.	74
2	1	Ranganathan, S. R.	54
3	2	Lancaster, F. W.	29
4	8	Soergel, D.	28

5	–	Fugmann, R.	27
6	3	Svenonius, E.	23
7	34	Aitchison, J.	22
8	–	Riggs, F. W.	20
9	–	Mills, J.	19
10	25	Austin, D.	17
	16	Neelameghan, A.	17
	5	Vickery, B. C.	17

Table 20.9.   Author citedness: OC-set B.

But for our purposes today, it's the data in Table 20.10 that are most informative, where the eight members of the CRG core are ranked by frequency of citations received from each citing document-set.

Set A: Rank	Set A: Freq.	Author	Set B: Rank	Set B: Freq
5	18	Vickery, B. C.	10	17
25	10	Mills, J.	9	19
25	10	Foskett, D. J.	19	12
34	9	Coates, E. J.	25	11
–	6	Farradane, J. E. L.	25	11
–	6	Palmer, B. I.	–	2
–	4	Kyle, B. R. F.	–	3

Table 20.10.   Author citedness: CRG.

I would venture that these data do not immediately reflect the place in the canon that is assured for each member of the CRG. What is going on, we might wonder, when Barbara Kyle, who contributed so much to the development of classification schemes for the social sciences in the 1950s and 1960s, is cited only four times in the entire published output (431 documents) of 35 of the world's experts in classification research?

My conclusion is hardly novel, but one that I think is worth re-stating. It is that we should remember that the revolution inspired by the members of the CRG was one with practical as much as theoretical repercussions. If we consider the legacy of the CRG, among the highpoints are real, useful schemes such as Thesaurofacet, PRECIS, and the 2nd edition of the Bliss Bibliographic Classification. The extent to which the CRG has influenced the field of knowledge organization may thus be quantified only if we have means of measuring the extent to which these schemes have been used in operational contexts, and have improved the performance of systems that support the provision of access to information. Clearly, that kind of means is not supplied by citation analysis!

But despite its limitations, there remain powerful reasons for engaging in quantitative analysis of this kind. For one thing, a citation study encourages historical thinking, characterized by a willingness to consider historical origins and patterns of influence when attempting to understand present-day principles and practice.

One primary intention of this talk is simply to contribute to attempts to re-ignite interest in the group itself and its unparalleled body of work. Although CRG meetings are still held at regular intervals, its younger members are few. At a time when facet analysis is increasingly attracting attention both within and beyond the traditional classification-research community as the most promising approach to the problems of organizing electronic documents, we may reflect with a sense of irony on the fact that Coates, Foskett, et al., are all long retired from professional work. If the CRG is not subsequently to be viewed as a distinctively twentieth-century institution, some form of renewal is surely to be encouraged.

A content analysis of the CRG's oeuvre, including an assessment of the continuing utility of individual ideas and principles established by its members, was beyond the scope of this study. We did not even attempt to analyze the content-based or context-based nature of citations to the CRG, as others have done, for instance, for citations to Ranganathan. But it is sincerely intended that at least the limits of the purely quantitative approach presented here have been thrown into appropriate relief, and that it will be helpful in the writing of a comprehensive work of a more qualitative nature—perhaps in time for 2002, the year of the group's 50th anniversary.

21
New

October 26, 2012

This talk was given in response to papers delivered at SIG/CR 2012: 23rd ASIS&T SIG/CR Workshop on Classification Research (Baltimore, MD, October 26, 2012), and was published in slightly different form in **Bulletin of the American Society for Information Science and Technology** *39, no. 3 (2013): 28–32. The workshop chairs were Kathryn La Barre (University of Illinois at Urbana–Champaign) and Joseph Tennis (University of Washington). Ten full papers were presented, with fifteen minutes allocated to each, along with nine "lightning talks" of seven minutes each and a doctoral mini-symposium in which five Ph.D. students introduced their research projects. Fran Miksa (University of Texas at Austin) and Shawne Miksa (University of North Texas) collaborated on a keynote panel, and Marjorie Hlava (Access Innovations, Inc.) provided a second keynote presentation. Full papers are available in* **Advances in Classification Research Online** *at https://journals.lib.washington.edu/index.php/acro/issue/view/999.*

Given the workshop's topic, I thought it might be interesting to categorize the innovations—literally, the new things—that I think we heard about during the presentations and follow-up discussions. I believe that the results are indicative of the vibrancy, the richness, and the complexity of the classification research field right now.

If I had to pick the one big theme of the day—and this should not be surprising given the thrust of the original call for papers—it would be the utility of *new approaches* with a historical focus. It is very appropriate that, in the year of ASIS&T's 75th anniversary that we should consider it important to remember and learn the many lessons taught by the past. Simply to lump all the historically-oriented approaches in a single category, however, would serve only to hide the variation in the kinds of histories that are being constructed, and in the innovations being made among them. In his keynote "Observations on historical aspects of classification theory," for instance, Fran Miksa's emphasis was on the history of ideas about classification, whereas both David Dubin (University of Illinois at Urbana–Champaign) and La Barre focused on different aspects of the history of the field of classification research. Presentations by Melissa Adler (University of Wisconsin–Madison) and K. R. Roberto (University of Illinois at Urbana–Champaign) were concerned with the histories of the concepts and terms that are the elements of classification schemes, and crucially with the primary role played in shaping those histories by the decisions and actions of particular individuals. Grant Campbell (University of Western Ontario) talked about changes in classificatory structures over time, while Tennis's interest was in the history of conceptualizations and definitions of classification. All these speakers prioritized the temporal, but in rather different ways.

More generally, I think we are continuing to see growth in the use of humanistic approaches (all imported from other disciplines, of course, but I'm not sure it could be any other way). When there is talk at the SIG/CR workshop of "the classificationist's gaze," you know things are going rather well in that direction. In this context, Daniel Martínez-Ávila (Universidad Carlos III de Madrid) and Richard Smiraglia's (University of Wisconsin–Milwaukee) integration of a phenomenological approach with discourse-analytic methods is a very interesting development, and it was a disappointment that neither speaker could attend on the day.

Many *new theories* and understandings, or relatively recently-developed ones, were introduced in the papers accepted for the workshop: theories of the ways in which power structures are unavoidably reflected in classification structures (Patrick Keilty, University of Toronto; Melodie Fox, University of Wisconsin–Milwaukee); of how folksonomies have emancipatory potential (Keilty); and of the cultural, social, historical specificity of definitions of classification (Tennis), of classification schemes (lots of people), and of classification practices (Eva Hourihan Jansen, University of Toronto). We learnt that standardization is not always beneficial, since its effects include undesirable decontextualization (Jansen); that personal classificatory practice is heavily influenced by social factors (Kyong Eun Oh, Rutgers University); that user-generated folksonomies are more similar to top-down schemes than previously thought (Andrea Scharnhorst, Royal Netherlands Academy of Arts and Sciences, & Smiraglia); that classification (and thus information retrieval) based on analysis of the probability, or "likeliness," with which a searcher will judge two objects to be related at any given moment is effective (Charles van den Heuvel, Royal Netherlands Academy of Arts and Sciences, & Smiraglia); and that, in any given domain, many different classification structures are possible, and many of those are potentially equally useful in different ways—in other words, there is no single correct classification, even in science (Rebecca Green, OCLC Online Computer Library Center, Inc., & Giles Martin, independent consultant).

Similarly, we were treated to presentations of several *new models*: of the cognitive processes involved in classifying—in lumping and splitting (Oh), for example—and in learning how to classify (Shawne Miksa); of the relationship between classifying, as the act of assigning labels to classes, and other cognitive activities such as counting and writing (Tennis); of knowledge organization systems as artificial languages rather than as hierarchical trees (Scharnhost & Smiraglia); of classes as situated in rhetorical space (Fox); and of the relationship between bibliographic/documentary classification and the scientific classification of naturally-occurring phenomena (to which both Dubin and Green & Martin alluded).

Hlava reminded us how the explanatory role of theory is significant not only for the design of new kinds of classificatory structures, but also for new kinds of uses of those structures—*new applications* of theory to practice, in other words—in systems designed for the improvement of search, retrieval, and related tasks. Meanwhile, Nicholas Weber, Andrea Thomer (both University of Illinois, Urbana–Champaign), and Gary Strand (National Center for Atmospheric Research) demonstrated the use of what Birger Hjørland calls pragmatic classification—in which classes are identified on the basis of usage—for identifying the elements in a metadata schema for climatology; while Jansen reviewed the use of the concept of "boundary object" to understand classification practices. Such work may be characterized as the application of otherwise well-understood methods in *new domains*.

Did we hear about any *new methods of building* classificatory structures and knowledge organization schemes? Methods that prioritize the needs of specific groups (e.g., Martínez-Ávila & Smiraglia) and that involve crowdsourcing (e.g., Jane Greenberg, Angela Murillo, both University of North Carolina at Chapel Hill, and John Kunze, California Digital Library) were discussed, and part of Adler's contribution was her account of the history of methods of dealing with new topics and subjects. But these probably should not be counted as innovations.

It is similarly difficult to identify, among the contributions to the workshop, any *new principles* for the construction of classification schemes. Smiraglia's domain analysis (not presented) shows that we're comfortable with a plurality of methods and approaches, and what is more, comfortable with the extent to which those approaches are compatible if not complementary. We may well still seek principled answers to questions like the following: Should classification schemes be theory-driven or based on empirical observation? Should classification researchers in the information sciences (broadly defined) be concerned with classification of natural kinds, or just of artifactual kinds? Whatever new principles are proposed, which of them (if any) reach the status of ethical principles? The possibilities might include principles that emphasize flexibility and pluralism (Campbell), that recognize that classification practices should be participatory, and classification schemes thus user-centered (Adler), and that require that all voices should be heard in the construction of classification schemes (Fox; Roberto). These latter proposals essentially would be a re-affirmation of the principle of user warrant—viz., the terms and structures that are used by the members of groups who share a social identity are the ones that should be included in classification schemes (Roberto). Greenberg, Murillo, and Kunze further suggested that there should be full participation in the evaluation of candidate terms/concepts for inclusion in classification schemes, thereby giving participants a sense of ownership.

In alignment with the already-noted emphasis on the temporal and historical, the *new method of analysis* of the moment seems to be ontogenesis. This method derives from Tennis's suggestion that we can and should explore "the life of the subject over time"—an empirical method that enables better understanding of the factors that influence the course of a classification scheme's development (e.g., Fox; Scharnhorst & Smiraglia). Campbell wants to combine ontogenetic analysis with principles of flexibility and pluralism, partly in order to predict future changes in classification schemes. Martínez-Ávila & Smiraglia talk about new extensions of discourse analysis as methods of ontogenetic analysis that "[reveal] knowledge as artificially constructed by social factors." Workshop participants were also introduced to methods of analyzing the discourse of domains to identify terms for inclusion in specialized vocabularies (Christine Marchese, Nassau Community College, & Smiraglia), and the use of diaries and interviews rather than direct observation as a way of collecting data about personal classificatory practices (Oh).

New empirical data that were reported in workshop papers included Smiraglia's data (not presented) on citedness, rates of self-citation, and disciplinary association of classification researchers; Elizabeth Milonas's (Long Island University) data that will inform the designers of the faceted search features of web search engines; Oh's data on the ways in which people organize personal files, which leads her to propose a new model of such practice as a five-stage process, which is intended to be useful for designers of new tools and interfaces supporting such practice; the results of Scharnhorst and Smiraglia's ontogenetic analysis, showing the gradual evolution of intension over time; and Fran Miksa's findings from his investigations of ancient, medieval, and Islamic classifications. *New methods of presenting data* included Scharnhorst and Smiraglia's visualizations of classifications over time, and Lori Ann Rung Hoeffner (Adelphi University) and Smiraglia's visualizations of the results of domain analyses.

Workshop participants heard much about *new methods of evaluation*. With respect to methods of evaluating the field of classification research, Dubin pointed to the ever-increasing specialization of scholarly communities, and asked, Is that a sign of success, or an indication that we're missing the opportunities for progress that come with interdisciplinarity? Jansen discussed critical-analytic methods of evaluating the theoretical frameworks that underlie classification research; Hoeffner and Smiraglia's method of evaluating domains uses coherence as a criterion; Green and Martin demonstrated the need for effective methods of evaluating and choosing among different scientific classification structures; and Milonas's study of the relationship between expert inspection and users' perceptions of usability could even be considered as a contribution to the literature on the evaluation of methods of evaluation! Several of these methods apply *new criteria for evaluating* classification schemes (and other products of classification theory and research) and/or classificatory practices.

From Habermas (via Martínez-Ávila & Smiraglia), we're reminded that theory is used to predict, to explain or understand, to emancipate, and to deconstruct. I think we're clearly seeing a shift towards the latter half of this list in our prioritization of criteria for evaluating the products of classification research. Greenberg, Murillo, and Kunze additionally propose the use of sustainability as a criterion for evaluating classification schemes.

The potential for *new definitions* of the nature of classification, of classification theory, and of classification history, was mentioned by both Fran and Shawne Miksa. Dubin considered the relationship between aboutness and topicality, and asked, is a topic a thing, or a concept? Possibly *new methods of creating definitions* included domain analysis and bibliometrics (Smiraglia), and methods based on the kind of phenomenon being classified (Tennis). Echoing the parallels drawn by Fran Miksa between the history of writing and the history of classification, Tennis asked, are counting and writing themselves kinds of classification? Fran Miksa reminded us that people became interested in the classification of the elements of knowledge (i.e., subjects) only relatively recently, and that the classification both of physical objects and of informational entities has a longer history. Steven MacCall's (University of Alabama) model of the relationships between works, texts, and artifacts (rather than the more familiar combination of works, expressions, manifestations, and items) could be viewed as a specification of *new kinds of objects* to be classified; Lei Zhang and Hur-Li Lee (University of Wisconsin–Milwaukee) advocated for genre as a *new dimension* or facet by which objects are to be classified.

Accompanying new principles and practices come *new problems* to address. These include not only the problems that are due to "life happening" and to the fact that the information explosion has only just begun (Hlava), but also those that emerge as unintended consequences of the application of innovative methods. The crowdsourcing of tags for use as class labels, for instance, may lead to undesirable results such as a "tyranny of the majority" or a "Matthew effect" in which less-popular classes are less likely than more-popular ones to grow in popularity in the future. Questions about the extent to which such methods are "fair" or "just" may be conceived as having an ethical dimension. I'm not sure that the ethical ramifications of the decisions made by classification-scheme designers (as distinct from those made by classifiers) were adequately covered at this particular workshop.

Did workshop participants characterize classification research as having any *new goals*? Fran Miksa proposed a framework for understanding how the goals of designers of classification schemes have changed over time, distinguishing among the pragmatic, scientific, and aesthetic functions of such schemes that have been prioritized in different ways in different periods and cultures. Shawne Miksa provided a list of questions that serves well as a comprehensive statement of the various goals of classification research—one stand-out being the goal of creating "living" classification schemes. Tennis's emphasis on the temporal reminded us of the importance of the goal of understanding the dynamic intensions and extensions of concepts, and Hoeffner and Smiraglia demonstrated the value of classificatory practices in defining the boundaries of a domain or discipline. Otherwise, the assumptions that appeared to underpin much of the work presented were that classification is a means to the end of resource discovery, and thus that the appropriate goal of classification research is to contribute to improvements in the design of retrieval and access systems.

Neither was it clear that any radically *new paradigms* or theoretical frameworks were identified on the day. Certainly, several speakers made reference to a (seemingly ongoing) battle between positivists and constructivists, and this tension was explored in different ways in different papers (e.g., by Jansen, and by Martínez-Ávila & Smiraglia). The closest we came to something that amounts to a whole new way of thinking about classification research, I think, was Campbell's suggestion that classification schemes should be understood as living, breathing organisms that change rhythmically over time. To my mind, however, the most valuable innovation of the day was Fran Miksa's conception of the history of classification theory. He distinguished among three historical periods—we might call them the periods of unificationism, specialism, and pluralism, although Miksa didn't use these labels himself—in a framework that provides an illuminating backdrop to the current turn in classification studies towards the generation of theories, principles, and methods that emphasize both the cultural and historical specificity of classification practices, and their emancipatory function.

Rebecca Green and Giles Martin explained that "A rosid is a rosid is a rosid," and in doing so received special commendation in the 1st Annual SIG/CR Award for Best Workshop Paper Title. But the winner of this prestigious new award was K. R. Roberto, for his paper, "Description is a drag, and vice versa." Kathryn La Barre drew praise for her reference to Mr. MITS (the "Man In The Street"), as did Jane Greenberg for her analogy between toothbrushes and metadata standards (we all think they're great, but ideally we'd like one of our own), and Andrea Thomer for her realization that hours in climate centers are like cigarettes in prison. (At least, I think that's what Andrea said … .)

Since we heard about so many different aspects of classification research during the workshop, we might have been forgiven at the end for reeling and asking afresh, what is classification research? or what *should* it be? or even what *can* it be? My personal response is that there is little need for concern. Classification research is "all of the above," and more. So long as it stays that way, the field is in excellent shape.

E
Vocabularies and folksonomies

22

International standards, national traditions: Vocabulary control in archival science

August 6, 2004

This talk was given at SAA 2004: Annual Meeting of the Society of American Archivists (Boston, MA, August 2–8, 2004) as part of a panel session on "Speaking of records … The challenges of archival language." The panel chair was Richard Pearce-Moses, and speakers were Jean E. Dryden, Jonathan Furner, and Richard Pearce-Moses.

By way of introduction, I'm going to begin by saying a few words about InterPARES, an international research project in archival science that I'm sure will be familiar to many of you. Then I'll concentrate on the specific aspect of the InterPARES project that is particularly relevant to the theme of today's session—its terminological database—and I'll talk about its structure, and the opportunities and challenges that we face in attempting to build such a structure using the international standards that are available.

I'm actually going to start with a couple of very basic definitions, not as examples of the kind of definitions that appear in the InterPARES vocabulary, but simply as a quick way in to a description of the objectives of the InterPARES project as a whole. So, a *record* is a document that (a) participates in or results from the activity of an individual or organization, and (b) constitutes the primary source of knowledge about that activity—a document that is increasingly likely to be generated in electronic form. *Preservation* is the physical and intellectual protection of records through time. The motivation for the InterPARES project may be understood in terms of recognition of the significance of a variety of obstacles to the long-term preservation of electronic records. These obstacles include the obsolescence of the software and hardware that are used to create, process, and provide access to electronic records; the fragility of the various kinds of media on which records are stored; the hybridity of formats of the components of records; and the ease with which electronic records may be manipulated and potentially tampered with.

This last problem is particularly significant, since archivists are concerned to preserve *authentic* records, that is, records that can be proved to be what they purport to be, and that are free of any tampering or corruption. Given this concern, we must have a means of evaluating the authenticity of a record at any time—an activity that becomes problematic in the electronic environment, since electronic records do not have physical form in the way that nonelectronic records do. On what principles and criteria should we base our assessments of the authenticity of electronic records?

So the aim of InterPARES—an international research project on Permanent Authentic Records in Electronic Systems—is to formulate principles and criteria for the development of policies, strategies, and standards that will guide archivists in the long-term preservation of authentic electronic records.

InterPARES is distinctive in its internationalism and multidisciplinarity. Its active participants include scholars and practitioners from many countries around the world, and these are not limited to the archivists that one might expect, but include computer scientists, librarians, and artists, humanists, natural scientists, and social scientists from a variety of domains.

The current InterPARES project is actually the second. The objectives of InterPARES 1, which was conducted over a three-year period between 1999 and 2002, were to establish: 1. a set of conceptual requirements for the authenticity of electronic records of various types; 2. a body of methods for selecting and preserving electronic records; 3. an intellectual framework for the development of policy relating to such preservation; 4. a portfolio of instruments for the assessment of existing records; and 5. a glossary of terms—a precursor of the current terminological database that I'll have more to say about in a minute.

The objectives of InterPARES 2, meanwhile, are to continue to establish methods of, and policies for, guaranteeing the reliability, accuracy, and authenticity of electronic records, but to focus especially on complex records such as those typically created by experiential, interactive, and dynamic systems in the course of artistic, scientific, and e-government activities—and the work of the project members is structured accordingly. Reaching an understanding of the more-complex policy issues is another priority, as is the construction of a thesaurus of terms, as we'll see.

InterPARES researchers have made use of a variety of methods of data collection and analysis and hypothesis formulation, including surveys, case studies, and grounded theory, and as one might expect, diplomatics, whose applicability to the electronic environment has been demonstrated by its specialized use in the assessment of the authenticity of records independently of context. I have classed these methods as "traditional" in the sense that they have all been used before in similar studies.

Some other methods may be less familiar, the most important being that of modeling. InterPARES analysts have modeled both activities, such as records creation, recordkeeping, selection and preservation, and the entities that participate in such activities. The modeling of activities involves decomposing them into a hierarchy of successively more specific sub-activities, and the identification of the entities that constrain or motivate those activities, or that are required or produced by them. The modeling of entities involves identifying their characteristic attributes, and the relationships between them, as well as the classification of entities by entity type, such as Agent, Event, Object, and so on.

Modeling of these kinds is similar to conceptual analysis. An adjunct to conceptual analysis is terminological analysis, which involves the consistent, rigorous definition of all the terms that are used to denote the activities, entities, attributes, and so on, that are identified at the modeling stage.

For example, some of the entities identified as participants in the particular activity that is labeled "Manage Chain of Preservation" are as follows. Constraining entities include the juridical system, the current state of technology, the mission of the preserver, and the concepts and principles of archival science. Motivating entities include information about documents, about the context of documents, about technology, and about the records creator. Required entities include a creator, a records manager, and a preserver. And produced entities include sent records, preserved records, and documentation about destroyed records.

This activity, "Manage Chain of Preservation," happens to be the top-level activity of one model that is the result of taking an approach based on a document lifecycle framework. By taking such an approach, the analyst is essentially assuming that it is most useful to consider the process of records management as one that follows the life of documents from creation through recordkeeping to selection and preservation.

Other frameworks or archival paradigms have been suggested over the years, including the records continuum model associated with Australian theory and practice. By taking these alternatives into account, it may eventually be possible to develop a unified model in which separate emphases on the document lifecycle, business functions, and the records continuum are integrated.

I'm spending time on this, because I think it's essential background for understanding the kinds of problems faced by any designer of a prescriptive tool such as the InterPARES vocabulary. Differences of opinion about the utility of archival paradigms—differences that of course have been voiced, and in some cases reconciled to a greater or lesser extent, over many years—are reflected at a more prosaic level in disagreements about the definitions of basic terms such as "record" and "archives," about the role of the archivist, and about appropriate criteria for selection and appraisal. If the InterPARES vocabulary were primarily a purely descriptive tool, it would be enough for such disagreements to be noted without judgment. But instead its function is to accurately reflect the judgments made by InterPARES researchers, and its construction is thus driven by the project's modeling activity.

With that rather lengthy preamble, I'd now like to move on to take a closer look at the InterPARES terminological activity, beginning with the question: What is the point of spending so much time in developing a vocabulary like ours? Fundamentally, our purpose is to ensure that all communication and dissemination among InterPARES researchers and between InterPARES researchers and the world is conducted as effectively as possible. We want to help authors, readers, and intermediaries such as indexers select and use terms in a consistent manner, such that authors end up using terms in the ways that are expected by their readers; such that readers end up finding the documents that they want; and such that readers end up interpreting documents in the ways intended by their authors.

The designers of any controlled vocabulary face challenges of many kinds. In the first place, there is potentially a conflict of purpose. On the one hand, the task of the designer might be conceived as one of determining current usage, and then ensuring that that usage is described in the definitions included in the vocabulary. On the other hand, the function of the vocabulary might be conceived as one of prescribing how terms are to be used in the future. In practice, both description and prescription are involved in identifying multiple current usages and designating certain of these usages as the ones that are to be preferred.

The terms that are used in any technical domain are often very specific, and it is no different in archival science. Many terms have different meanings or different shades of meaning in different domains or in different sub-fields, and these differences need to be identified accurately and precisely.

Archival science is also characterized by profound differences of approach and principle that divide along geographical lines: there are many points on which Australians, Canadians, Americans, and the Dutch (for example) will strongly disagree, and picking one's way through this minefield of cultural differences is fraught with difficulty.

The existence of a variety of vocabulary-construction standards, which occasionally contradict one another on vital points, is an undesired complication. The standards that we have generally relied upon most often are two that give guidance specifically for thesaurus construction. These are ISO 2788, the *Guidelines for the establishment and development of monolingual thesauri*, 2nd edition, published by the International Organization for Standardization in 1986; and ANSI/NISO Z39.19, the *Guidelines for the construction, format and management of monolingual thesauri*, published by the American National Information Standards Organization in 1993.

Finally, in this list of challenges, we find facet analysis. Facet analysis of the kind that is necessary in constructing a thesaurus is no simple matter. And we'll come back to that in a moment.

Okay. We typically talk about the vocabulary as if it's made up of four separate tools—a register, a dictionary, a glossary, and a thesaurus—but in fact each of those four words simply denotes a different view of the same database, as we'll see shortly.

We've built it as a database comprising two linked files, one in Microsoft Access format and one using a program called TCS-8, where TCS stands for Thesaurus Construction System. TCS-8 is helpful in the definition and presentation of hierarchies of terms.

The core data elements that go to make up each record in the terminological database including the following: the qualified term, which itself is made up of term, part-of-speech, facet, and domain; the definition, which itself is made up of sense, and source; the approval status, as either a preferred or non-preferred sense; and the contextualization in the thesaural hierarchy, as either a narrower or a related term.

We define a qualified term as a composite of a term and the three qualifiers associated with it in a dictionary record—that is, its part of speech (e.g., "noun"), its facet (e.g., "object"), and its domain (e.g., "archival science"). Given that, in ordinary language, a single term may have multiple senses, and different terms may have the same sense, two simple aims of our controlled vocabulary are to disambiguate homonyms (which is achieved through the use of qualifiers), and to collocate synonyms (which is achieved by defining links between non-preferred and preferred terms).

The dates of edits of the database and the identities of editors are automatically recorded, and weekly reports to the InterPARES terminology team are automatically generated. Selecting the Register view of the database displays audit data.

So, Table 22.1 shows you what dictionary records look like. By the way, there's an unintended complication here because I'm using the word "record," in the phrase "dictionary record" to indicate an entry or row of the file, at the same time as using "record" as my example of the term that's being defined in each row. Sorry about that!

Here we have three dictionary records. In the first field, we have the term being defined (and in all these three cases, that term is "record"); in the second, the part of speech (again, in all three cases, the part of speech is "noun"); in the third field, the facet to which the term belongs (again, in all three cases, the facet is given as "object," which indicates that the term in question refers to a kind of object, rather than a kind of agent, or a kind of property); in the fourth field, we have the domain in which the term is commonly used with the definition given; in the fifth field, we have that definition; and in the last field, we have a note of the source of that definition, where each note refers to a particular publication.

Term	Part of speech	Facet	Domain	Sense	Source
record	n.	object	archival science	A document created or received and maintained by an agency, organization, or individual in the pursuance of legal obligations or in the transaction of business.	IP
record	n.	object	archival science	Document created by a physical or juridical person in the course of practical activity.	UBC
record	n.	object	computer science	A grouping of interrelated data elements forming the basic unit of a file.	SAA

Table 22.1. Dictionary records: Example.

In summary, selecting a dictionary view of the database retrieves records for all defined terms, and presents one record per definition. Each qualified term may be defined in more than one record.

Table 22.2 gives an example of the way the glossary view looks. The points to note here are that there is only one record per qualified term—and that record is the one that contains the sense that has been approved as an InterPARES-preferred sense. So, of the two senses that were recorded in the dictionary for the qualified term "record–noun–object–archival science," only one appears in the glossary.

Term	Part of speech	Facet	Domain	Sense	Approved?
record	n.	object	archival science	A document created or received and maintained by an agency, organization, or individual in the pursuance of legal obligations or in the transaction of business.	Yes
record	n.	object	computer science	A grouping of interrelated data elements forming the basic unit of a file.	Yes

Table 22.2. Glossary records: Example.

Table 22.3 shows a representation of the thesaural view of some records. In each case, the additional data that is displayed indicates a second term to which the given term is linked, along with the type of that link—where NTG, for instance, stands for "Narrower term—Generic," to indicate that a record is a type of document, and an active record is a type of record, and so on.

Term	Facet	Subfacet	Link type	Linked term
record	object	[none]	NTG	document
record	object	[none]	RT	archives
active record	object	records by level of activity	NTG	record
reliable record	object	records by level of reliability	NTG	record

Table 22.3. Thesaurus records: Example.

One of the basic distinctions between the thesaural view, then, and the other three views lies in its presentation of the hierarchical relationships among terms. Such relationships may be of a genus–species variety, such as that between "record" and "active record," of a whole–part variety, such as that between "archives" and "record," or of a class–instance variety, such as that between "archive" and any name of a particular archive (as opposed to a particular kind of archive).

Another basic distinction between the thesaural view and the other three views lies in its presentation of the relationships among facets. Facets are the fundamental categories among which terms are classified. One option—one that we did not take—would have been to use disciplines or fields as facets. We might, for example, have chosen to classify terms under headings such as "Record creation," "Arrangement and description," and "Appraisal." Instead, we chose to classify terms under headings that denote the fundamental kinds of things that the terms refer to. In similar thesauri in other fields, facets such as "Objects," "Actions," "Agents," and "Properties" are common, and we embarked on the design of our thesaurus accordingly. But we faced (and continue to face) several problems.

Firstly, there are difficulties in assigning particular terms to facets. Should "date of receipt" and "authenticity" really be assigned to the same facet ("Properties"), for instance?

Secondly, questions remain about our choice of facets. Proposals for additional facets that are more or less persuasive include "Disciplines," "Concepts," "Events," "Systems," and "Principles."

Figure 22.1 shows a screenshot of a portion of the database as it is presented in the TCS program. The layout here is very similar to the way in which the thesaurus will eventually be accessible to all users over the web. I'm not sure how much detail you'll be able to make out here, but the term highlighted on the left is "evidential value." The system of indentation on the left indicates the hierarchical relationships between "evidential value" and other terms; it is a member of the subfacet "properties of objects," which itself is a member of the "Properties" facet. The sense of "evidential value" appears in the panel on the right, and various search facilities, including an option to search on this term in external databases such as the web or other InterPARES documents, are available bottom left.

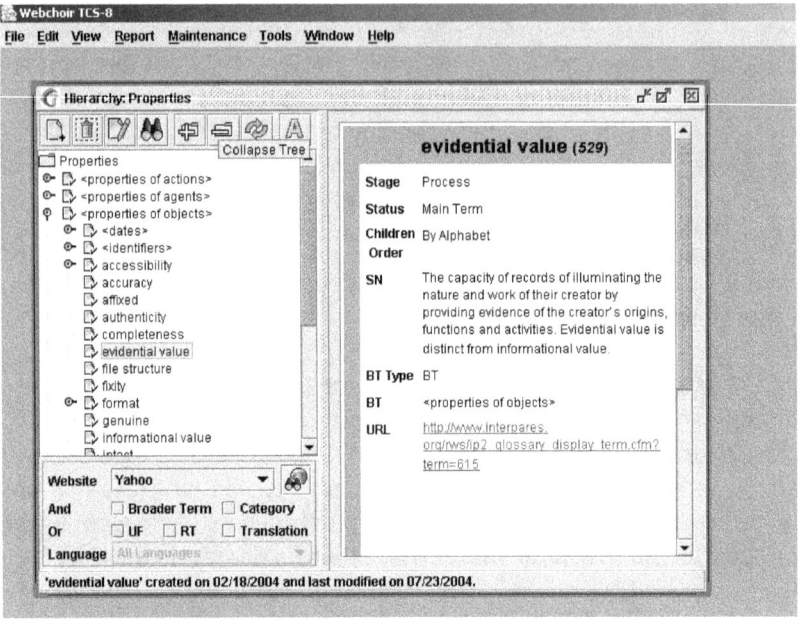

Figure 22.1. TCS-8 example.

There are several issues remaining to be resolved, and our work on the terminological database continues. When populating the vocabulary with new terms, which external sources should be consulted? What procedures and criteria should be used in such selection? Should compound terms (such as "reliable record") continue to be selected, and, if so, how?

As I asked earlier, is the set of facets currently in place the one that is most useful? And how should terms most usefully be categorized within facets?

How should we effect a reconciliation of the conflicting recommendations in the various standards as to the form of terms—singular or plural, infinitive or gerund, and so on? How can we adjudicate fairly between differences of opinion about the most useful prescription of definitions?

And perhaps most pressingly at this point, how are the tools to be evaluated, not only with respect to their compliance with international standards, but also with respect to the degree to which they meet the requirements of their users (of which there are several groups, each with a different set of needs)?

We are often reminded by distinguished members of the archival profession that the process of deciding what is worth remembering and what is not is essentially a political process. I'd like to conclude by making what is probably an obvious point: the process of prescribing the meanings of terms in the name of standardization is also a political one. It seems to require neutrality or impartiality on the part of the lexicographer, but such neutrality is impossible. The only criteria on which we can usefully evaluate a controlled vocabulary are its internal consistency, simplicity, and utility, and it is on these bases that we continue to try to improve InterPARES terminology.

I'd like to recognize the members of the InterPARES terminology team for all their hard work, especially our lexicographer Naomi Cull at Toronto, our database administrator Jean-Pascal Morghese at UBC, and our graduate student researcher Nadav Rouche at UCLA.

23
Collaborative indexing of cultural resources: Some outstanding issues

July 8, 2006

This talk was given at Digital Humanities 2006: The First ADHO International Conference (Paris, France, July 5–9, 2006). A paper with the same title as the talk, co-authored with Martha Kellogg Smith and Megan Winget, was published in **Digital Humanities 2006: The First ADHO International Conference**, *edited by Chengan Sun, Sabrina Menasri, and Jérémy Ventura (Paris: Université Paris–Sorbonne), 69–71.*

The old way

Today I'm going to be talking about a kind of subject indexing called collaborative indexing, specifically with respect to cultural resources such as museum objects. But I'm going to start by showing you three examples of a more traditional kind of indexing, to put the later discussion into context. These examples are portions of the catalog records for three objects in the collection of the Getty Museum in Los Angeles. The records are made available to the public on the web, and are constructed in accordance with the guidelines developed by the Visual Resources Association (VRA) and to be published by the American Library Association (ALA) later this year: *Cataloging cultural objects* (CCO). In fact, they are examples taken directly from CCO. (Representatives of the Getty have had much input in the development of that standard.)

Here [Slide #2][1] we see an image of the *Lansdowne Herakles*, so called because the statue used to be in the collection of the Marquess of Lansdowne. In ancient Greek mythology, the first of Hercules' twelve labors was to slay the Nemean lion and bring back his skin. Here, the figure of Hercules is in contrapposto, with the shoulders and arms twisting off-axis from the hips and legs. This posture is very characteristic of the work of Polyclitus, a Greek sculptor active in the fourth century BC. The metadata provided in the caption accompanying the image give details of (i) the title given to the work depicted, (ii) the work's creator, (iii) the date of creation of the work, (iv) its medium, and so on.

On this next slide [Slide #3][2], the same image is accompanied by a short description supplied by a curator, and two sets of subject terms—some descriptive of the *kinds* of objects depicted, and some identifying the names of the *particular* objects depicted. These terms represent expert knowledge of the circumstances in which the work was created and the identity of the objects depicted. The terms were assigned by experts, and chosen from among the terms appearing in strictly controlled vocabularies, those vocabularies themselves having been created by experts. On the slide, the occurrences of these terms are underlined to indicate that, in an online catalog, they would be hotlinked to the controlled vocabulary from which they were taken.

Here [Slide #4][3] we have an image of a painting that might appear, on first glance, to depict a fairly ordinary vase of flowers. If we look more closely, however, we will see that the flowers are drooping and decaying, and are being eaten by insects. The painting is an example of Pronkstilleven, a kind of still life fashionable in the Netherlands in the 1650s ("pronk" means "ostentation"), and is intended to represent the transience of life through its symbolic references to Ecclesiastes 1:2: "Vanitas vanitatum omnia vanitas" (translatable as "Vanity of vanities, all is vanity" or "Utterly meaningless, everything is meaningless"). Again, the description and subject terms given here [Slide #5][4] represent expert knowledge of iconography, of symbolism, and of kinds of

---

1 https://litwinbooks.com/books/information-studies-and-other-provocations/

2 Ibid.

3 Ibid.

4 Ibid.

objects such as specific kinds of flowers. A third category of subject—interpretation—is introduced here in addition to the description and identification we saw earlier.

In this third example [Slide #6][5], we have a photogram by Man Ray that, as it happens, was created here in Paris. Photograms are photographic images made by placing objects directly on to the surface of photo-sensitive paper and then exposing the paper to light, thus producing a negative image without the use of a camera. Ray called his photograms "rayographs," and his style was to use objects that are difficult to identify, placed in unusual juxtapositions. Ray often moved objects during the exposure period, and varied the exposure time given to different objects in a single image. In this case, the accompanying description and subject terms reflect a fairly subjective interpretation of what is important to say about this abstract artwork and its subjects [Slide #7][6].

The new way

Indexing cultural resources involves identifying and specifying their subjects so that resources (or information about them) can be found and enjoyed by people interested in specific subjects. The general problem relating to indexing is that it's very labor-intensive and therefore very costly. Many cultural resources are not texts whose subjects may be indexed automatically. But manual indexing by subject experts is frequently neglected because of its high costs. Even when manual indexing is carried out, one might argue that it is not done very well, since the language used by subject indexers often turns out not to be particularly comprehensible to museum visitors. This violates a principle that is the key to effective information retrieval—the principle that consistency between indexers and searchers be maximized.

A solution that has been proposed is for traditional indexing to be supplemented (if not necessarily replaced) by collaborative indexing. This method is called "collaborative" simply because, in most implementations, it is possible for any given resource to have been indexed by multiple people. It's interesting to note that traditional indexing, since it often represents a consensus reached by a team of experts, is often

---

5   https://litwinbooks.com/books/information-studies-and-other-provocations/

6   Ibid.

more deliberately collaborative than so-called collaborative indexing. The more distinctive feature of collaborative indexing is the fact that the indexers engaged in collaborative indexing need not be experts: they may be members of the viewing public. Another term that has often been used to capture this essence is *user-generated* indexing.

A more detailed characterization of collaborative indexing that contrasts it to traditional indexing is as follows:

- It's collaborative—just in the sense that any given record or description of a resource is potentially representative of the work of multiple people.
- It's distributed: No single person is required to index all resources; no single resource needs to be indexed by all people.
- It's dynamic: The description of a given resource may change over time, as different people come to make their own judgments of its nature and importance.
- It's instructive: The descriptors supplied by indexers may be analyzed with a view to learning about the kinds of aspects of works that are interesting or significant for those indexers.
- It's democratic: Indexers are not selected for their expertise by collection managers, but are self-selected according to indexers' own interests and goals.
- It's empowering: People who might in the past have been accustomed to searching databases by attempting to predict the descriptors used by "experts" are now given the opportunity to record their own knowledge about resources.
- Above all, it's cheap: Indexers typically volunteer their efforts at no or low cost to collection managers.

I'm sure many of you will be familiar with the first two applications of collaborative indexing I'm about to use as examples (Del.icio.us and Flickr). Maybe fewer will know the third (Steve). Let's take a quick look at each of these.

Here [Slide #12][7] is a tag cloud of the most popular single-word tags or descriptors assigned by users of Del.icio.us to web pages that they've

---

7   https://litwinbooks.com/books/information-studies-and-other-provocations/

bookmarked. The larger the word's size in the cloud, the more pages it's been assigned to. Note the lack of opportunities to browse here. The arrangement of tags is alphabetical, not classified. No attempt is made to control for synonyms or homonyms, for example. For proponents of tagging and folksonomies, that's the beauty! "Ontology is overrated!" (For that is their battle cry.)

Here [Slide #13][8] is Flickr's home page … and [Slide #14][9] a cloud of the most popular tags. *Paris* is just off the screen. If you click on *Paris*, this [Slide #15][10] is what you see—photos recently uploaded by Flickr users and tagged with that term.

Steve [Slide #16][11] is the idiosyncratic name for the wonderful project run by Jennifer Trant out of Canada which aims to study the applicability of tagging in the art museum context by building a community of interested parties and allowing them to share their ideas, tools, and data. Several papers by Trant and her collaborators at New York's Metropolitan Museum of Art are available at http://steve.museum/. One of the participants in Steve is Cleveland Museum of Art, which for a while now has been encouraging visitors to its website to "Help others find …" the works documented in its catalog records. Here [Slide #17][12] is an example work. You click on the "Help others find me" link, and assign terms to the work just by typing them in a text-entry box [Slide #18][13]: "… [P]lease use the box below to type in words and phrases that would be meaningful to you if you were searching for [this art object]." Other participants in Steve use similar methods to gather user-generated descriptors.

This feature of Cleveland's digital museum may be conceived as one more in a long line of recent projects where the interactivity of the web is exploited in a such a way that visitors are encouraged to engage more actively with, and thus derive more value from, the objects in museum collections. The Victoria & Albert Museum in London invites

---

8   https://litwinbooks.com/books/information-studies-and-other-provocations/
9   Ibid.
10 Ibid.
11 Ibid.
12 Ibid.
13 Ibid.

visitors to "tell stories" about its objects [Slide #20][14], and these stories are both collected and made available via the web [Slide #21][15]. Tate Britain visitors are invited to "write their own labels" for its objects [Slide #22][16], and again this is done using a web form [Slide #23][17]. In the U.S., visitors are invited to produce their own audio tours for museums [Slide #24][18], and these are distributed via podcasts [Slide #25][19].

So why is all this happening right now? Well, clearly the technology for "social computing" is in place. There's also a growing recognition in the museum sector that, if museums are truly to benefit what are often extremely diverse communities of users, more than lip service must be paid to the principles of the "new museology" that emphasizes social justice and social inclusion. And we are now in an era when the Library of Congress (among other institutions) is seriously considering doing away with expert subject indexing on the grounds of its high cost. "Library economy" was the old name, in Melvil Dewey's time, for what came to be known as library science. It would be interesting to speculate as to what Dewey—first and foremost a businessman concerned with efficiency of operations—would have made of the Library of Congress's plans.

So, the bottom line is an important motivation. But the ultimate goal, of course, is to improve the quality of visitors' engagement with resources. Some proponents of collaborative indexing would argue that the very act of describing and recording what one sees in a work is in itself beneficial to the individual. Other proponents focus more on the value that is to be derived by others—i.e., by future searchers—from the indexing supplied by a given individual. In that case, visitors' engagement is improved indirectly through the intermediate improvement of access to those resources. And a third group of researchers are most interested in finding out what they can about what is important to visitors by analyzing patterns in the sets of index terms that visitors generate.

---

14   https://litwinbooks.com/books/information-studies-and-other-provocations/.

15   Ibid.

16   Ibid.

17   Ibid.

18   Ibid.

19   Ibid.

On a complementary dimension, the quality of any cultural information system may be evaluated by considering its performance in relation to three imperatives, each of which corresponds to a separate aspect—cultural, political, economic—of the complex mission of contemporary cultural institutions. Firstly, how effectively does the system allow its users to find the resources in which they have an interest, and to derive optimal value from those resources once found? Secondly, how broadly and inclusively does the system serve all sections of its parent institution's public? Thirdly, how well does it do at delivering maximal quality at minimal cost? Justifications of the collaborative-indexing approach tend to proceed by drawing attention to the ways in which it can be viewed as responding to one or other of these three imperatives.

Evaluating collaborative indexing: What do we know?

I would now like to turn to the main argument of this paper, which is that, although collaborative indexing shows promise as a method of improving the quality of people's interactions with those resources, several important questions about the level and nature of the warrant for basing access systems on collaborative indexing are yet to receive full consideration by researchers in cultural informatics. Specifically, we suggest that system designers look to three cognate fields—classification research, annotation studies, and iconographical analysis—for pointers to criteria that may be useful in any serious estimation of the potential value of collaborative indexing to cultural institutions.

Classification research

In classification research, for example, it has long been argued that indexers and searchers benefit from having the opportunity to browse or navigate for the terms or class labels that correspond most closely to the concepts they have in mind, rather than being required to specify terms from memory. Indexer–searcher consistency, and thus retrieval effectiveness, can be improved to the extent that a system allows indexers and searchers to identify descriptors by making selections from a display of the descriptors that are available to them, categorized by facet or field, and arranged in a hierarchy of broader and narrower terms so that the user can converge on the terms that they judge to be of the most appropriate level of specificity. Current implementations of systems based on collaborative indexing shy away from imposing the kind of vocabulary control on which classification schemes and thesauri are conventionally founded. The justification usually proceeds along the lines that indexers should be free, as far as possible, to supply precisely those terms that they believe will be useful to searchers in the future, whether or not those terms have proven useful in the past. Yet it remains an open question as to whether the advantages potentially to be gained from allowing indexers free rein in the choice of terms outweigh those that are known to be obtainable by imposing some form of vocabulary and authority control, by offering browsing-based interfaces to vocabularies, by establishing and complying with policies for the specificity and exhaustivity of indexing, and by other devices that are designed to improve indexer–searcher consistency.

Just to put some of these remarks into context, here [Slide #31][20] is the Tate's top-level display of subject categories. The searcher can browse this structure by clicking on *Nature*, for example, then [Slide #32][21] *animals: mammals*, then [Slides #33, #34][22] *lion*, to see the 65 works indexed by that term. Here [Slide #35][23] is one such work of local interest, by Conroy Maddox. If you click on the "Subjects" tab [Slide #36][24], you can then click on any of the terms assigned to this work to see a list of other works indexed by that term. For example, the term *Paris–non-specific* has been assigned to 46 works. This is fairly simple stuff, of course: there's nothing groundbreaking about this approach. But that's the point. It's what subject searchers have come to expect. These screenshots show the kind of browsing opportunities that system designers can provide with a bit of vocabulary control and classified structure. These are opportunities that are more helpful to most users than a tag cloud—there's no doubt about that. The question is: How can the folksonomies constructed by collecting user-generated index terms be integrated with the structures that already exist for the organization of terms assigned by experts?

Just for interest, here [Slide #37][25] is the online interface to the iconographical classification scheme Iconclass. Searching on the keyword

---

20 https://litwinbooks.com/books/information-studies-and-other-provocations/.
21 Ibid.
22 Ibid.
23 Ibid.
24 Ibid.
25 Ibid.

lion points you to several locations, and you can see the detail here [Slide #38][26]. The class code 25F23 refers to the animal itself, with no other context. You can use this interface to search directly in collections indexed using Iconclass [Slide #39][27]. Great stuff!

Annotation studies

Researchers in the human–computer interaction (HCI) community are continuing to develop an agenda for work in the emerging subfield of annotation studies, focusing on ways to improve interfaces that support annotation behavior of a variety of kinds, in a variety of domains. In this research, an annotation is commonly considered as evidence of a reader's personal, interpretive engagement with a primary document—a form of engagement that is not so different from that which cultural institutions seek to encourage in their patrons. A cultural annotation system that allowed patrons not only to supply their own descriptions of an institution's resources, but also to add comments and to build communities around personal collections, could be envisaged as a vital service that would help patrons interact with and interpret those resources, largely outside the authority and control of curators and other specialists. It remains an open question as to whether a system that allows patrons to supply their own descriptions of institutions' resources is most appropriately evaluated as a tool for creating and accessing personal annotations, as a tool for sharing and accessing collaborative descriptions, as a retrieval tool pure and simple, or some combination of all three. Unfortunately, our understanding of the purposes and intentions of users of systems based on collaborative indexing is still spotty, and further research in this area is necessary.

Theories of iconographical interpretation

Another relevant subfield of library and information science is that which is concerned with the effective provision of subject access to art images, and commonly invokes the theory of iconographical interpretation developed by the art historian Erwin Panofsky. Panofsky distinguished three layers of meaning corresponding to three levels of art-historical research: the levels of *pre-iconographical description*

---

26   https://litwinbooks.com/books/information-studies-and-other-provocations/.

27   Ibid.

of natural subject-matter, *iconographical analysis* of conventional subject-matter, and *iconological interpretation* of intrinsic meaning. The standard application of Panofsky's theory in library and information science is through the work of Sara Shatford, Karen Markey, and Elaine Svenonius, which distinguishes firstly between the *ofness* and the *aboutness* of an artwork, and secondly between *generic* and *specific* ofness. You'll recognize how these categories of generic ofness, specific ofness, and aboutness correspond to the three categories of index terms—description, identification, and interpretation—that were assigned to our earlier examples.

Questions that relate to the aboutness of a work include, what is its meaning? What does it express? What do the objects, events, etc., depicted in the work symbolize? How may the work be interpreted? Moreover, what were the intentions of the work's creator? And how has the work been interpreted historically? Questions relating to the ofness of a work include, for figurative works, what are the *kinds* of objects and activities depicted in the work? What are the names of the *particular* objects, events, places, and periods depicted in the work? And, for non-representational works, what is the form and function of the work?

Current implementations of art-museum systems based on collaborative indexing focus on eliciting generic terms for (what Panofsky calls) pre-iconographic elements, i.e., pictured objects, events, locations, people, and simple emotions—the assumption apparently being made that such terms are those that will be most useful to searchers. There is very little evidence supplied by studies of the use of art image retrieval systems, however, to suggest either that pre-iconographic elements are indeed what non-specialists typically search for, or that generic terms lead non-specialist searchers to what they want. We do know from analyses of questions that visitors ask in museums that non-specialists typically do not have the specialist vocabulary to specify precisely what they are looking for. This does not necessarily mean, however, that searchers always default to using pre-iconographic terms whenever they wish to get more complex themes and ideas, nor that searches for higher-level elements using pre-iconographic terms will be successful. In other words, will searchers who are interested enough in certain subjects to know to use terms like "contrapposto," "Nemean lion," and "Vanitas" be well served by visitors' descriptions of the kinds of objects they see depicted in works? Of course, if the aim of a particular implementation of collaborative indexing is directly to engage visitors by allowing them to interact with works through the act of indexing, there might not seem to be a problem—especially if collaborative indexing is conceived as a complementary activity to expert indexing. But the proponents of collaborative indexing often promote it either as (i) a productive source (even, potentially, an alternative source) of index terms that will support future retrieval, or (ii) a good way of learning about what visitors are interested in. As yet, there isn't sufficient evidence to allow us to evaluate those claims.

Conclusion

There are other questions to be addressed. Given the distributed nature of collaborative indexing, for example, how can it be ensured that every resource attracts a "critical mass" of index terms, rather than just the potentially quirky choices of a small number of volunteers? Given the self-selection of indexers, how can it be ensured that they are motivated to supply terms that they would expect other searchers to use? Empirical, comparative testing of the utility of different prototypes—focusing, for example, on forms of interface for elicitation of terms, or on algorithms for the ranking of resources—is undoubtedly an essential prerequisite for the future development of successful systems based on collaborative indexing. But it is also important, we argue, that the results of prior research in a variety of cognate fields be taken into account when addressing some of the more problematic issues that we have identified.

24

Social classification: Panacea or Pandora?

November 4, 2006

This talk was given as a welcome to the 17th Annual ASIS&T SIG/CR Workshop on Classification Research, at ASIS&T 2006: 69th Annual Meeting of the American Society for Information Science and Technology (Austin, TX, November 3–8, 2006). The workshop chairs were Jonathan Furner and Joseph T. Tennis. The program included a keynote by Joseph Busch, nine full paper presentations, and twelve poster presentations.

What is social classification, and why should we care?

What's in a name? I know there are considerable differences in the denotations and connotations of the terms in Table 24.1. But it's almost as if we could have taken one term from the list on the left, and one from the right, and we would have quite a nifty "Topic 2.0" for today's program. "Collaborative indexing," anyone? "Democratic description"? "Mob metadata"? Anyway, we went with "social classification," even though that raised some people's hackles since that term has already been used to mean something quite different. And here we are.

Everybody's doing it, it seems. (Although: *are* they, really? More on that later.) The reason SIG/CR is excited is because—you know those tags that Flickr users and Del.icio.us users are creating in their millions?— they're *index terms*! And it's not too much of a stretch to think of them as *labels for classes*! Folksonomies? They may be faux, but they're still -xonomies! Fact is, you've people—regular people—*blogging* about taxonomies, hierarchies, facets, controlled vocabularies, pre-coordination, *Ranganathan* ... What's up with *that*? Any which way you look at it, this is a big opportunity for the classification research community, because suddenly a lot of people are interested in our history, in our perspective, in our expertise, and in collaborating on research that improves our understanding of classification.

audience-derived	annotation
collaborative	arrangement
community	bookmarking
cooperative	cataloging
crowd	categorization
democratic	classification
distributed	description
dynamic	documentation
folksonomic	indexing
inclusive	metadata
mob	ordering
public-created	organization
reader-assigned	ranking
social	recordkeeping
user-generated	representation
visitor-produced	tagging
wikified	taxonomy

Table 24.1. "Social classification" and its variants.

Whence comes the "social" in social classification? Well, here is a much simplified view of what's happening, contrasting the bad, boring, old way with the new, exciting, social way. In the old way (Figure 24.1) you had a single indexer—human or automated—assigning a number of

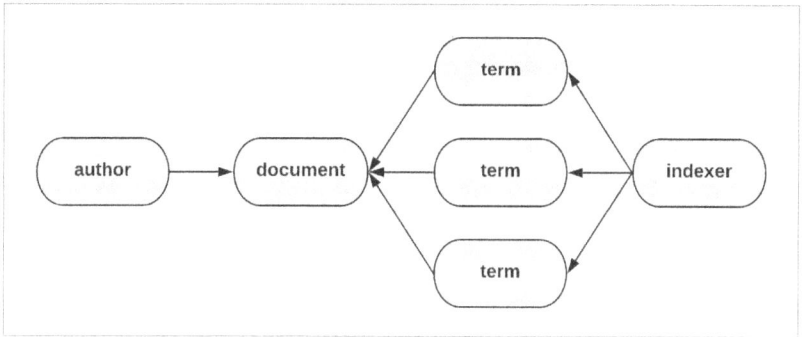

Figure 24.1. The old way.

terms with any given document in a collection. In the new way (Figure 24.2) we have *multiple* indexers assigning terms to given documents in a collection. And those multiple indexers? You know, they don't like to be told what to do. They don't like their vocabulary to be controlled, like in the bad old days.

Actually, you might decide that there are, conveniently, seven wonderful aspects of social classification.

- Social classification is *collaborative*—if only in the sense that any given record or description of a resource is potentially representative of the work of multiple people.

- It's *distributed*: No single person is required to tag all of the resources in a given collection. At the same time, no single resource needs to be tagged by all of the people in a given community.

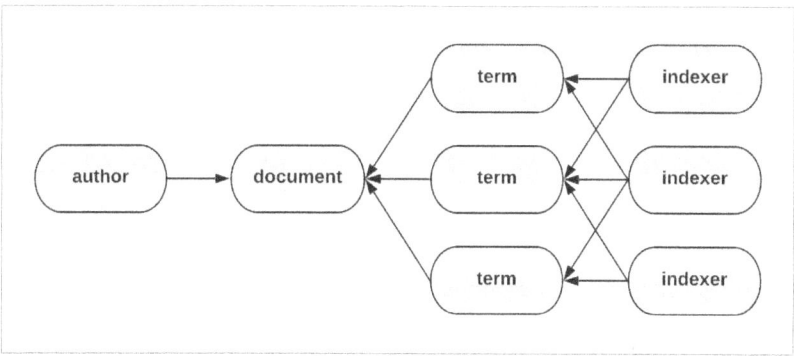

Figure 24.2. The new way.

- It's *dynamic*: The description of a given resource may change over time, as different people come to make their own judgments of its nature and importance.

- It's *instructive*: The descriptors supplied by taggers may be analyzed with a view to learning about the kinds of aspects of resources that are interesting or significant for the members of the taggers' community.

- It's *democratic*: Taggers are not selected for their expertise by collection managers, but are self-selected according to taggers' own interests and goals.

- It's *empowering*: People who might in the past have been accustomed to searching databases by attempting to predict the descriptors used by "experts" are given the opportunity to record their own knowledge about resources.

- Finally, and above all, it's *cheap*: Taggers typically volunteer their efforts at no or low cost to collection managers.

Does social classification work?

So, what's the problem that we need to solve, today? (I'm only half joking.) The big question, I think, is "What factors will determine whether or not systems that implement social classification are successful?" Here, of course, we might immediately want to distinguish between success measured in terms of sheer popularity, and success measured in terms of how well a system actually works, how well it actually does what its designers want it to do, i.e., how well it performs its function. Trouble is: It's often quite difficult to determine what that primary function is, because social classification systems are typically multifunctional. People use them differently depending on whether they're focusing on personal goals, or wanting to help other people (or both at the same time); and depending on whether they're focusing on creating descriptions of resources, or using descriptions to find stuff; and depending on whether their interest is simply in access to resources (or to information about resources), or in some form of deeper engagement or interaction with those resources. And this is before we've even started to consider all the different kinds of document that can be classified socially, all the different kinds of context that social classification systems can be used in, and all the different ways in which people's tagging activity can be analyzed with a view to understanding those people's behavior.

Another way of putting the same question is to ask "How do (or how *should*) social classification systems help their users get the stuff done that they want to get done, or even pass their time in the way they want to pass the time—easily, cheaply, quickly, and well?" Essentially this is your basic *evaluation* question, and the thing about most of the existing literature on social classification is that it doesn't provide much in the way of empirical data that would allow us to answer it—especially the last part. How does the *effectiveness* of social classification systems compare, for instance, with that of more traditional systems? Despite all the hype, we still don't really know.

Many researchers, in the HCI community for instance, are starting to move beyond questions about interface design, and ask questions about the kinds of *infrastructure* that need to be built if social classification systems are to become truly useful on a global scale. Much of the talk about infrastructure focuses on its *socio-economic* components—for example, figuring out the right kinds of incentives to offer in return for taggers' voluntary efforts. As classification researchers, we need to focus on deciding what the *linguistic* infrastructure should be like.

For instance, if (as is often claimed) the key to effective information retrieval is that indexers are enabled successfully to predict the terms used by searchers, and vice versa, then how can vocabulary control, policies on specificity and exhaustivity, hierarchical arrangement, categorization by facet, browsable displays—all the good old-fashioned *fiber* of predefined classification schemes—how can all this good stuff be integrated with social classification systems in such a way that the benefits that accrue from *not* imposing any control—the low cost, the DIY factor—aren't lost?

Here's the problem restated one final time. Actually: two final times. Can we expect taggers to think like searchers? Or, in fact, *should* they think like searchers, and if so, how can we encourage them to do so? And the bottom line: Social classification may be wonderful in all those ways mentioned earlier. But does it—can it—ever *work*?

25

User tagging of library resources: Toward a framework for system evaluation

August 23, 2007

This talk was sponsored by the Classification and Indexing Section of the International Federation of Library Associations and Institutions (IFLA), and was given at the World Library and Information Congress (WLIC 2007): 73rd IFLA General Conference and Council (Durban, South Africa, August 19–23, 2007). A paper with the same title as the talk was published in International Cataloguing & Bibliographic Control *37, no. 3 (2008): 47–51.*

The Ann Arbor District Library's OPAC

My topic today is user tagging of library resources. To give you a quick idea of what that involves, I have a few screenshots of the web-based interface to the online public-access catalog (OPAC) of resources offered by the Ann Arbor District Library (AADL), a large public library system in the state of Michigan in the United States. I have no connection with Ann Arbor, but this library was one of the early adopters of user tagging technology, and the features offered by this service are pretty representative of the kinds of features that are being offered increasingly frequently by public and academic libraries in the

U.S. and beyond. Although, I have to say it's not a great example of what Patrick Danowski, in his talk earlier this week, characterized as a library "going to where the users are." AADL still expects its users to come to where the library is.

This [Slide #2][1] is the basic search page—you can type in a search term in the box, or click on one of the links at the bottom to see the items that are grouped into certain predefined categories (new items, or "hot" items, and so on), or even click on one of the so-called *tags* listed on the right. More on those tags in a minute. First, let's imagine we click on the "Hot Books" link, and this [Slide #3][2] is what we get—a list of the most requested items in the catalog, unsurprisingly headed at this time (August 2007) by the latest installment in the Harry Potter series.

If we click on the book title, we see the full record, of which this [Slide #4][3] is the top part. (I'm not sure why the diacritic in the illustrator's name isn't handled well here—it may be a Safari issue.) The important thing to note here is the list of terms given just below the main entry. These are the tags that have been assigned by library *patrons* rather than by library staff, and I know you won't be able to see these, so I'll read them: *harrypotter* (all one word, in lower case), *21july2007* (again, all one string with no spaces), *fantasy*, *voldemort* (the name of a character in the book), *HarryPotter!* (with an exclamation point and no space), *Harry Potter* (two words), *kill*, *death*, *rowling* (the author's last name), *7* (the numeral, presumably to indicate that this book is the 7th and final installment in the series), *final*, *last*, *magic*, *deathly*, *hallows* (the last two words lifted from the title). You might be thinking: Hmm, some of these tags are a little … idiosyncratic? Especially so, if you're familiar with the more traditional methods of describing the content of library resources that are used by library staff.

Further down the record, for instance, we can see [Slide #5][4] the Library of Congress Subject Headings (LCSH) that have been assigned to this item, including the authorized forms of the main character's name (*Potter, Harry*) and the main place name (*Hogwarts School*), plus

---

1 https://litwinbooks.com/books/information-studies-and-other-provocations/.

2 Ibid.

3 Ibid.

4 Ibid.

four topical terms (*Wizards*; *Magic*; *Schools*; *England*) and a genre term (*Fantasy fiction*), none of which are already included in the title.

Both the tags and the LCSH terms are hotlinked. If we click on the tag *magic*, for instance, we see [Slide #6][5] a list of all items that have been assigned that tag by patrons.

So now if we turn our attention to the list of tags on the right hand side, these are the tags that happen to have been assigned by library patrons in general to the largest number of resources. (These are not necessarily the tags that have been assigned most *frequently*, by the way, since it's possible, of course, for the same tag to be assigned multiple times by different people to the same resource.) I'll read the top ten tags: *fantasy*, *manga*, *animé*, *shonen jump*, *time travel*, *shonen*, *ghosts*, *half-demons*, *demons*, *shape-changing* ... I'm sure you can see a pattern emerging here!

The system provides other ways of navigating this list of tags, such as a tag-cloud feature, but there is no structure to the list other than that which is produced by the relative popularity of the tags. In other words, this list is a *folksonomy*, one that emerges over time as the result of many people's tagging activity.

You might have noticed the tiny icon of a baggage tag next to the list of tags as they appear in a record. If, as a library patron, you were to click on that icon, this [Slide #7][6] is what you would see—a simple text-entry box that allows you to type in the tags you wish to assign to a resource. With this system, patrons may act not only as searchers, but also as taggers.

Tagging and user tagging

Now, we might wish to distinguish between the general term "tagging" and the more specific term "user tagging." "Tagging" can refer to any act of assigning a tag, term, heading, or code, to a resource with the dual intention of *describing* that resource and thereby providing future *access* to that resource. "User tagging" refers to tagging done by users rather than by others. In this sense, tagging includes the work traditionally done by indexers and catalogers, whose primary task is

---

5   https://litwinbooks.com/books/information-studies-and-other-provocations/.

6   Ibid.

the description of resources, whereas user tagging is limited to the activity of those who are interested also (or even primarily) in seeking access to resources.

So in the bad old days, this is how indexing or subject cataloging was done: An expert, whose job it was to tag, would assign a relatively small set of tags, typically chosen from a strictly controlled set of candidates, to each of the resources in a collection.

In the brave new world, regular people—non-librarians, by golly—can go ahead and assign as many tags as they like, from off the tops of their heads, to as many resources as they like. Obviously there's a whole range of possibilities for hybrid systems that take advantage of both kinds of practice. But it's this new way that's called user tagging— or social classification, or collaborative indexing, or mob metadata.

Lots of people (and I'm one of them) think user tagging is great, for all these reasons: User tagging is *user-oriented*, it's *empowering*, it's *democratic*, it's *cheap*, it's *collaborative*, it's *distributed*, it's *dynamic*, it's *instructive*. Hey, these are all good things! Nobody could argue with that, right?

And applications of user tagging can be found, of course, in non-library contexts, such as systems for organizing bookmarks of web pages, digital images, and art museum records—as well as in academic libraries, public libraries, and systems for organizing personal library collections. I'm sure some of you will have heard Stephen Abram the other day, characterizing LibraryThing as the second largest library in North America.

In the library world, applications of user tagging are often dealt with under the banner of "Library 2.0," about which we've heard so much at this conference. (Although, I was a little concerned to hear in one session that Library 3.0 is here already, so, if your library has not yet upgraded to 2.0 you might prefer to wait a few weeks for the new version.) One of the defining characteristics of Library 2.0 that Patrick Danowski mentioned in his talk was that it links people to people, not just people to information. This is admirable, of course, but is it so new? The implication is that Library 1.0 was somehow *not* about building community or providing space or allowing people to create, nor about helping people to engage with their own and other cultures. But since when was Library 1.0 merely about supplying information rather than about learning, cooperation, community, or fun?

More specifically, user-tagging features are typical of instances of "OPAC 2.0," where catalog users are encouraged to participate not only in searching activities, but also in activities that contribute to the *creation* of the very metadata that makes searching possible. And there are some very exciting possibilities that are being mined by enterprising developers: the blog/OPAC mash-up mentioned here is just one example.

Does user tagging work? How can we tell?

Here's the main point of this presentation, though. We know—or, at least, we're fairly certain that we know—that user-tagging services are cheap and empowering and democratic, and all those other good things. But: *we don't really know whether they work*. And part of the problem is that *we don't really know how to tell whether they work*. If we look around, we won't find many empirical evaluations of, for instance, the effectiveness of retrieval from collections of user-tagged resources. Of course, that might be because retrieval effectiveness is simply the *wrong thing* to be measuring if we want to know how well these services work. In which case: What's the *right thing*?

If we look at the history of the methodology of evaluation of information systems, we'll see that, in general, the success with which a system operates may be defined in one of two ways—either in terms of the sheer *popularity* of the system with its users, or in terms of the level at which the system *performs its functions* (i.e., does what it's supposed to do). The point is that popularity and performance are only ever contingently related. Good performance is neither a necessary nor a sufficient condition for popularity, and vice versa. In the remainder of this presentation, I'm going to assume, rather arbitrarily, that it's performance rather than popularity that we're interested in.

I'm going to suggest that, if we're to design a conceptual framework for the reliable evaluation of user-tagging services, we need to get very straight our answers to two basic questions. Firstly, on what *criteria* may the performance of systems be judged? And secondly, what methods may we use to *measure* the extent to which systems meet those criteria?

One fairly common approach to answering the first question is to assume that the choice of criteria should be based on a determination of the functionality of systems—in other words, that systems are designed and developed with the *intention* that they perform certain functions, and are used with the *expectation* that they perform certain functions, and therefore should be evaluated on the basis of how well they perform those particular functions.

A second step in this approach is to recognize that, in practice, the functionality of systems ultimately depends not on those intentions of system designers, but on those expectations of system users, and so the choice of criteria for evaluation should be made on the basis of the *reasons* that people have for deciding on particular occasions to use particular systems. If we know what kinds of goals people have, what their intentions and expectations are, and what motivates them to make use of a given system, then we can evaluate that system on the basis of how well it allows people to achieve their goals.

Thirdly, we need to keep in mind that individual systems may vary greatly in functionality, but that it will surely help if we can identify a few general dimensions of variance, and perhaps establish a taxonomy of system types.

Toward a taxonomy of library implementations of user tagging

The construction of a taxonomy is one thing I tried to do in the accompanying paper. We can distinguish user tagging systems in libraries according to the type of parent institution (academic, public, school, etc.), the type of user to whom the tagging tool is directed (expert or novice, professional or layperson, etc.), the type of resource to which tags may be assigned, and the type of access (full or partial) offered to the content of resources.

Some more interesting dimensions, perhaps, are the functionality of the tagging service itself, the functionality of the associated search service, the goals of the implementers of the service, and the motivations of its end-users. I'm going to focus today on the last two of these, beginning with the goals of *implementers*, which may include any or any combination of the following:

- to engender a sense of community among library users in separate locations;
- to help library users identify others with whom they share interests;
- to engender a sense of empowerment among library users who may not otherwise feel involved in library activities;

- to encourage library users to engage with and understand the resources they tag;
- to improve the effectiveness of retrieval of records and discovery of resources (by allowing users to take account of the recommendations of other users);
- to improve the effectiveness of personal rediscovery of resources (by allowing people to bookmark resources that they like);
- to help users find out which resources and topics are currently popular;
- to help users demonstrate and share their knowledge;
- to improve the entertainment value of, and thereby the level of user satisfaction with, the search experience; and
- to reduce the costs normally incurred in manually cataloging the resources in a collection.

There may well be others. Pam Gatenby talked the other day of the library manager's motivation to ensure that the library stays relevant and visible in its community; Stephen Abram spoke of the need to "enchant" the user. The main point is that implementers' goals are not likely summarizable in a single statement, which accordingly greatly complicates the evaluation question.

If we look at the potential motivations that library *users* may have when deciding to use a tagging service, we can identify many that correspond directly to implementers' goals. For their part, end-users may wish to partake of that sense of community just mentioned, to identify others with whom they share interests, to partake in that sense of empowerment, and so on. Again, an important distinction to be made is that between the motivation to improve the effectiveness of other people's searches (by recommending resources that one thinks might be of interest of others), and the motivation to improve one's own future searches (by bookmarking resources that one predicts one might like to find again).

In fact, when we look at the kinds of mental model that individual people may have of the ways in which tagging services can help them achieve their goals, we can initially distinguish between the user with an *individualist* motivation who focuses on personal goals, and the user with a *social* motivation to help other people achieve their objectives. (In reality, of course, this distinction is blurred because one's wish to help others may itself be the result of a calculation that helping others is likely to be the most effective way of improving one's own circumstances.)

We can also distinguish between the *intrinsicalist* who enjoys their tagging activity as an end in itself, and the *instrumentalist* who sees it simply as a means to the end of finding resources. And again, we can distinguish between another sort of intrinsicalist whose ultimate goal is to engage deeply with the resources in a collection (whether their hope is to be informed or to be entertained), and the instrumentalist whose goal is simply to complete a particular task that may be less a matter of personal interest than a matter of professional duty.

Criteria for evaluation

So where does this analysis of functions, goals, and motivations get us with regard to the selection of appropriate evaluative criteria? On the face of it, given the range of motivations that people may have for using tagging services, the range of *criteria* proposed in the extensive literature on evaluation frameworks for information systems may seem comparatively narrow. One convention in that literature is to distinguish between effectiveness, efficiency, cost-effectiveness, and usability, which correspond roughly to how well, how quickly, how cheaply, and how easily system users can get their jobs done. Another convention is to privilege *effectiveness* as the criterion that really matters, as there's not much point doing a job quickly, cheaply, and easily, if it's done badly. And a third convention is to distinguish between methods of arriving at supposedly *objective* measurements of these values, and methods of determining people's *perceptions* of how good systems are.

It's debatable how far almost fifty years of tests have got us in clarifying, once and for all, the nature of the relationship between the quality of the results of any process of resource description such as tagging, and the level of effectiveness of retrieval from collections of tagged resources. And this is significant, because it means that there are many aspects of the resource description process that are still contested matters. Should tags be generated automatically or manually? How useful to taggers and searchers is access to some sort of vocabulary of candidate terms whose forms are controlled and whose relationships are represented by a faceted and hierarchical structure?

Many of us in the library world accept, of course, that indexer–searcher consistency is a good indicator of retrieval effectiveness, and that this observed correlation is reliable evidence in support of the provision of controlled vocabularies.

There's no law that prevents the implementation of a user tagging service in tandem with a controlled vocabulary. But in practice, most tagging services are based on the *folksonomic* model, in which taggers' choices of terms are not constrained in any way (at least in theory). The claim is often made that the folksonomies that emerge reflect more accurately the actual consensus of opinion of end-users of tagged resources. The argument in favor of tagging without vocabulary control then tends to run as follows:

- taggers are drawn from the same population as searchers;
- taggers tend to use the same terms to tag resources as searchers use to look for resources; and so
- high levels of tagger–searcher consistency (and thus high levels of retrieval effectiveness) are assured.

Here's the rub: *None of these claims have been conclusively shown to be true.* Empirical tests are required to demonstrate the soundness of this argument. And, in any case, it's an argument that will only interest us if we accept that measurement of retrieval effectiveness is the appropriate way to evaluate the performance of tagging services.

Against *that*, I'll just point out the following:

- different kinds of users have different *motivations* for making use of tagging services (not just social motivations to help others find resources);
- different kinds of users have different perceptions of the *functions* of tagging services (not just resource discovery); and
- evaluation of the success with which systems perform any of their multiple functions may be based on a variety of different criteria (not just retrieval effectiveness).

Conclusion

Ingrid Parent mentioned in her talk the other day that she'd heard practicing bibliographers talk about the idea of wiki bibliographies as "madness," but that, well, the times they are a-changing and "we have to take into account what our users are saying"—meaning, presumably, that we have to take into account what tags people assign to resources, given the chance. The rhetorical question here is, *Why* do we have to? Do we have to because we know that, if we take those tags into account we will be providing a better service, however that may be measured? (I don't think we do know that.) Or do we have to because we know that, if we take those tags into account we will be able to provide a service at lower cost? Ingrid talked about the need to *simplify* description practices. Complicated description practices are only bad if they're expensive or if they produce results that are of low quality or utility. The questions remain: Is it possible to simplify description practices while maintaining the quality and utility of the results of those practices? And what methods can we use to measure levels of quality and utility while maintaining the reliability and validity of those methods?

With the advent of user tagging, evaluation of OPAC performance has itself become more complicated. But that fact should not be used as an excuse for forgetting what we have known for decades, which is that evaluation—in whatever form it takes—is a necessary condition for system improvement.

26
Twenty tall tales about tagging

September 17, 2009

This talk[1] was given at the 5th Annual OCLC Digital Forum West: Convergence: Where metadata and access meet for digital discovery and delivery (Los Angeles, CA, September 16–17, 2009) as part of a panel on "'Not your typical tagger': Content description by content producers." The panel chair was Murtha Baca, and speakers were Jonathan Furner, Karen Smith-Yoshimura, and Luiz Mendes.

What's a tall tale, you might ask? Well, it's what in England we might call a likely story, by which of course we would mean an unlikely story—sort of like a myth, or an assumption that some people make some of the time, that (despite being dubious in some more-or-less obvious way) sometimes doesn't get questioned, or compared with the evidence, in the way that perhaps it ought to. My aim today is simply to call out a few of what I think are the taller tales, and invite you—us—to consider exactly how tall we think they are. And I want to do that just because I think that if we can reduce the average height of the tales told about tagging, we can build better systems, provide better services, and all that good stuff.

---

[1] See slides at https://litwinbooks.com/books/information-studies-and-other-provocations/.

I gave a version of this talk about a year ago, and then it was called "*Ten* tall tales about tagging." So on the face of it we don't seem to be doing too well in terms of tale-shortening. But I think I might have miscounted back then.

These quotes are a few years old now—I should find more recent ones—but they are representative of sentiments that you do still find quite widely expressed. My goodness! "There's a revolution happening on the internet that is alive and building momentum with every passing tag." (Kroski 2005, quoted in Abbas & Graham 2006).

But, wait, "Despite a considerable amount of attention in academic circles as represented in various blog posts … , little academic research work has been invested in tagging systems to date." (Marlow et al. 2006). And "The literature of tagging is largely opinion-based [rather than evidence-based] … and the topic is largely absent from academic literature." (Speller 2007). This situation is changing a little bit—apart from anything else we have the work of the ongoing Steve project on tagging in art museums—but you know there are still a lot of opinions out there and it's sometimes difficult to sort out what we think we know from what we know we know. Difficult, but as I hope to show today, absolutely necessary.

A few quick clarifications just before we dive into the tall tales. What's the difference between tagging and user tagging? I quite like to retain a distinction, to be honest, if only to emphasize that tagging, the more general term, can essentially be understood as a synonym of resource description, which covers quite a wide range of practices undertaken in support of resource discovery or the provision of access to resources. User tagging is then the kind of tagging that is done when the population of describers (or at least the population of *potential* describers) is roughly equivalent to the population of access-seekers (or at least the population of *potential* access-seekers).

And why do people like user tagging so much? Well, typically it's because they conceive of user tagging as being empowering, or democratic, or fun, or some such thing. For content providers, of course, the major upside of user tagging is that it's fairly cheap compared with other methods of resource description. The question is, "Is user tagging a free lunch, or do we get what we pay for?"

So the archetypical characterization of user tagging is that it is something done by people who do not earn their livelihood from doing that thing, using computers to create links between three kinds of entities: themselves, certain words or phrases, and resources of various sorts. These resources might be digital objects (such as web pages, digital images, or videos) or digital records, either of concrete objects (such as books, paintings, or people) or of abstract objects (such as editions, texts, or works). And the reason for participating in this practice is typically understood to be in order to improve resource discovery or resource rediscovery, whether by the tagger or by others, although research continues to indicate that individual motivations to tag, as well as institutional motivations to offer tagging services, may be multifaceted, subconscious, unobservable, and generally complex in lots of ways.

And the archetypical characterization of a folksonomy is that it is something that emerges from multiple acts of tagging, that can be exploited or studied in many of the same ways in which controlled vocabularies can be exploited or studied, but that is relatively weakly structured, relatively weakly controlled, and relatively flexible. A folksonomy can be used as a kind of search thesaurus, allowing searchers to recognize rather than requiring them to recall, "without [their] needing to know an often outdated, Anglo-centric controlled vocabulary that librarians and users alike do not always know or understand" (Abbas & Graham 2006). Does the mere fact that a folksonomy emerges from the bottom up rather than being imposed from the top down necessarily mean that it works better than other tools for resource discovery? Good question. Cards on the table: I don't think so.

Here's tall tale #1. Tagging is good! Right? Of course it is, it's fantastic! Millions of people, contributing their wisdom and expertise every day, for free, for goodness' sake! Well, the reality is we don't really know when (or even whether) tagging really does help us do what we want to do. Can you guess what tall tale #2 is?

You got it. Tagging is bad! Right? Of course it is, it's horrible! Hoi polloi, clogging up our beautiful systems with their mistaken beliefs and their bad judgments and their misspellings and their prejudices, for goodness' sake! Well, once again, the reality is: we don't really know when (or even whether) tagging really *doesn't* help us do what we want to do.

(#3) Oh, and just in case anyone wants to say well, it's understandable that we don't know any of this, because tagging is new! Of course some of the operational tagging services are quite new I suppose (if you're like me and think that any year beginning with a 2 still counts as recent). But the concept of tagging, if not the name, is most definitely not new, and there's a long tradition of work on user-centered indexing, democratic indexing, and so on, that's well worth looking at for insight into the origin and impact of many of these tall tales.

(#4) Some people try and tell us, oh you're talking about *indexing*? Well, tagging is something that's quite different from indexing. All that fuddy-duddy library-school stuff about indexing? Not relevant here, thanks anyway. Hmm, well, if tagging is anything, I think a form of indexing or resource description is precisely what it is, and that means that concepts of indexing quality, indexing consistency, specificity, exhaustivity, retrieval effectiveness, recall and precision, and so on, are highly relevant. In fact, if we are going to demonstrate the value of tagging for resource discovery, then it has to be done in these terms.

(#5) Similarly, some people say, oh you're talking about indexing languages? About vocabularies? Well, folksonomies are totally different from indexing languages. All your fancy-pants information "science" about the importance of vocabulary control and facet analysis and hierarchical structure? Not where the action is, not what the people want. Well, once again, I think that if we ever want to evaluate folksonomies, then it's going to have to be as indexing languages that we evaluate them. Maybe it will turn out that uncontrolled languages have particular advantages in particular circumstances. Maybe it won't.

Tall tale #6: Folksonomies are necessarily unstructured. No, they're not necessarily unstructured. Many, probably most, *are* very weakly structured, in the sense that they lack browsable links between semantically-related terms. But is there anything about the concept of folksonomy that precludes such structure being built into a folksonomy? I'll tell you: No.

Tall tale #7: Tagging is necessarily uncontrolled. No, it's not *necessarily* uncontrolled. Many tagging services, probably most, *do* impose very little control over the form and content of the tags supplied by users. But is there anything about the concept of tagging that precludes such control being built into a tagging service? You know what: No.

(#8) Now, sometimes you might get the impression that tagging is all about resource description—that we tag stuff in order to describe that stuff. But this is an instance of the *means* assuming more importance than the *end*. We tag stuff in order to help ourselves or others to *find* or re-find that stuff. In the same way, it's fair to say that library catalogers don't assign subject headings with the aim of describing the subjects of those books accurately, precisely, and comprehensively—they assign subject headings with the aim of making those books findable by those who would look for them. It's not about getting the description correct—it's not as if any objectively correct description exists, and it's not as if there exists any particular person who could make a ruling as to whether a description is the correct one or not—it's about making a best guess as to which tags will be used in the future by people for whom the resource in question will be relevant.

(#9) But here's a thing. It's not the case that tagging is *always* about resource discovery. I'm conscious that in my quick characterization of tagging earlier, I was probably guilty of giving the distinct impression that people's motivations to engage in tagging activity are generally to do with making it easier, either for themselves or for others, to find stuff. But we do know that sometimes, in certain circumstances, some people tag *because they like tagging*. And sometimes this liking for tagging is related to the learning—about resources, about the cultures in which those resources were created, about other taggers, about one's own values—the learning that taggers do when they tag.

(#10) Okay, so now we're finally getting closer to one of the ideas on which this session is based, the idea that there is a useful distinction to be made between the "expert" tagger, or the content provider as tagger, and (for want of a better word, and one that I'll say something more about in a minute) the "novice." Tall tale #10 is the assumption that every tagger is an expert, all the time—or in other words that content expertise is not distributed unequally among taggers. I'm not sure anyone really believes this one, but maybe a fairer way of putting it would be to say that, even if it is accepted that content expertise is distributed unequally among taggers, it is still not useful to distinguish between content experts and others, because that would hurt the benefits to be derived from treating the population of taggers as a democratic body. One tagger, one vote, anyone?

Which brings us to tall tale #11: The crowd is always right. Oh, wouldn't the world be a better place if that were true? Actually, the crowd is sometimes wrong.

(#12) You might be thinking, come on, you said yourself that there's no higher authority who can lay down some sort of gold standard of correctness for resource descriptions—so how does it make any sense to talk about a crowd of taggers being "right" or "wrong"? All that matters is the result of the vote. Taking note of that result is as good a way as any of arriving at a resource description that is useful. But even this argument is based on the implicit assumption that individual taggers act independently of one another. And of course we know that assumption to be incorrect. Individual taggers are necessarily, unavoidably, understandably influenced by the prior activity and judgments of other taggers. It's a universal, very well-understood phenomenon: you're aware of the judgment made on some issue by someone else; all other things being equal, you're more likely to make the same judgment rather than some different one. The Matthew effect: the probability that a particular resource will be cited in the future is directly proportional to the number of times it has already been cited. The probability that a particular tag will be assigned to a particular resource in the future is directly proportional to the number of times that tag has already been assigned to that resource. The rich get richer. The popular get more popular. It doesn't *necessarily* make the rich or the popular any better or more useful or more relevant.

(#13) So, if we shouldn't necessarily listen to the crowd, why shouldn't we listen to the experts? Well, there's quite a good argument why we shouldn't, actually, but it takes unpacking, and there's several tall tales wrapped up inside it. Basically, the argument is one that takes seriously one of the ideas that we started with, which is that user tagging is something that is done, for good reason, by a population of taggers that is *the same population* as the population of people seeking access to the tagged resources. This is supposed to be the whole point—that taggers will use the same words (or at least the same kinds of words) to tag as the words (or kinds of words) that searchers will use to search. And a related assumption is that, since the content experts are not typically members of that population of searchers—they might be curators or educators or historians or librarians or archivists in the employ of the cultural institution, rather than members of that institution's public—they are actually unqualified for this particular task. Not unqualified to describe the resources—of course not—they are supremely qualified for that, no question. But rather less qualified than members of the public are to predict the terms that those same members of the public will use to look for the stuff that they're interested in. *That's* the first tall tale.

(#14) Of course, it's also possible to go rather too far in the opposite direction, to claim that some potential taggers have no content expertise, and to use that as an argument for preventing those taggers (and, if it is considered to be impossible to isolate those particularly lacking in content knowledge, maybe even preventing all members of the public) from contributing to resource descriptions. So it's important to recognize that in fact every tagger is sometimes an expert, and specifically is always an expert on the question of which terms they themselves are likely to use as search terms in the future.

Tall tale #15 is the tale that good tagging is accurate tagging, and we've already touched on this one a couple of times. The aim of tagging is not to create an accurate description of the resource or of the context in which it was created. If that's anyone's job, it's the job of the professional interpreters employed by the institution. One primary aim of tagging is typically to make stuff findable. In the jargon of the field, we say that indexing that successfully supports access, discovery, retrieval, that is high-quality indexing, is indexing that is effective.

(#16) You might be thinking, well, isn't that just another way of saying that good tagging is accurate tagging? Because surely tagging that's effective is tagging that is accurate? Well, no, not really. The best way of characterizing effective tagging is to point out that it's tagging that is consistent.

(#17) Aha, you might say, I see where you're going. You're going to say that it's important that different taggers exhibit high levels of consistency in their judgments as to which tags are assigned to which resources, and that we can use inter-tagger consistency as a surrogate measure of tagging quality, just like people in library science used to make similar arguments about the relationship between inter-indexer consistency and retrieval effectiveness. Hmm, well, no, I'm not going to say that, actually. What is actually important are the levels of consistency observable between taggers on the one hand and searchers on the other. If taggers are doing a good job of predicting the terms, or the kinds of terms, that searchers actually use in practice to find the stuff that they want, then we can say that the products of taggers' activity are good.

(#18) Oh, okay, you might say, well then I can tell you that tagger–searcher consistency is necessarily high, because taggers and searchers are drawn from the same population, and *we know that* people always use the same kinds of terms to tag as they do to search. And then I would say, No! We don't know that! We'd really, really like to know whether or not to accept this particular tall tale, and it's good that lots of great people are working on that.

(#19) One complicating factor that is making that work particularly interesting is the recognition that past searching activity might not be the best guide to future searching activity. You might imagine that we could take a look at the kinds of terms that people have used in previous searches, and then base an evaluation of the products of tagging on a measurement of the consistency between those kinds of tags and the kinds of terms used by searchers to find tagged resources. But searchers' choices of kinds of search terms are influenced by their beliefs (which may or may not be accurate) about the kinds of terms that have been assigned as tags, about the kinds of terms that have been assigned to other fields in the record, about the kinds of terms that have proved effective as search terms in the past, and so on. Nothing is ever simple, unfortunately.

And so we come to tall tale #20. Which is that there are 20 tall tales. No, wait … .

To wrap up, then, I'm just going to summarize a few of the points that are most relevant to the issue of tagging by content providers. First of all, what is the most useful way of categorizing groups of taggers? We've seen that the binary distinction between so-called "experts" and so-called "novices" is probably not so helpful. There are people who tag who tag as part of their professional work. There are automatic tagging systems. There are people who tag by assigning tags to resources that they themselves have created. And there are people who tag by assigning tags to resources that they've accessed in some way. These categories certainly overlap—any individual could be a member of more than one group, at different times or at the same time. The important thing to note is that any member of any group could meaningfully be characterized as an expert in some way.

The big issue is one of evaluation. Presumably if we're supporters of tagging, we're interested in tagging being good. But how do we measure goodness of tagging? How can or should we identify which tags are good and which tags aren't? One hypothesis is that good tags are the ones that are supplied that by good taggers. Obviously this just shifts the focus from tags to taggers, and the question becomes, How can or should we identify which taggers are good. The hypothesis might be, well, good taggers are those who are deemed to have supplied good tags in the past. Sounds a bit circular, doesn't it? But we could restate this by saying, okay, good taggers are those who have a good reputation for tagging.

So how can we measure reputation? We have to ask people. Who do we ask? Well, we have two basic options: Either we could ask the crowd, or we could ask those with good reputations. Circular again. Perhaps we could ask the crowd first, and then ask those who turn out to have good reputations, Google-style. Or we could start off with the currently-recognized authorities—the content providers. At what level of granularity should we discriminate between the objects of our reputation scores? Again, we have two basic options: We could discriminate among individual taggers, or we could discriminate among groups. At the extreme, we might simply choose to distinguish between tags supplied by content providers and tags supplied by members of the public. Job done? Maybe, maybe not. We'll just have to see how things go.

So I'm going to conclude with a few observations, none of which is earth-shattering or new, but I think they're worth restating nonetheless. Some things we know are: that different kinds of user have different motivations for making use of tagging services; that different kinds of user have different perceptions of the functions of tagging services; that any assessment or evaluation of the success with which systems perform any of their multiple functions may be based on a variety of different criteria; and that the design of evaluative tests must take these complexities into account if the tests are to tell us anything helpful.

Meanwhile, we know that different kinds of user can make different kinds of contributions to tagging services, and that the best implementations of such services will be the ones that give the widest range of different user groups the fullest opportunities to make their best contributions. The big challenge, of course and as always, is the one of providing effective incentives to tag while keeping costs down.

References

Abbas, June, and Jennifer Graham. 2006. "So, let's talk about tagging, user-defined/supplied descriptors ... A research and curricular agenda." *Proceedings of the American Society for Information Science and Technology* 43.

Kroski, Ellyssa. 2005. "The hive mind: Folksonomies and user-based tagging." *Infotangle* [blog]. http://web20bp.com/13z2a6019/wp-content/uploads/2013/03/The-Hive-Mind-Folksonomies-2005.pdf.

Marlow, Cameron, Mor Naaman, Danah Boyd, and Marc Davis. 2006. "HT06, tagging paper, taxonomy, Flickr, academic article, to read." *Hypertext '06: Proceedings of the 17th Conference on Hypertext and Hypermedia*, 31–40.

Speller, Edith. 2007. "Collaborative tagging, folksonomies, distributed classification or ethnoclassification: A literature review." *Library Student Journal.* http://citeseerx.ist.psu.edu/viewdoc/download?doi=10.1.1.90.5964&rep=rep1&type=pdf.

27
Children's tagging of artworks

May 4, 2011

This talk was given at the 2011 GSE&IS Dean's Circle Champagne Reception (Los Angeles, CA, May 4, 2011), hosted by Aimée Dorr.

It's an honor to have the opportunity to tell you a little bit about the project we've been working on at the UCLA Lab School because I know how much really amazing work is being done there by my colleagues in the Education department. I'm in the Information Studies Department, which we call IS for short, I teach on the Master's program in Library and Information Science and in the doctoral program in information studies, and my specialty is an area that's sometimes known as cultural informatics. One of the things I'm interested in is how art museums can provide better access through their websites to information about the objects in their collections, so it's quite fitting that we happen to be gathered here at the Fowler museum today. I'm just going to spend a few minutes to talk about some of the kinds of issues that the designers of art museum websites have to take care of, to ensure that their users have a good experience while visiting the online counterparts to the physical museums. In particular, I'm going to say a few things about the specific issue we wanted to explore, which is how children's experience of art museum websites might be improved, and about the results of the project that we worked on with students from the Lab School.

So, we know from previous studies that there are almost as many different reasons for visiting art museum websites as there are visitors!

But one of the very common reasons that people seem to have, is to find out more about the museum's art—either to find out more about the works that they looked at when they visited the museum itself, or to find out more about the artworks that they hope to see when they next visit the museum, or even, in the case of somebody accessing the web on a mobile device while they're walking around the museum, to find out more about the artworks that they're looking at right there and then. Maybe you can remember a time when you went to the Getty's website, or lacma.org, or the Fowler's website, with that kind of motivation, what we in IS would call an information need. Now, usually, the way that museums deal with this kind of information need is very simple and straightforward and it's entirely what you might expect—somebody builds a database or catalog; each record in that catalog corresponds to a different artwork and contains a description of that artwork, including details of the artist who created it, the date and place of creation, and so on; and then online access to that catalog is provided via some kind of search engine on the museum website, where visitors to the website can type in words, the search engine checks to see if those words appear in any of the catalog records, and the records which do contain those words are displayed to the user.

The trouble is, we also know from previous studies that it's quite often the case that these kinds of searches fail, that people don't find what they're looking for, and they come away disappointed, which is bad for them of course and also bad for the museum, because after a few disappointments like that people might not be too bothered about coming back to the museum, let alone the museum's website. Why is that? What is it about the set-up that is preventing people from finding what they want? Well, our hypothesis—nothing too earth-shattering—is that it doesn't have too much to do with the search engine technology, like I say that's all fairly straightforward—it's got a lot more to do with the descriptions of the artworks that are recorded in the catalog, and with the mismatch between the kinds of words that are often used in those descriptions, and the kinds of words that are often used by museum visitors to describe the works they're looking for.

We speculated that children, especially kids between the ages of 8 and 10 years old, are especially badly served by the kinds of descriptions that are routinely used in catalog records for artworks. These children are old enough, of course, to think of words to describe the artworks they see, to think of words to describe the artworks they want to see, to spell those words and to type them into search boxes. Again, we know from previous studies that many kids of that age, and in fact many people of all ages, tend to describe their information needs for artworks by using words that name the things depicted in artworks, or by using words that name the kinds or properties of things depicted in artworks. These things might be activities, events, periods, people, or places, but often they're just the objects that you see represented in pictures. So, for example, if you're a kid looking for more information about a painting that you saw in the museum yesterday which happened to be a picture of a man with a gun and a dog, you're quite likely to use the words "man" and "gun" and "dog" or variations thereof as your search terms.

Unfortunately for these kids, these happen not to be the kinds of terms that are routinely included in the catalog descriptions of artworks. Those records are usually created by gathering together descriptions written by museum curators, art historians, and other scholars or professionals, who often have other audiences in mind when they're writing. Instead of writing for children, or even for adult museum visitors, these experts often write for fellow researchers and other relatively well-informed viewers. And even when they do write for wider audiences, they tend to focus on details of art-historical style, genre, and technique, or details of the cultural contexts in which artists work and the variety of interpretations of individual artworks that are possible, rather than focusing on naming the things that are depicted in the images. And this is entirely understandable, because their purpose when writing is not so much to make the artworks findable, but to help viewers engage with the art once they've found it.

So what's stopping the designers of museum catalogs from including in their records the kinds of words that would help children find the works they're interested in? Well, until recently, it was pretty clear that the main obstacle was one of cost, and the fairly low priority accorded to findability. You can't get computer programs, yet, that can cheaply and quickly analyze digital images of artworks across a range of styles and genres and reliably identify the kinds of things they depict. So you have to get real living humans to do that job. It's simple but time-consuming and tedious, and in the past the assumption was that people would prefer to be paid to do it. But over the last few years, another option has emerged, which is for museums to collect words-that-describe-artworks from the museum visitors themselves, or from the museum website visitors themselves. This is called tagging: you look at an image of an artwork on your computer, you think of a word or phrase that describes some aspect of the artwork, you type that word or phrase in, and the museum collects all the words and phrases that different people suggest for that particular artwork, and then adds to the catalog record those words and phrases (or maybe just the most frequently suggested ones or the ones that meet some other predefined criteria). These words and phrases are called tags. The idea is that, so long as you, as the tagger, find this a fun thing to do, the museum can build descriptions-that-help-people-find-objects at very low cost.

Now, there are quite a number of interesting open questions about this idea. There are technical questions about the precise ways in which systems should be set up to collect the best kinds of tags. There are social questions about the precise ways in which museums can motivate or provide incentives to would-be taggers. But the one standout question we were interested in is, can we be sure that the kinds of words we can collect from children are better candidates for inclusion in catalog records than the ones we can easily collect from existing curatorial descriptions? Is our intuition correct, that the descriptions we might build from children's tagging activity make stuff more findable than do existing catalog descriptions? So this was the question we decided to address with our study that we did in collaboration with the Lab School.

Thanks to the arrangements made by teacher Jan Cohn and her wonderful staff at the school, my graduate student researcher Ben Lee Handler took 108 8–10-year-old children for a tour of the Los Angeles County Museum of Art given by LACMA educators headed by Mary Lenihan. Half of the kids were taken on a "virtual" tour of selected works at the Lab School; the other half were taken on a "live" tour of the same works at the museum. Half of the children in each tour group were asked to tag the works, simply by talking about the works in small groups for a few minutes as part of the regular tour experience, and writing down their chosen tags using pencil and paper. The tags were collected and added to LACMA's online catalog records. Some of the results of the tag-collection stage of the project can be seen on the handout. On each side of the paper, you'll see a reproduction of one of the ten works we focused on. You can see we have an otherwise untitled "anthropomorphic burial urn" from Colombia, and Thomas Hart Benton's "The Kentuckian." To the right of each image, you'll see a so-called cloud of the words included in the existing catalog record, where the size of each word in the cloud indicates the frequency with which that word occurs in the record. Then, below each image, on the bottom left, you'll see a corresponding cloud of the tags suggested for that image by the children—again, the size of each tag represents its frequency. The main thing to notice at this point is how different those clouds are.

Back to the project: A few days after being given the museum tour, all the children were asked to use LACMA's online catalog to search for the works they'd seen. Remember that half of the kids had tagged, half of them hadn't; half of them had actually been to the museum, half of them hadn't. We recorded the words they used as search terms, and the cloud on the bottom right of the burial urn page shows that set of terms. Then we analyzed the data with a view to answering our main research question, Can children's tags be used to improve searches? Our argument was that we could answer this question by comparing the proportion of search terms that matched tags, with the proportion of search terms that matched words from the original catalog records. All other things being equal, if more search terms matched tags than catalog words, then we would expect searchers to find more of what they wanted if tags were used to describe the artworks rather than or in addition to the words that appear in the original catalog records. We realized that it would be important to isolate the influence of prior tagging activity on selection of search terms, and that's why we designed the study so that, while all of the children carried out the search task, only half of them participated in the tagging task. We argued that, if it were to turn out that even the non-taggers' choice of search terms matched tags more frequently than they matched catalog words, then that would be a clear indication that adding tags to the catalog records would improve findability.

And that's exactly what happened. The answer to our main research question, you might not be too surprised to hear, was an unequivocal "Yes! Tags can be used to improve searches." Whereas only a quarter of the search terms used by those children who had not participated in tagging matched words in existing catalog records, a whopping two-thirds of the search terms used by those children who had not participated in tagging matched the tags that were suggested by those who had.

On that positive note, and given the time, I'll take the opportunity to stop! Of course, this particular finding only raises further issues that we don't have time to look at today, some technical, some social, some of which we explored in our project, some of which are on the agenda for future research. If you're interested in hearing more about this line of work, I'll be very pleased to talk to you.

F
Information retrieval and scholarly communication

28
Bibliographic relationships, citation relationships, relevance relationships, and bibliographic classification: An integrative view

November 17, 2002

This talk was given at the 13th Annual ASIS&T SIG/CR Workshop on Classification Research, at ASIS&T 2002: 65th Annual Meeting of the American Society for Information Science and Technology (Philadelphia, PA, November 18–21, 2002). The workshop chairs were Clare Beghtol, Jonathan Furner, Barbara Kwaśnik, and Jens-Erik Mai. A paper with the same title as the talk was published in Advances in classification research, Vol. 13: Proceedings of the 13th ASIS&T SIG/CR Classification Research Workshop, *edited by Clare Beghtol, Jonathan Furner, Barbara Kwaśnik, and Jens-Erik Mai (Medford, NJ: Information Today, 2004), 42–50.*

The proposition

The basic idea that I hoped to get across in the submitted paper was this—that it's my belief that certain kinds of relationship between bibliographic entities that are not typically treated as shared-characteristic relationships ought to be so. In our few minutes of presentation time today, however, we were encouraged to concentrate on describing the research agenda that we envisage for the future. The agenda proposed here is motivated by the recognition that the normative claim I'm making—that we ought to treat these relationships in a certain kind of way—might be more persuasive if I could justify it on an empirical basis.

In this context, then, I'm assuming a rather general goal—that as classificationists we wish to improve the performance of library catalogs, or, if you prefer, information access systems. And I'm stating my proposal in the form of a hypothesis—namely, that the performance of an information system will improve if the system is designed so that co-indexing, co-citation, co-relevance relationships are all treated as shared-characteristic relationships, and so that searchers are offered the opportunity to exploit any or any combination of those relationships as sources of evidence of the relatedness of documents, and by extension as sources of evidence of the relevance of documents to individual information needs.

What I'm saying is that, if we are to accept or reject the claims that I started with, we need to test the hypothesis by setting up, in the tradition that began at Cranfield, an experimental comparison—of a system that "does," as it were, and a system that "doesn't."

Bibliographic relationships

A minimum amount of explanation of some of the terms that are being used here is probably necessary. What are co-indexing, co-citation, and co-relevance relationships? What, for that matter, are shared-characteristic relationships? And why should we—as people interested in classification research—care?

Indexing, relevance, citation

Figure 28.1 is the first of two diagrams that hopefully do some of the explanation. Here the relationships that are represented are plain indexing, relevance, and citation relationships.

Taking the *indexing* relationship first: This is a relationship between two bibliographic entities, identified by a person—an indexer—but the entities are not of the same type. One is a document, the other is a term. One thing that we can infer from this relationship is that the two entities are both members of the same class, that is, the abstract topic or subject that both document and term may be said to be "about."

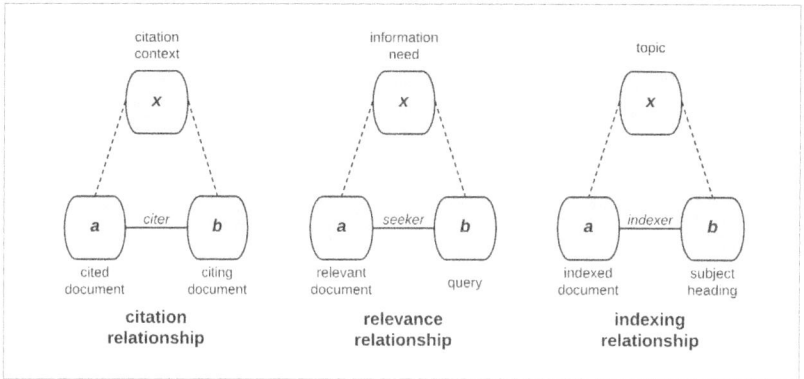

Figure 28.1. Citation; relevance; indexing.

Similarly, turning to the representation of the *relevance* relationship, we see that the relationship is between two entities of different types, one a document, the other a query. The relationship is identified by a person—a searcher. And we may infer from the existence of the relationship that the two entities are both members of the same class, that is, the information need that both document and query may be said to be "about."

Finally, we see that the *citation* relationship can be modeled as a relationship between two entities that are usually considered as the same type, but that are here distinguished in a directional sense. Again, we may infer from the existence of the relationship that the two entities are both members of the same class, that is, the citation context that both cited and citing document may very loosely be said to be "about."

The basic point I hope to make is that there are certain useful analogies that we can draw between the three kinds of relationship.

Co-indexing, co-relevance, co-citation

Here (Figure 28.2) is a different diagram, this time showing co-indexing, co-relevance, and co-citation relationships. In these cases, the relationships that we start with are the class/member relationships, between document and subject, that we inferred from the previous diagram. If two documents are found by this method to be members of the same class, then we can infer in the opposite direction that they are related. Two documents judged to be indexed by the same term are said to be *co-indexed*. Two documents judged to be relevant to

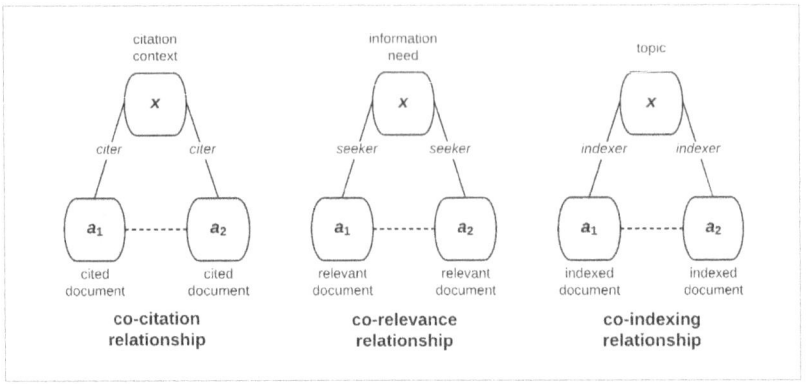

Figure 28.2. Co-citation; co-relevance; co-indexing.

the same need are said to be *co-relevant*. And two documents judged to be citable with respect to the same citation context are said to be *co-cited*.

Again the point here is to draw an analogy between the three kinds of relationship—an analogy that I suggest should be interesting to classification researchers, since normally we are concerned only with co-indexing relationships.

Shared-characteristic relationships

Turning now to the question, "What is a shared-characteristic (S-C) relationship?": The term derives from Barbara Tillett's taxonomy of seven types of relationship between bibliographic entities: equivalence, derivative, descriptive, whole–part, accompanying, sequential, and shared-characteristic relationships. At this point, I won't go into any more detail about the differences between these relationships. Suffice to say only that this taxonomy has proved very useful for modeling the structure of library catalogs, both actual and proposed.

Tillett defines S-C relationships as those that "hold between bibliographic entities that are not otherwise related but coincidentally have a common author, title, subject, or other characteristic used as an access point in a catalog." In other words, I would suggest, these relationships may be inferred from the recognition that two entities are members of the same class. Also, it should be noted that they are bi-directional (or, you might prefer, non-directional), like equivalence relationships, but unlike all the others in Tillett's taxonomy. What is interesting about the usage of Tillett's taxonomy is that very little attention seems to have been paid by the subject classification community to the fact that topical relationships are essentially subsumed in this category.

I have a suggestion of a way in which our understanding of S-C relationships might be modified. Tillett and others talk about the characteristic that is shared in each case being a property of the bibliographic entities—that is, the documents in question—themselves. I don't think I agree. I suggest that the characteristic that is shared is a property of events in which those entities are involved. The kind of event I mean is the one that occurs when somebody decides that a document is about something, or that it's relevant, or citation-worthy. It's not the case that a document is about something. Aboutness doesn't inhere in a document. It's subjective, and has to be decided by someone. So the events I mean are decision-acts carried out by particular people at particular times.

One of the characteristics that may be shared by a pair of indexing events is the judgment that the two documents involved are members of the same class. Similarly, one of the characteristics that may be shared by a pair of relevance judgments is the judgment that the two documents involved are members of the same class. And one of the characteristics that may be shared by a pair of citations is the judgment that the two documents involved are members of the same class.

Rationalism/empiricism

In other words, my contention is that co-indexing, co-citation, and co-relevance relationships are S-C relationships. But they have not yet been recognized as such in the literature. Now, I could continue to attempt to provide further justification on *rationalist* grounds, by appealing to logic and consistency and completeness and so on. Instead, a more effective means of proceeding might be to attempt to justify my argument on *empirical* grounds, perhaps by demonstrating that the performance of information access systems might be improved if the three kinds of relationship in question were treated as S-C relationships.

You may well ask, "What would such a system be like?" Well, it would be one in which our understanding of the value of classification for information retrieval is not limited to the classification of documents by their *content*, but encompasses also the classification of documents by the *approval* that has been expressed for those documents in the past, and the classification of documents by the *contexts* to which they have been assigned by citers. In such a system, documents would then be rankable not only by the strength of co-indexing, but also by the strength of co-relevance and co-citation.

Clearly, such systems exist. We're all familiar with the recommender systems that rank objects by the extent to which their approval profile matches that of other objects historically approved by us, and with link-analytic search engines such as Google and CiteSeer. But where is the rigorous experimental testing of the effectiveness of different ranking algorithms, and of different combinations of ranking algorithms?

Specifically, where is the data that will allow us to draw one or other of two possible conclusions? We may find that it is possible to develop a system that successfully manages to select the most appropriate ranking algorithm in a particular circumstance by analyzing characteristics of that circumstance. Alternatively, we may find that it is more beneficial to allow the searcher to maintain control over the selection of the ranking algorithm that appears to match their particular requirements on a given occasion.

Recommendations

Whatever the result, my recommendations are as follows:

- that, as classification researchers, we broaden our definition of classification so that it includes not just content-based, but also approval-based and context-based classification;
- that we develop taxonomies of bibliographic relationships that take into account not just indexing and co-indexing relationships, but also relevance, citation, co-relevance, and co-citation relationships; and
- that we urgently conduct evaluations of the comparative effectiveness of offering searchers the opportunities to exploit such relationships.

29

A unifying model of document relatedness for hybrid search engines

July 11, 2002

This talk was given at ISKO 2002: 7th International Conference of the International Society for Knowledge Organization (Granada, Spain, July 10–13, 2002). A paper with the same title as the talk was published in Challenges in knowledge representation and organization for the 21st century: Integration of knowledge across boundaries: Proceedings of the Seventh International ISKO Conference, *edited by María J. López-Huertas (Würzburg, Germany: Ergon, 2002), 245–50.*

Introduction

In this talk, I hope to do three main things:

- Firstly, I'm going to introduce a conception of a field of inquiry that I call "document network analysis."
- Secondly, I'm going to present the outlines of a simple model, a way of understanding some of the data that are typically manipulated by network analysis systems such as web search engines. In doing this, I'm going to recap some of the basic assumptions and procedures of information retrieval that I know

will be more than familiar to many of you. But I'm going to do it in a way that highlights some important aspects that I believe deserve more clarification than they typically receive.

- And thirdly, reversing the generally accepted run of things, I'm going to conclude with a hypothesis that I believe should drive future research.

Document network analysis

Document network analysis is the term that I think is most useful in denoting the intersection of four related fields of inquiry—information retrieval, knowledge organization, hypertext, and bibliometrics.

Individually, these fields have varying goals. But ultimately I think their commonality consists in three things:

- firstly, in their primary concern with documents, and with classes of documents, and the document-related behavior of human and mechanical agents;

- secondly, in the assumption that such documents do *not* exist independently of one another; in fact, they're inter-related in all sorts of complex ways;

- and thirdly, that these inter-relationships may be modeled using the established mathematical techniques of graph theory and matrix algebra.

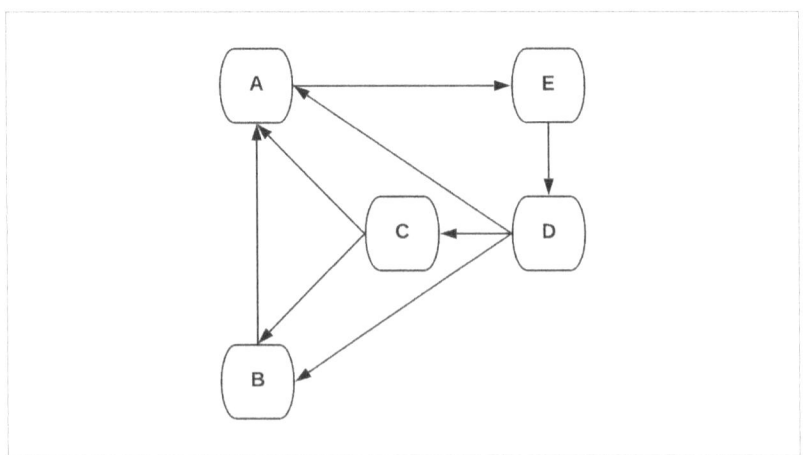

Figure 29.1. Example of a small document network.

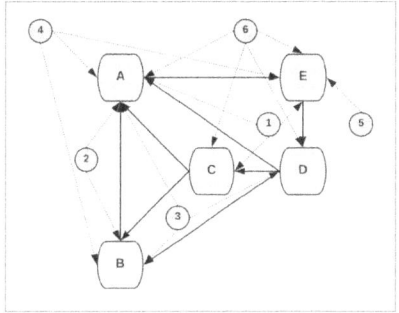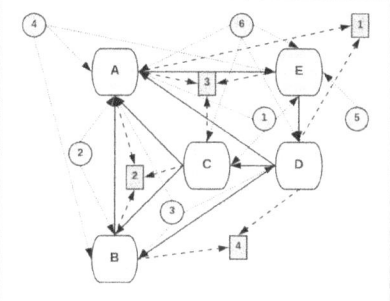

Figure 29.2. Example of a small document network (augmented).

Figure 29.3. Example of a small document network (augmented again).

So here (Figure 29.1) we have a diagrammatic representation of a network of five *documents*, each document represented by a node A through E, and each relationship of *adjacency* between documents represented by an arrow, or link.

Here (Figure 29.2) the same network is augmented by the representation of six human *judges*, one through six, each relationship of *approval* between a judge and an approved document also represented by an arrow.

And here (Figure 29.3) the same network is again augmented by the representation of four index *terms* or subjects. This time each relationship of *content* between a document and an assigned or extracted term is represented by an arrow.

The matrices in Figure 29.4 capture the same information as the diagrams, but in a form more amenable to computation. The existence of a relationship of content, approval, or adjacency, is indicated here by a "1," and an absence by a "0." You can imagine, perhaps, how non-binary data can instead be used to indicate the strength of the relationship between a particular pair of objects.

	M1: Document–term content matrix						M2: Document–judge approval matrix								M3: Document–document adjacency matrix						
	Terms						Judges								Docs						
		1	2	3	4			1	2	3	4	5	6			A	B	C	D	E	
	A	1	1	1	0	3	A	1	1	1	0	1	1	5	A	0	0	0	1	1	1
	B	0	1	0	1	2	B	0	1	1	1	0	0	3	B	1	0	0	0	0	1
Docs	C	0	1	1	0	2	C	1	0	0	0	1	0	2	C	1	1	0	0	0	2
	D	1	0	0	1	2	D	1	0	1	0	0	1	3	D	1	1	1	0	0	3
	E	0	0	1	0	1	E	0	0	0	1	1	1	3	E	0	0	0	1	0	1
		2	3	3	2	10		3	2	3	3	1	4	16		3	2	1	1	1	8

Figure 29.4. Matrix representation.

The CCC model of retrieval

Assumptions

Two fundamental assumptions underlying the design of any document retrieval system are these:

- One is that the searcher s is able, if requested at any given time t, to supply an expression of a personal *preference ordering* over the set of documents of whose existence she is aware. This preference ordering represents the varying and relative degree to which s approves of each document at time t.

- Another assumption is that the primary task of the system is, again if requested at any given time t, accurately to predict the structure of the preference ordering that would be expressed by s if s were in possession of complete knowledge about the universal set of documents. In other words, the task of the system is to make a *recommendation* to the searcher, in the form of a list of documents, ranked in order of the degree to which they are predicted to meet with the approval of the searcher.

The retrieval process

In general terms, the procedure by which agents (human or mechanical) collaborate in order to produce such preference orderings may be modeled as follows.

In the stage of *document classification*, agents evaluate the degree to which each document is a member of each of a number of pre-defined or dynamically-defined classes. The result is a set of document statements, each statement taking the form of a set of attribute/value pairs, each value indicating the degree to which the document is a member of the class indicated by the attribute.

In the stage of *query formulation*, agents specify the extent to which they personally approve of each class. The result is a set of query statements, each expressing a single agent's judgments in the same attribute/value format as that used for document statements and representing a personal preference ordering over classes. In many situations, agents select pre-existing documents as queries.

Thirdly, in a stage of *document/query comparison*, each preference ordering over classes is translated into a preference ordering over documents by conducting a mathematical comparison of the query statement and all document statements.

Three kinds of classification

Taking each stage in this procedure in turn, and looking first at the stage of classification, we may distinguish in general between three kinds of classification, on two corresponding bases: firstly, by the kind of classes to which each document is assigned; and secondly, by the primary role of the agent doing the classifying.

Classification by content

One kind of classification is that done through analysis of content. The classes to which documents are assigned are conceived as concepts, and the role of the classifier is commonly conceived as indexing—i.e., identifying the concepts covered in the textual content of each document, and representing those concepts by appropriate terms.

Classification by chronology

Another kind of classification is that done through chronology. (Admittedly, I chose this term for want of a better term beginning with "c." It's very important, of course, that it begins with a "c." I originally used the term "collaboration" here, but that wasn't quite right either.) In this case, the classes to which documents are assigned are conceived as judges (i.e., previous searchers), and the role of the classifier is conceived as tallying—i.e., identifying the judges who have rated each document in the past.

Classification by context

A third kind of classification is that done through analysis of context. In this case, the classes to which documents are assigned are conceived as other documents, and the role of the classifier is conceived as citing—i.e., identifying target documents to which the source documents are considered to be related.

I think it's fairly important to recognize that the common result of evaluating documents in any of these three ways is an evidentiary record or representation of various agents' judgments of the extent to which particular documents are members of particular classes.

Content, collaboration, and context

This enumeration of three kinds of classification corresponds to my original CCC model of retrieval systems, that I introduced in an article written in the summer of 2001 that's currently still under review at *JASIST*. This distinguishes between traditional content-based systems that characterize documents as sets of terms, collaboration-based systems that characterize documents as sets of judges, and context-based systems that characterize documents as sets of other documents.

Two kinds of query

Turning now to the stage of query formulation, we may distinguish in general between two kinds of query, on three corresponding bases: firstly, by the extent to which classes are differentiate in the query by level of approval; secondly, by the relative size of the user group to which the query selector will be assumed by the system to belong; and thirdly, by the nature of the preference ordering over documents that may possibly be derived from the query.

Universal queries

One kind of query is that in which all classes are approved to an equal, maximal level. In other words, the preference ordering expressed over classes by such an *unstructured* query has a single level. The searcher specifying a query of this kind will be treated by the system as a member of a single, large, undifferentiated, homogeneous group, and the system will find it possible to derive from such a query only *universalized* document rankings—i.e., those that may vary only over time and not by searcher.

Personal queries

A second kind of query is that in which some classes are approved at a higher level than others. The ordinal number of a preference ordering expressed over classes by such a *structured* query is greater than one. The searcher specifying a query of this kind will be treated by the system as a unique individual, and the system will find it possible to produce *personalized* rankings that may vary from searcher to searcher as well as from time to time.

Three kinds of ranking algorithm

Turning, finally, to methods of comparing query statements with document statements, we may distinguish in general between three kinds of ranking algorithm. Methods of each kind depend on the results of the classification and query formulation stages described above being recorded for manipulation in matrix form, each row of a matrix corresponding to a single set of attribute/value pairs, as was displayed on an earlier slide.

Ranking by similarity

In the first place, a range of formulae exist for the calculation of the degree of similarity between such sets of attribute/value pairs. One formula that is commonly used in IR applications is the cosine coefficient. Use of such a formula can produce a simple ranking of documents headed by those that are most similar to the given query.

In Figure 29.5, for example, the degree of similarity between every pair of rows in our original document/document adjacency matrix is recorded in a coupledness matrix. And below, the degree of similarity between every pair of columns is recorded in a co-citation matrix. Given the query document B, for instance, we may rank other documents by the extent to which they are bibliographically coupled with B, in this order: C, with a score of 0.71; D, with a score of 0.58; and then E and A, both scoring 0.

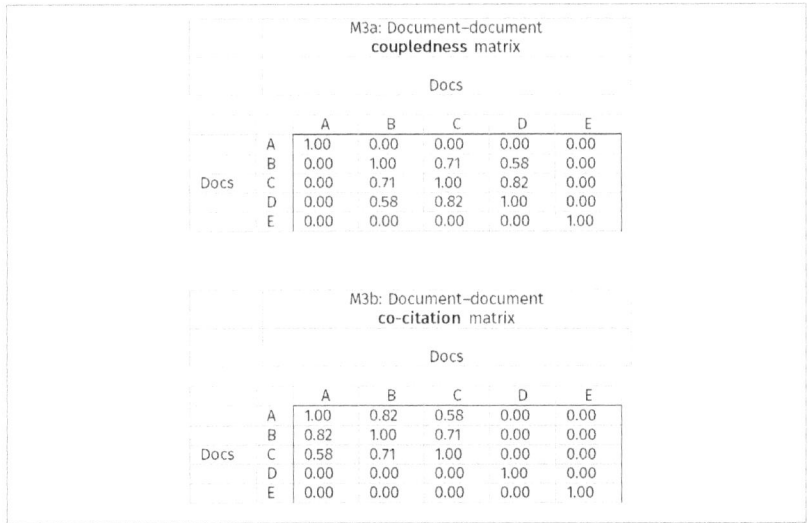

Figure 29.5. Similarity matrices (cosine) derived from adjacency data.

Ranking by proximity and centrality

On the other hand, representation of data in matrix form opens the door to more-complex analytical techniques based, for example, on the determination of shortest paths, or the derivation of eigenvectors. Use of these techniques can produce different rankings headed by those documents that are most proximate to the given query, or by those that are in one or other sense the most central or authoritative in a given group.

So here (Figure 29.6), for example, is a matrix of values representing the forward distance between each document and every other one in the network. Given the query document B, we may rank other documents by the extent to which they are proximate to B in this order: A, E, D, C.

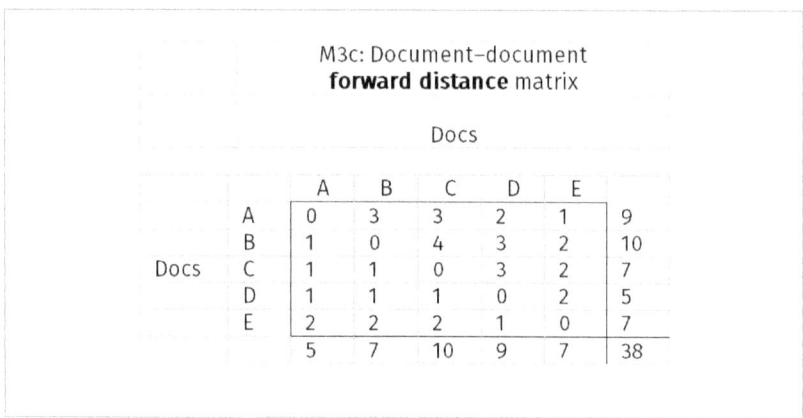

Figure 29.6. Proximity (distance) matrix derived from adjacency data.

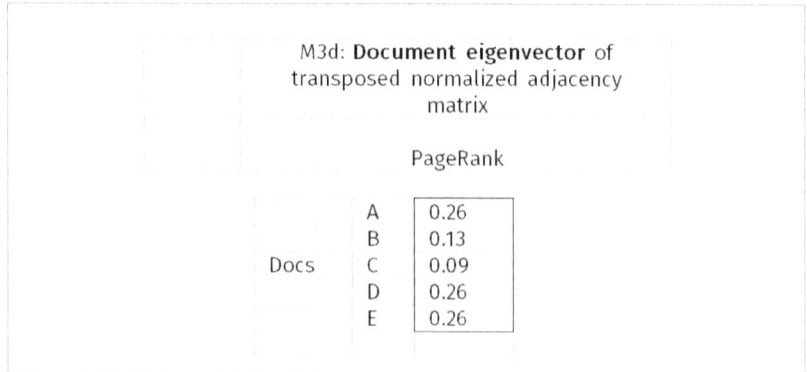

Figure 29.7. Centrality scores (Google's idealized "PageRank") derived from adjacency data.

Then here (Figure 29.7) is a single vector of values representing the idealized "PageRank" score that Google's ranking mechanism would assign to each document, determined by calculating the dominant eigenvector of a transposed normalized version of our original adjacency matrix. Documents may thus be ranked in order of their "PageRank" score as follows: A, D, and E at the top with 0.26, followed by B, and then C.

Possibilities for hybrid systems

So, we have briefly reviewed three kinds of classification, two kinds of query, and three kinds of ranking algorithm. All sorts of combination of these types of method are possible to implement in a single system. Moreover, it's also possible to use any kind of universalized ranking to weight any kind of personalized ranking, throwing up further possible combinations.

Content-based systems

For example, in a simple content-based system, both the length of documents and the frequency of occurrence of terms may be used in weighting personalized rankings of documents that otherwise express the degree to which they are co-indexed with a query. (Remember that the universalized rankings are derived from summations of the rows or columns of the original content matrix; personalized rankings may be derived from similarity matrices produced by applying similarity coefficients to pairs of those rows or columns.)

Collaboration-based systems

Similarly, in a simple collaboration-based system, both the absolute popularity of documents and the indiscrimination of judges may be used to weight personalized rankings of documents in order of the degree to which they are co-approved with a query. Both universalized and personalized rankings are calculated in the same manner as before, but with different results due to starting with a different set of base data.

Context-based systems

Turning to context-based systems, we find a number of possible bases for universalized rankings, ranging from simple counts of citivity and citedness, to more-complex "PageRank," authority, and hub scores, as well as a number of possible bases for personalized rankings—for example, coupledness, co-citation, and both forward and backward distance.

Are radically hybrid systems the most effective?

Which all brings me finally to my central point today. Even a system such as Google, for all its apparent success, offers the searcher a limited palette in the sense that it fixes on a particular combination of elements of the kinds I've been talking about, involving just a single method of universalized ranking ("PageRank"), and a single method of personalized ranking (co-indexing).

The idea is that there seems to be no *a priori* reason why any individual system should not aim to offer as many different combinations of such elements as the searcher might wish for, in any conceivable context. Why not construct a hybrid system that takes advantage of *all* possible sources of evidence of document relatedness, that allows searchers to personalize the rankings derived from these sources in any way they like, that allows searchers to weight these personalized rankings in any way they like, and to do either whenever they like?

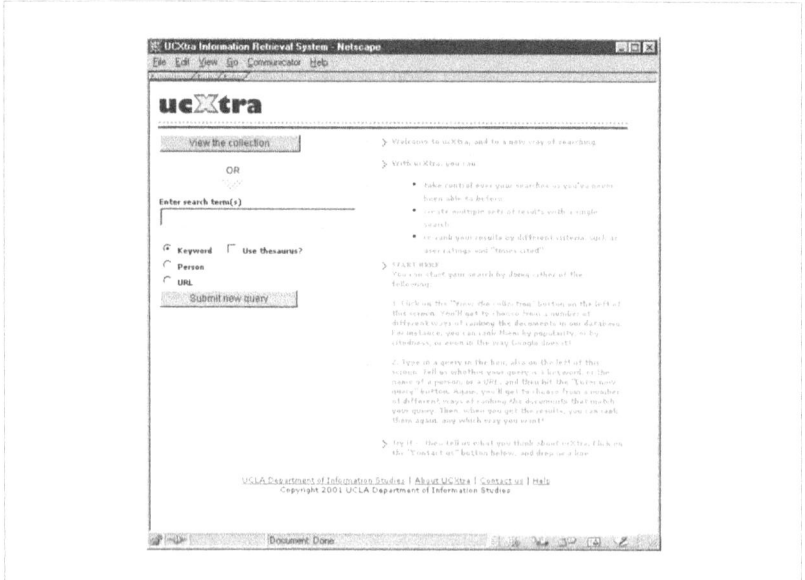

Figure 29.8. UCXtra: Initial screen.

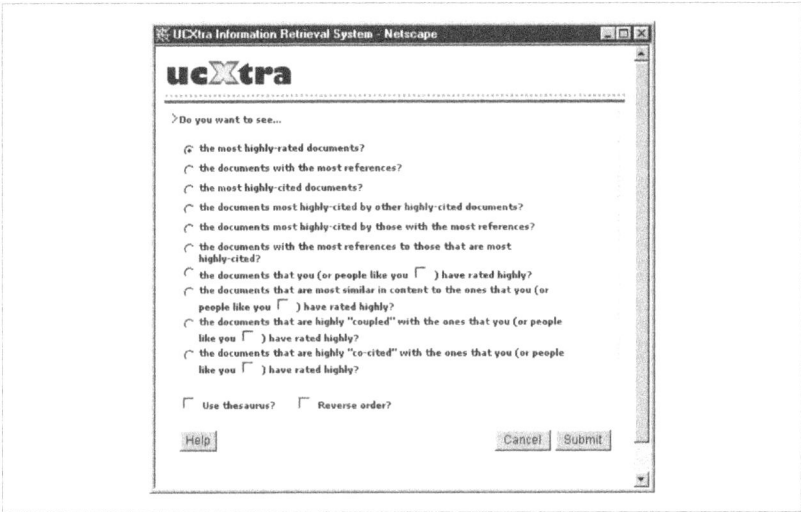

Figure 29.9. UCXtra: "View the collection" pop-up.

The interface problem

Of course, one major problem then becomes the design of an interface that appropriately expresses the capabilities of the system in an immediately comprehensible manner, and this is something we're still wrestling with in the design of our hybrid system, UCXtra.

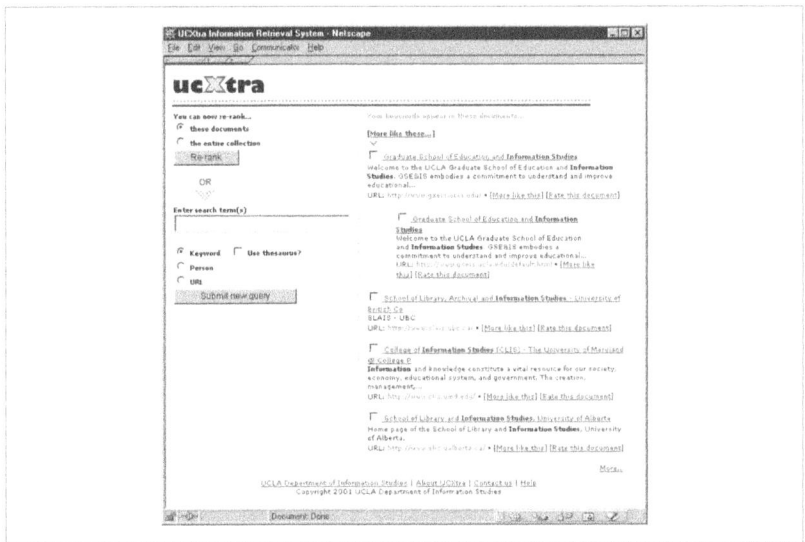

Figure 29.10. UCXtra: Results screen.

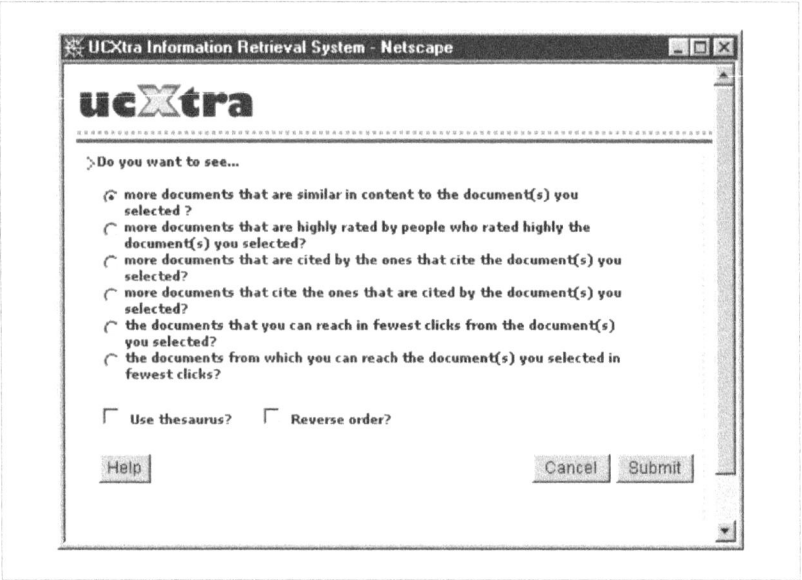

Figure 29.11. UCXtra: "More like this" pop-up.

These screenshots (Figures 29.8–29.11) are too small to see properly, I think, but the impression you'll get, perhaps, is that they're very wordy. For example, there aren't going to be too many users who will be comfortable with the question, "Do you want to see more documents that cite the ones that are cited by the document(s) you selected?" Some sort of visual interface is likely to be a partial solution here.

Conclusion

As I hinted at earlier, I'm going to conclude at this point with the hypothesis that continues to drive the development of UCXtra, which is in two parts:

- firstly, that searchers benefit from being afforded the *opportunity* to exploit multiple sources of evidence of documents' class membership;
- and secondly, that they benefit additionally from being allowed to maintain *control* over the ways and combinations in which such sources are exploited.

30

The serials crisis and what we can do about it: New roles for the library and for faculty

March 11, 2003

This talk was given at a meeting of the Committee on the Library, Academic Senate, UCLA (Los Angeles, CA, March 11, 2003), and published in a slightly different form in Voice of the Faculty: Newsletter of the UCLA Academic Senate *11, no. 3 (2003).*

Faculty and students at UCLA enjoy access to one of the finest library collections in the world. When the Association of Research Libraries ranks university libraries in the U.S. and Canada on the basis of an index designed to measure their relative size, ours comes in at seventh place. In terms of current subscriptions to serials (journals and periodicals), UCLA ranks second only to Harvard. In 2000–01, the library subscribed to 94,824 journals, a large proportion of which are conveniently made available to library users in electronic format as well as (or sometimes instead of) in print.

Of course, this embarrassment of scholarly riches doesn't come cheaply. The price of an annual subscription to a single journal can often top $10,000. An institutional subscription to the journal *Brain Research*, for instance, published by the market leader Reed Elsevier, will cost $19,971 in 2003. And the average annual increase in journal subscription prices—an increase that may be conservatively estimated at around 7–10%—continues to outstrip the general rate of inflation. Given that many academic libraries, including our own, are simultaneously struggling to implement sweeping budget cuts, it's not too surprising that the journal collection is often among the first of a library's resource areas to feel the pinch. The result? Reductions in the levels of access to the literature enjoyed by library users, and a corresponding downturn in the quality of service provided by the library.

The serials crisis—old news to long-suffering librarians—has recently begun to be exacerbated by what some are referring to as the permission crisis. The nature and severity of the permission crisis has become clear only in the few years since libraries began to license the contents of electronic journals from publishers. When a library pays a subscription fee for the electronic version of a journal, it is usually merely a license that is being paid for, rather than permanent ownership. The distinction becomes relevant when any decision is made as to who may view, copy, and distribute the contents of the journal in question. Under current licensing agreements, it is the publisher, not the library (and certainly not the author), that retains the authority to make any such decision; access to content is thus restricted to those library users who are expressly authorized by the publisher.

That publishers are able to wield such power is a result of the common procedure by which authors sign away the copyright over their own work to journal publishers, typically not in return for any direct payment, but in the expectation that their work will receive wide dissemination. Many scholarly authors are starting to realize, however, that this basic wish—for wide dissemination of their work—cannot be granted as long as the traditional business model for scholarly publication remains in place. Under this model, whereby authors typically give away their work for free to third-party publishers, the dual result is that (i) authors are prevented from distributing their own work, and (ii) readers are prevented from accessing that work, either through prohibitive costs or by lack of authorization.

Many active participants in the scholarly-communication process—authors, reviewers, editors, librarians, readers—are working together to build the infrastructure of a new system for the distribution of scholarly papers. This new system is based on the Principle of Open Access: the conviction that authors should retain the right to offer access to their work, free-of-charge, to all interested readers (and, correspondingly, that authors should not be forced to relinquish copyright over that work simply in order to ensure its distribution among a limited audience).

It is the emergence of the Internet as a delivery system for electronic documents that has made it possible for us even to contemplate building such an infrastructure. Once an electronic version of a scholarly paper is stored on a networked computer, readers at multiple remote locations may download an electronic copy of that paper (and print off a hard copy of that electronic copy). All that prevents authors and readers from taking full advantage of this capability are the twin barriers, erected by the commercial journal publishers to whom authors give away their papers, of cost and authorization. Some users can't afford to pay the subscription fees that journal publishers charge; some users don't happen to be affiliated with the institutions (e.g., university libraries) that pay those subscription fees on behalf of their members. But many commentators have argued that, with the emergence of the Internet, scholars no longer have any reason to sustain any arrangement with third-party publishers that only results in the imposition of unnecessary restrictions on would-be readers. The electronic delivery of scholarly papers can instead be organized by the institutions that employ authors, at a much lower cost to those institutions than the cost of subscribing to multiple printed journals each year.

The University of California, for example, has recently been active in its support for the eScholarship program, an initiative of the California Digital Library (CDL). Under the eScholarship banner (and amongst many other related accomplishments), the CDL has built a centralized store—the eScholarship Repository—for archiving pre-prints of faculty publications. This collection of draft versions of journal papers, conference papers, and research reports is not only fully searchable on its own, but is indexed by various specialized search engines that index other e-print archives maintained by institutions beyond UC. Submitting a paper to the eScholarship Repository is voluntary, easy, and free-of-charge for all UC faculty. The ultimate goal for such repositories is that every faculty member submits a version of every paper and report that they write, so that the entire research output of the university is fully accessible and searchable by all.

The eScholarship Repository does not itself offer a peer-review service to authors. Yet, other than the barriers set up by commercial journal publishers to protect their own profits, there is nothing to stop authors from depositing copies of peer-reviewed articles in such a repository. And there is nothing about peer review that makes it necessarily the preserve only of printed journals, or of journals run by commercial publishers. Another initiative of the eScholarship program is its launch of *Dermatology Online Journal* (DOJ), a peer-reviewed e-journal that joins hundreds of similarly prestigious, frequently-issued, ISI-indexed journals already established in fields ranging from architecture to zoology. Even once an article has been published in DOJ, for instance, the author retains the right to deposit that article in as many e-print archives around the world as is desired—since CDL, unlike a commercial publisher, has nothing to gain from imposing any kind of restriction of access to that article.

It's important to recognize that initiatives such as the two briefly described above can only really succeed if, as faculty, we lend our individual, practical support. Fortunately, there are many ways in which we can support the open-access model, and help our libraries avert the serials crisis. We can resolve to self-archive our papers in the eScholarship Repository; we can encourage our colleagues to do so; if our department is not currently an institutional member of the repository, we can enroll it. We can submit our papers for publication in open-access, peer-reviewed e-journals; if no such journals exist in our field, we can launch one; if, in the course of such a launch, we incur costs we can't otherwise bear, we can ask the agency or institution funding our research to cover those costs. We can serve as editors and reviewers only for open-access e-journals; we can withdraw our services from those journals that restrict access. If we must publish in a restricted-access journal, we can ask to retain the copyright to our own work (or at the very least ask to retain the right to self-archive our own work). We can publicize amongst our colleagues the existence of open-access journals and archives in our field, and promote the benefits of supporting them.

These and other options for faculty action have been the focus of lively discussion in recent meetings of the Academic Senate Committee on the Library. Most importantly of all, it is abundantly clear that we must continue to support the work of our librarians, whose responsibilities include the maintenance of the institutional e-print archives, instruction of faculty and students in the use of those archives, development of the tools that allow us to search indexes of those archives, and continued development of one of the finest collections of serials (whether in print or electronic format) in the world.

Index

aboutness, 83, 95-97, 114, 153, 155, 232, 258, 299
adjacency, 303, 307-9
admissibility, 66
agent[s], 88-9, 90, 102, 163, 239, 243, 245, 302, 304-5
aggregation, 114, 136
algorithm[s], 12, 259, 300, 307, 309
American Documentation Institute, 45
American Library Association (ALA), 249
American National Information Standards Organization, 241
annotation studies, 255, 257
anthropology, 87, 190
approval, 242, 300, 303-4, 306
Archival and Manuscripts Control (AMC), 167, 168
archival data modeling, 161-2, 165-9, 173-4
archival resources, 164
archival science, 167, 169, 237, 240-44
Aristotle, 109, 138, 140, 156
artifacts, 26, 31, 118, 129, 142, 163, 232
    documentary, 144, 146
    human, 97, 114, 190, 194
Association of Research Libraries, 313
attitudes, 50
attributes, 139-40, 144, 186, 190-1, 239
attribute-value pairs, 215, 216, 307
Australian theory, 240
authenticity, 67, 68, 146, 238-9, 245
authority control, 201-2, 217, 256
authority data, 164

Bates, Marcia, 17, 75, 210, 218
Beals, Ralph, 42-4
Bearman, David, 166-7, 174-5
behavior, 31, 40, 46, 174, 257, 264, 302
    information-seeking, 29, 35, 40
beliefs, 16, 29, 33, 35, 279, 284
    relevant and non-relevant, 50, 103
    true and false, 50, 54, 55
Bernier, François, 192
bibliography[ies], 17, 40, 46, 47, 149, 181, 203, 275
bibliology, 27, 37
bibliometrics, 40, 232, 302
Blumenbach, J. F., 193
Boulding, Kenneth E., 29
boundary object, 229

Briet, Suzanne, 130, 131
British Library, 167
Brookes, Bertie, 75, 79
Brookes' Fundamental Equation of Information Science, 79
Buckland, Michael, 129-33
Bureau of Canadian Archivists (BCA), 166

California Digital Library (CDL), 315
Carlyle, Allyson, 114
cataloging, 168, 273
    concept of, 158
    subject, 154, 155, 270
Cataloging Cultural Objects (CCO), 117-22, 124-26, 249
categorization, 85, 89, 102, 146, 148, 186, 189, 262, 265
category theory, 127-8
census, 186-89, 191
Center for Documentation and Communication Research (CDCR), 42-3
certification of authenticity, 146
Chisholm, Roderick, 138
citation analysis, 108, 197-01, 213-5, 217, 226
citing document-set (CD-set), 216-21, 225
classical race theory, 192-3
Classification Décimale Universelle, 179-81
classification schemes, 31-2, 36, 98, 179, 185, 188, 256
Classification Research Group (CRG), 197, 199-201, 213, 215
classification theory, 201, 205, 210, 218, 228, 231-33
classifier[s], 82, 92, 232, 305
Cleveland Museum of Art, 253
Coates, Eric J., 199, 212, 214, 225-6
cognitive turn, 29, 37
coherence, 24, 79, 92, 93, 231
conceptual analysis, 6, 33, 74, 84, 239
conceptual model[s], 114, 119, 126, 163, 173
Conceptual Reference Model (CRM), 166, 170, 173, 174
concrete object[s], 140-42, 144, 148, 279
content analysis, 17, 45, 212, 226, 305
continuants, 128, 148
controlled vocabularies, 241-2, 247, 250, 275, 279
Cook, Michael, 167, 169, 174
crisis, 83, 313, 314, 316
critical race theory (CRT), 186, 192-3
crowdsourcing, 230, 232
Cull, Naomi, 247

cultural imperialism, 53
cultural stewardship, 4-6
cultural studies, 20, 87
Custer, Benjamin, 181

data model[s], 136, 161-9, 173-4
Day, Ron, 131, 132
declarations, 128, 146-7
Del.icio.us, 252, 261
describers, 278
descriptors, 252-3, 255, 264
Dewey Decimal Classification (DDC), 179-81, 184-5, 191-94
Dewey, John, 46
Dewey, Melvil, 181, 254
Dialog's RANK command, 197-8, 216-19, 221
diplomatics, 239
discourse analysis, 174, 186, 231
discourse-analytic methods, 228
Document Academy (DOCAM), 127, 148
document acts, 128, 145-6, 148
document-as-meaning, 134, 143-4
document-as-medium, 133, 143-4
document-as-message, 133-4, 143
document classification, 304
document lifecycle framework, 240
document network analysis, 301-3
document statements, 304-5, 307
document theory, 144-5, 148
document/query comparison, 304
documentalists, 27, 111, 114
documentation, 129, 165
documentation movement, 129, 179
domain analysis, 186, 195, 230, 232
Don Quixote, 110, 112-3, 122-24
dualists, 125

Egan, Margaret, 27, 28, 37, 39-47, 216
eigenvectors, 308
eliminativism, 193
entities, 95, 109-14, 120-22, 142, 145-47, 152-54, 166, 173, 232, 239-40, 279
   bibliographic, 94, 295-99
   physical, 136, 146
   quasi-abstract, 128, 146, 149
entity-types, 112, 115, 119, 152-3, 158-9, 169, 239
epistemology, 33-4, 40, 49-51, 71, 78
   Egan's Social (SE), 79, 103
   social, 27-29, 32-37, 39-43, 47-52, 55, 216
eScholarship Repository, 315-6
ethics, 10, 25-6, 51, 80, 104
event[s], 4, 16, 24, 65-67, 70, 128, 132, 148, 152, 158, 170, 174, 239, 245, 258, 299
evidence, 3, 51, 54, 63-72, 130-36, 175, 201, 296, 310, 312
evidence theory, 71-2
exhaustivity principle, 188-9
Experts Group on Archival Description (EGAD), 161, 174
exploitation, 53
expressions, 31, 35, 71, 87, 90, 112, 115, 121-24, 136-7, 142, 232
expressives, 147

facet[s], 98, 101, 232, 242-46, 255, 262, 265
analysis, 102, 200, 212, 214, 226, 241, 280
faceted search, 231
fairness, 52, 92
Fallis, Don, 103

FictionFinder, 123
Fidel, Raya, 91
field of inquiry, 18, 26, 49, 301
findability, 289, 291
flexibility, 230
Flickr, 252-3, 261
Floridi, Luciano, 26, 103
folksonomy[ies], 6, 228-9, 253, 256, 262, 269, 275, 279-80
fonds, 164-5, 167-9, 173
Fontaine, Henri La, 129, 179, 181
format[s], 118, 135, 137, 238, 242, 304, 313, 316
Foskett, Douglas J., 41, 186, 200, 204-14, 222, 225-6
FRAR (Functional Requirements for Authority Records), 153
FRBR (Functional Requirements for Bibliographic Records), 71, 107-14, 112, 120-26, 136-7, 148, 151-3, 157-59, 166, 170, 173
Fricker, Miranda, 54
FRSAR (Functional Requirements for Subject Authority), 151, 153

genre, 6, 17, 232, 269, 289
Goodman, Nelson, 108, 113, 147, 155
goodness, 16, 25, 84, 284
Google, 300, 310
graph theory, 302
Green, Rebecca, 94, 99, 219, 229, 231, 233
Greenberg, Jane, 230, 232, 234

Habermas, Jurgen, 232
Hensen, Steven L., 166
hierarchy[ies], 70, 102, 113, 122, 125, 157, 159, 189, 239, 242, 262
   Lowe's, 140, 143-4, 148
   of terms, 242, 255
Hjørland, Birger, 186, 211, 229
Hunter, Eric, 200, 213

iconclass, 256-7
iconographical analysis, 255, 256-9
indiscernibility, 85-6
individuation, 87, 114
informatics, 12, 17, 117, 124, 255, 287
information retrieval (IR), 6, 37, 71-2, 83, 155, 229, 251, 265, 299-02
   applications for, 307
   systems for, 25, 35, 64, 71, 93, 97, 154
   theory of, 159
information theory, 70, 155
information use studies, 35-6
informatism, 77-79
informatology, 78
injustice, 11, 53, 54
instance[s], 60-1, 76-8, 87-8, 96-99, 112-3, 123-26, 140, 152
instantiation, 87, 96-7
Institut International de Bibliographie (IIB), 129, 132, 179, 180
instrumentalist, 274
interface problem, 311-2
International Council on Archives (ICA), 135, 161, 166-7, 173
International Council on Museums (ICOM), 165, 166
International Federation for Documentation and Information (FID), 180-1
International Standard Archival Description (ISAD), 166-7
InterPARES (international research project on Permanent Authentic Records in Electronic Systems), 237-40, 242-3, 245, 247

Index

intersectionality of attributes, 190-1
intrinsicalist, 274
Invitational Meeting of Experts on Descriptive Standards (IMEDS), 166-7
item[s], 61, 64, 71, 87, 112, 121-23, 136, 152, 157, 159, 164, 168-9, 174, 232

justice, 10-1, 49, 51-5, 92-3, 254

Kant, Immanuel, 109
knowledge domains, 15
knowledge organization (KO), 36-7, 40, 81-87, 90-94, 97-100, 102-3, 186, 214-5, 224, 226, 230, 302
Kuhn, Thomas, 15, 33, 223
Kunze, John, 230, 232
Kyle, Barbara, 199, 206-08, 210, 214, 225

La Barre, Kathryn, 228, 233
Lee, Hur-Li, 232
Leibniz, Gottfried, 84, 86
liberal race theory, 193
library cataloging theory, 107
Library of Congress, 181, 254
Library of Congress Classification (LCC), 180, 181
Library of Congress Subject Headings (LCSH), 268, 269
LibraryThing, 270
linguistic infrastructure, 265
Linnaeus, 192
Los Angeles County Museum of Art (LACMA), 290
Lowe, E.J. (Jonathan), 128, 138, 140-43, 156

MacCall, Steven, 232
manifestation, 64, 71, 112, 122-3, 152
Markey, Karen, 198, 258
Martin, Giles, 229, 231, 233
materiality, 129, 132-34, 145
matrix algebra, 302
Matthew effect, 232, 282
McIlwaine, Ia C., 200, 213-4, 219
meaninghood, 134
megatype, 113, 124
Menard, Pierre, 112, 113
metaphysics, 85, 104, 140
Miksa, Francis L., 232-3
Miksa, Shawne, 229, 232-3
Mills, Jack, 199-201, 205, 207-8, 214, 225
Mitchell, Joan, 99
modeling, 91, 95, 161-63, 165-67, 239-40, 298
modern race theory, 192-4
modes of orientation, 40
Morghese, Jean-Pascal, 247
multi-continental ancestry, 194
multidimensionality, 101-03
multifacetedness, 101-2
multi-racial ancestry, 194
multiraciality, 101
Murillo, Angela, 230, 232

National Archives of Canada, 166
National Information Systems Task Force (NISTF), 166, 167
network analysis systems, 301
neutrality, 55, 162, 247
non-linearity principle, 189

numbers, 141, 144, 184, 192

observed citation-set (OC-set), 216, 218
occurrents, 128, 148
ofness, 258
Olson, Hope, 99, 102, 186, 219
online public-access catalog (OPAC), 267, 271, 276
ontogenesis, 230
ontogenetic analysis, 230-1
ontological square, 140
ontology, 107, 109, 111-4, 124-5
open access, 179, 314, 316
oppression, 11, 52, 53
Otlet, Paul, 27, 37, 129, 179, 181

PageRank, 308-10
Palmer, Bernard I., 199-201, 207, 214, 225
Panofsky, Erwin, 257, 258
paradox of the ship of Theseus, 86
part-of-speech, 242-44
particulars, 118, 128, 138, 140-44, 149, 158
    abstract, 156
    concrete, 112, 152, 156
persons, 88, 90, 97, 99, 101, 164, 185
phenomena, 61, 132, 157, 229
    information-related, 16, 19, 22, 24
philosophy, 49-50, 85, 102, *see also* ontology
    of art, 85, 107, 109, 111, 124
    of cultural stewardship, 4, 6
    of documentation, 47, 85, 103, 111, 114
    of information, 6, 49, 61, 78-9, 103
    of knowledge organization, 85, 103-4
    of language, 49, 64, 70, 74, 78, 154
    of logic, 85, 151, 154
    of mind, 49, 78
    of race, 186
    social and political, 51, 85, 87
pluralism, 18, 115, 157, 230, 233
Popper, Karl, 75
powerlessness, 53
preference ordering, 304, 306
pre-iconographical description, 257
premise[s], 64, 65, 68-71
preservation, 78, 91, 129, 132, 238-40
preserver, 240
prioritization, 25, 101-2, 232
property, 140, 154-5, 159, 216
    cultural, 10, 53
    of documents, 95-6
    of events, 299
    of evidence, 68-9
    identity as, 82, 85, 88-90, 101, 140
property-instances, 140, 143
property-kinds, 140, 144
propositions, 50-1, 64-72, 75-6, 83, 141-44, 154-58
provenance, 168
psychology, 33, 37, 40, 87
    cognitive, 27, 29, 36

quality, 84, 109, 133
quantitative analysis, 201, 212, 226
query formulation, 32, 304, 306-7
query statements, 304-5, 307
query[ies], 306, 309

319

racially mixed people, 101, 183, 185, 187-8, 191-2
racism, 186, 194
radical constructionists, 190, *see also* social constructionists
Ranganathan, S.R., 41, 132, 198-200, 211-2, 214, 216, 222-24, 226, 262
Ranganathanian theory, 200, 214
rankings, 149, 306, 308-10
reality, 19, 22, 29, 65, 79, 92, 102
    models of, 82, 93-4
    nature of, 16, 18
    representation of, 97, 100, 163
    social, 128, 145-48
records continuum model, 240
records manager, 240
relations, 86, 95, 98-100 102, 139, 141, 163
relation-types, 97-9
relevance-value, 50
Renear, Allen, 87, 114
repositories, 164, 166-7, 315
resource data, 164
resource discovery, 233, 275, 278-81
Roberto, K. R., 228, 233
Root, Maria, 191
Rouche, Nadav, 247
Russell, Bertrand, 33
Ryle, Gilbert, 154-5

sameness/difference, 88
Searle, John, 145-47
self-identity principle, 191
semiotics, 129
sentence[s], 60-1, 64, 70-1, 75, 124-5, 142, 155, 157
separatism, 157
seriality, 114
series, 164, 169, 174
sexual orientation, 88, 101, 190
Shatford, Sara, 258
Shera, Jesse, 27-32, 34-37, 39-45, 47, 103, 210, 216, 218
sign[s], 130-34, 145, 148
signhood, 134
similarity, 85-6, 97, 103, 307, 309
Smiraglia, Richard, 87, 108-9, 229-33
Smith, Barry, 127-8, 140, 145-48, 156
social computing, 254
social constructionists, 190, *see also* radical constructionists
social epistemology, 27-8, 32-4, 36-7, 40-3, 47, 49-51, 53, 55, 79, 103, 216
Social Sciences Citation Index (SSCI), 41, 197, 201-03, 217-8
Society for American Archivists (SAA), 166, 167, 243
Society of Archivists, 167
sociology, 27, 32-36, 40, 46, 186
specificity principle, 189
speech acts, 18, 128, 146, 148
standardization, 179-80, 228, 247
standards, 12, 134, 165, 173-75
    archival, 162, 169-70
    descriptive, 166-69
    international, 237, 238, 246
    library, 169
    metadata, 6, 180, 234
    vocabulary-construction, 241
statement[s], 65-68, 70-1, 154, 158
    document, 304-5, 307
    query, 304-5, 307

Steve [project], 252-3, 278
Stevenson, Charles, 124
structure[s], 35, 97, 138, 167, 256, 304
    of document networks, 35, 103
    knowledge, 29, 36
    of library catalogs, 298
    of work-instantiation, 96, 97
subject authority files, 158
subject ontogeny, 186, 195
sustainability, 232
Svenonius, Elaine, 79, 95, 99, 108, 198, 211, 219, 224-5, 258

tagging, 267, 269-72, 275-6, 278, 282
TCS-8, 242, 246
Tennis, Joseph T., 91, 186, 228, 229, 232
Thesaurofacet, 226
thesaurus, 222-3, 239, 241-2, 244-5, 279
Thesaurus Construction System (TCS), *see also* TCS-8, 242
Thomer, Andrea, 229, 234
Thompson, Warren, 44
Thomson ISI, 108, 109
Tillett, Barbara, 99, 108, 298, 299
token[s], 75, 112-14, 124, 125, 142, 144-6, 148, 157
topicality, 232
Trant, Jennifer, 253
trope[s], 139-40, 143
truth-value, 50, 65, 71
type/token distinction, 125, 148
type/token model, 114
type/token relationships, 125

UCXtra, 310-12
Union française des organisms de documentation, 130
unitarianism, 158
universal bibliographic control, 179, 180
Universal Decimal Classification (UDC), 179-81
Universal Declaration of Human Rights, 55
universals, 128, 138, 140-45, 149, 158
    abstract, 112, 156
utterance[s], 60-1, 64, 70-1, 124, 142, 157

vagueness, 101-03
Vickery, Brian C., 198-00, 203-08, 210, 211, 214, 224, 225
Victoria & Albert Museum, 253
Visual Resources Association (VRA), 117, 249
vocabularies, 231, 256, 280 *see also* controlled vocabularies

Weber, Lisa, 167-69, 174
Weber, Nicholas, 229
Williamson, Timothy, 102
Wittgenstein, Ludwig, 33
workhood, 61, 87
work-as-mental-object thesis, 112
work-as-physical-object thesis, 112
work-as-set thesis, 112
work-as-type thesis, 112, 113
Works, Expressions, Manifestations, and Items (WEMI), 112, 122-3, 125, 136, 232
world peace, 179

Young, Iris Marion, 53

Zeng, Marcia Lei, 152
Zhang, Lei, 232

www.ingramcontent.com/pod-product-compliance
Lightning Source LLC
Chambersburg PA
CBHW070808300426
44111CB00014B/2457